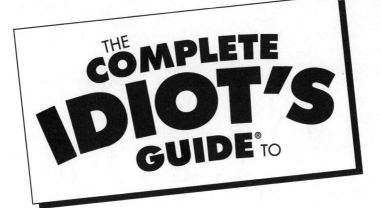

THE COMPLETE IDIOT'S GUIDE® TO

Difficult Conversations

by Gretchen Hirsch

ALPHA

A member of Penguin Group (USA) Inc.

This book is for Tom, Tyler, Trevor, Ryan, and Amanda.

ALPHA BOOKS

Published by the Penguin Group

Penguin Group (USA) Inc., 375 Hudson Street, New York, New York 10014, USA

Penguin Group (Canada), 90 Eglinton Avenue East, Suite 700, Toronto, Ontario M4P 2Y3, Canada (a division of Pearson Penguin Canada Inc.)

Penguin Books Ltd., 80 Strand, London WC2R 0RL, England

Penguin Ireland, 25 St Stephen's Green, Dublin 2, Ireland (a division of Penguin Books Ltd.)

Penguin Group (Australia), 250 Camberwell Road, Camberwell, Victoria 3124, Australia (a division of Pearson Australia Group Pty. Ltd.)

Penguin Books India Pvt. Ltd., 11 Community Centre, Panchsheel Park, New Delhi—110 017, India

Penguin Group (NZ), 67 Apollo Drive, Rosedale, North Shore, Auckland 1311, New Zealand (a division of Pearson New Zealand Ltd.)

Penguin Books (South Africa) (Pty.) Ltd., 24 Sturdee Avenue, Rosebank, Johannesburg 2196, South Africa

Penguin Books Ltd., Registered Offices: 80 Strand, London WC2R 0RL, England

International Standard Book Number: 978-1-59257-619-7
Library of Congress Catalog Card Number: 2007924614

09   08   07   8   7   6   5   4   3   2   1

Interpretation of the printing code: The rightmost number of the first series of numbers is the year of the book's printing; the rightmost number of the second series of numbers is the number of the book's printing. For example, a printing code of 07-1 shows that the first printing occurred in 2007.

Printed in the United States of America

Note: This publication contains the opinions and ideas of its author. It is intended to provide helpful and informative material on the subject matter covered. It is sold with the understanding that the author and publisher are not engaged in rendering professional services in the book. If the reader requires personal assistance or advice, a competent professional should be consulted.

The author and publisher specifically disclaim any responsibility for any liability, loss, or risk, personal or otherwise, which is incurred as a consequence, directly or indirectly, of the use and application of any of the contents of this book.

Most Alpha books are available at special quantity discounts for bulk purchases for sales promotions, premiums, fund-raising, or educational use. Special books, or book excerpts, can also be created to fit specific needs.

For details, write: Special Markets, Alpha Books, 375 Hudson Street, New York, NY 10014.

Publisher: *Marie Butler-Knight*
Editorial Director: *Mike Sanders*
Managing Editor: *Billy Fields*
Acquisitions Editor: *Michele Wells*
Development Editor: *Michael Thomas*
Senior Production Editor: *Janette Lynn*
Copy Editor: *Jeff Rose*

Cartoonist: *Richard King*
Cover Designer: *Kurt Owens*
Book Designer: *Trina Wurst*
Indexer: *Angie Bess*
Layout: *Brian Massey*
Proofreaders: *Aaron Black, Mary Hunt*

Contents at a Glance

Contents

Introduction

If it seems to you that you're involved in more difficult conversations than ever before, you're not alone. Civility lies at the heart of fruitful, rewarding, and enjoyable conversation, and in today's world, civility is under attack.

The pace and stress of modern life may conspire to make us abrupt and brusque in our dealings with others, and others may be equally short and ill-mannered with us. Polarization surrounding political and social issues means that discussion is often mean-spirited and aggressive. In short, difficult conversations seem to lurk around every corner.

If you've picked up this book, it's a pretty sure bet that you're dealing with some difficult conversations at work or at home—or both—and you need practical help in navigating these tough situations. You want real-life examples of what you can say and do today. This book provides them.

The topics in *The Complete Idiot's Guide to Difficult Conversations* are important, but they're offered with a light touch. I hope you'll profit from the strategies you'll find in these pages and that you'll enjoy the reading as well.

How to Use This Book

The Complete Idiot's Guide to Difficult Conversations comprises five sections. Using the table of contents, you can dip into any area of special concern immediately or read the whole book at your leisure. Here's what you'll find in these pages:

Part 1, "Conversation Basics," explores the role of words and nonverbal communication in every conversation, from the simplest to the most difficult. Part 1 is where you'll find information about how conversation differs from small talk and how space, time, eye contact, touch, gestures, and gender shape what you say and what you hear. There's a special emphasis on the role of listening with intention.

Part 2, "The Anatomy of Difficult Conversations," describes the reasons you may shy away from confrontation, how to confront others effectively, and what you should know about cross-cultural confrontation. You'll learn a simple three-step method that helps make confrontations productive rather than threatening.

In **Part 3, "Difficult Conversations for Everyone,"** you'll dive right into applying what you've learned. You'll deal with a gamut of issues ranging from touchy annoyances such as poor hygiene to major topics such as money, illness, death, and grief. You'll find just the help you need if you must be the bearer of bad news.

Part 4, "Conversation and Productivity," gives you the words and techniques to use in critical situations such as discipline, firing, substance abuse, and other concerns, both on the job and at home. Special chapters devoted to customer service highlight how to ask for, receive, and give the service that makes a business successful.

Part 5, "The Stages of Life," guides you through difficult conversations with children and teens, spouses, neighbors, and aging parents.

Extras

Keep your eyes peeled for extra information in boxes:

def•i•ni•tion

Succinct definitions for terms you might not know or need to review.

 Don't Do It!

Words and actions you definitely want to avoid in any conversation.

 Words to the Wise

Guidance and quick techniques to keep conversation positive.

Talking Points

Interesting facts and information about the topic being discussed.

Acknowledgments

My profound gratitude is extended to:

My agent, Janet Rosen, at Sheree Bykofsky and Associates, for suggesting me for this project.

Michele Wells, who guided me so compassionately through my initial panic; Mike Thomas, who was so positive about the process; Jan Lynn, for her efficiency in moving things forward; Jeff Rose, for his good questions and light touch; Trina Wurst, for her design expertise; and all the others known and unknown to me at Alpha Books. It's been a pleasure.

Kathy Baird, for her flexibility and kindness during the writing process—and the rest of the team at Ohio Wesleyan: Ann, Chris, Cole, Doug, Ericka, Ida, Margaret, Mark, Pam, and Sara.

My family, both immediate and extended, for their patience with long hours and slap-dash meals.

And you, for caring about conversation.

Special Thanks to the Technical Reviewer

The Complete Idiot's Guide to Difficult Conversations was reviewed by Keith Groff, Ph.D., Program Chair of Organizational Communication at Franklin University in Columbus, Ohio. Dr. Groff has been a USIA Fellow at Mansoura University in Al Mansoura, Egypt, and a USIS Fellow in the Eastern Europe English Teacher Training Program at Janus Pannonius University in Pecs, Hungary. He was a Fulbright Research/Teaching Fellow at Pontificia Universidade Catolica de Rio de Janeiro.

Dr. Groff taught at Harvard University in the Applied Linguistics ESL Program and served as Chair of the English/Writing Program at Eastern Oregon State University. At Holy Family University in Philadelphia, Pennsylvania, Dr. Groff was Associate Dean for Academic Affairs and Associate Professor of English. He also served as an Adjunct Professor of Applied Linguistics and English Composition at Boise State University.

Trademarks

Part 1

Conversation Basics

Conversation makes up a good part of everyday life, and it's disconcerting when any conversational exchange veers from pleasant to difficult. To protect yourself, it's good to know how a conversation is constructed, how the nonverbal elements of a conversation shade and modify the words you say, and how good listening affects you and your conversational partners. That's what you'll find in this part.

"You're a really good listener, y'know."

The Elements of Conversation

In This Chapter

- Talk vs. conversation
- The three parts of a conversation
- How space and time affect conversation
- A bit about culture

Difficult or baby-simple, all conversations have important details in common. Some details may seem surprising, but all are essential to good conversation. This chapter helps you differentiate conversation from other types of oral expression.

The Challenges of Conversation

"Conversations" of various types occur in every species, and some animals, such as dolphins and chimpanzees, have sophisticated systems of communication. But no matter what they say to one another, animals very rarely misunderstand each other. Their messages are clear and unmistakable.

On the other hand, human conversation is easily misunderstood because all the participants have to agree on the meaning of the words themselves and be aware of the context in which the words occur. At the same time, they have to read the tacit language of facial expressions, gestures, and body positions. Sometimes we attach too much importance to one facet of the conversation ("I don't like that tone of voice") while not attending to the message itself. Conversation in the twenty-first century is a complicated business, and conversing well is an art. How artful are you?

The quiz below will give you a baseline to measure your skill at conversation in general.

What's Your Conversation IQ?

For each of the following statements, circle the number that best describes you.

	Agree				Disagree
1. I learn something new in almost every conversation.	5	4	3	2	1
2. When I'm conversing with someone, I listen about as much as I talk.	5	4	3	2	1
3. I never violate a confidence.	5	4	3	2	1
4. I give whoever I'm talking to my full attention.	5	4	3	2	1
5. I'm curious about many topics.	5	4	3	2	1
6. I think it's more important to maintain a relationship than to prove I'm right.	5	4	3	2	1
7. I know something about conversational styles of different cultures.	5	4	3	2	1
8. I try to schedule important conversations at times and places that are convenient for the other person, as well as for me.	5	4	3	2	1
9. I like hearing a wide spectrum of opinions, and even if I disagree, I try to respect the other position.	5	4	3	2	1
10. I think other people are fascinating and that every person has an interesting story to tell.	5	4	3	2	1

Key:

40-50 points: You understand the purposes of conversation and are probably a rewarding conversational partner.

30-40 points: You're an adequate conversationalist.

20-30 points: You have a lot to learn about basic conversational skills.

Below 20 points: Does anyone talk to you?

More Than Talk

Although all human conversation is talk, not all talk is conversation. To have a real conversation, several components must be in place:

- At least one other person
- Civility
- Reciprocity
- Nonverbal elements
- Something new
- An interest in others
- Trust

At Least One Other Person

When we talk to ourselves, we may get very intelligent answers, but thrashing out issues aloud or rehearsing what we're going to say to someone in a particular situation qualifies as interior monologue, not conversation. Because conversation involves sharing ideas, there must be somebody else present, no matter how brilliant you are in your own head.

Civility

A conversation is an exchange by people with an interest in pleasant discourse. There may be disagreement in a conversation, and that disagreement may at times be heated, but if the conversation strays from civility— if name-calling, insults, and disrespect become part of the equation—then the conversation has degenerated into a *diatribe* or even to verbal abuse.

def•i•ni•tion

A **diatribe** is an extended verbal assault on another person.

Reciprocity

A conversation involves a back-and-forth interchange of words and ideas. If one person dominates the arena, the conversation becomes a lecture, presentation, oration, or one-person show in which the others involved serve only as an audience. Of course, some people are quiet by nature and choose to speak less than others, but the choice must be theirs. If they can't speak because another person is hogging the floor, then conversation has ceased.

> **Words to the Wise**
>
> Every conversation has at least four participants: you as speaker, you as listener, and the other person as both speaker and listener. All four of you need to be involved in the conversation.

Conversational partners can sense when the rule of reciprocity is being violated. The conversation feels out of whack, and one or both will usually try to put it back in balance with a phrase such as, "What you're saying reminds me …" or "I've been talking a lot. I want to hear about you now."

Nonverbal Elements

Conversation comprises not only words, but also gestures, facial expressions, body language, tone of voice, and volume. That's why e-mail, though certainly a form of communication, is not conversation. E-mail is pure, unmediated word, and it sometimes sounds brusque, snippy, and rude, even if the sender didn't intend to send that message. *Emoticons* are not a sufficient substitute for the whole panoply of subtleties that surround conversation. The telephone is a better medium because it allows the listener at least to hear the other's tone of voice, but body language is still lost, and with it, some degree of understanding.

> **def•i•ni•tion**
>
> **Emoticons** are the symbols used to convey emotions in text-based communication. The name is derived from the words "emotional" and "icon." Some common ones are :) and ;-).

Something New

Conversation results in a new idea, a new relationship, a new understanding of people or concepts, a new product or service, or a new appreciation for another's point of view. If nothing new arises, the conversation usually dies out.

The new thing can be mind-blowing (a business idea that will save the company) or mundane (your four-year-old suddenly understands why Erika doesn't want to play with her anymore), but an oral exchange that is simply a replay of old tapes can hardly qualify as conversation.

The "something new" requirement removes many types of communication from the realm of conversation. Asking for and receiving information or ordering someone to do something both involve communication, but they are hardly conversational.

A *debate* may appear to be conversational because it involves a discussion of opposing viewpoints, but it rarely brings about new understandings or ideas in the minds of the participants. In fact, debate encourages participants to hold fast to their current views, no matter what those on the other side may argue. In a conference room or living room, the only new thing created by debate is exhaustion.

Most of the time, something new arises from discussion or dialogue that allows for the candid expression of ideas in an atmosphere free of stress and threat.

def•i•ni•tion

A **debate** is disciplined, logical argument in which each person is entrenched in defending a specific position.

An Interest in Others

If you don't like people or really don't care much about what they think and believe, you won't be much of a conversationalist. Good conversation requires authenticity. You can't fake respect and regard for very long.

Some experts believe that conversation must involve a degree of humor or *repartee*. I disagree. Although witty, intellectual byplay is entertaining and certainly has a place in the conversational smorgasbord, not all conversations require it—and in some instances, it can be counterproductive. In addition, some people just aren't very fast on their feet; even if they aren't particularly witty, they nonetheless can be fascinating conversationalists.

def•i•ni•tion

Repartee is conversational banter that consists of quick, snappy retorts and wisecracks.

Trust: The Essential Ingredient

The most important conversational element is trust. Unless people feel comfortable sharing their thoughts and speaking their minds, conversation won't happen.

Conversational partners may chat about topics such as the weather, sports teams, or community news, but that type of exchange is more correctly called small talk.

There's certainly a place for small talk: at parties, sports events, or school functions, for example; and small talk is invaluable when people are breaking the ice and getting to know each other. But an endless stream of social chitchat gets boring in a hurry. People who can't move beyond surface banalities often find their conversational circle shrinking.

> **Talking Points**
>
> Understanding many points of view makes conversation more interesting and rewarding for everyone. Reading several newspapers or reputable blogs that present different takes on events can help you understand another person's perspective and keep conversation from becoming an exchange of prejudices and misinformation.

Conversation that involves self-revelation doesn't flourish unless people feel safe. For conversation to succeed, participants must know they won't be attacked or ridiculed, even if they are being called to account for a mistake or lapse in judgment; their confidences will be kept; their ideas will be fairly listened to and considered; promises will be honored; and differences, including those of race and culture, will be respected.

Here are some tips for fostering trust:

 ◆ **Delay if you must.** Don't attempt conversation if you are rushed, distracted, worried, or angry and cannot give full attention to your conversational partner.

 ◆ **Concentrate on the other person.** Multitasking may be efficient, but it's often just plain rude. If you answer your cell phone, check messages, or send e-mail while you're conversing with someone, it's a clear signal that the conversation you're having and the person you're having it with are very low on your list of priorities.

 ◆ **Listen with intention.** Listening is the most powerful thing you can do for another person. Not feeling fully heard is the reason many people become aggressive and rude, not only in conversation, but also in their daily lives.

A Conversation in Three Acts

Conversation generally consists of three phases: a beginning, which is concerned with building *rapport;* a middle, in which the conversational subject or subjects is discussed; and an end, when the partners begin to signal that the conversation is nearing its conclusion.

Different phases may be shortened or lengthened, depending on the circumstances. For example, a salesman who's meeting a client for the first time may spend most of the exchange in rapport building. He may open with some banter that disarms the prospect and ask questions that show an

interest in the potential client's concerns and issues. He may comment on the family pictures on the desk or the office décor, staying away from anything controversial or debatable.

On the other hand, two old friends meeting for coffee already have established considerable rapport. Phase one of their conversations may take no longer than a blink and consist only of nonverbal signals: a hug or warm handshake that confirms their previous intimacy.

The middle of the conversation moves to substance: the sharing of news, ideas, concepts, concerns, and advice and counsel. The salesman gets down to showing how his product or service can solve a problem for the prospect, and the friends might talk about an issue that's bothering one of them—a child in trouble, a work-related dilemma, or a marital concern. Friends also often "solve the problems of the world," discussing their viewpoints on political or social topics.

Just because conversation deals with issues of importance to the participants doesn't mean it can't be fun, light, and amusing. Conversation between co-workers, friends, parents and children, and spouses is often hilarious, with inside jokes, immediately understood references to past events, teasing, and byplay. If used appropriately, humor can lighten a serious atmosphere and relieve stress.

Body language often signals the end of a conversation. A participant glances at his watch or toward the door. If the cue isn't picked up, more direct communication ends things. "I'm sorry, but I have another meeting ... I'm on my way to the gym ... I have to pick up the kids ...." What's important about ending a conversation is that the cutoff not be abrupt and rude. Either set the timeframe at the beginning of the conversation or let the other person down gently as you reach the end of the time you have.

The Right Place at the Right Time

A conversation is greatly affected by the setting in which it's held. Suppose you've spent a great deal of company money on an advertising program that has failed miserably. And suppose the president wants to discuss that situation with you.

Where will the conversation have the greatest impact on you—in your office, the president's office, a conference room, or the lunchroom?

If you go to the president's office, it feels a lot like being summoned before the principal when you were in grade school. You'll be intimidated before the conversation even begins because you're on another's turf. Would your office be better? Maybe or maybe not. Your office is your territory, which might make you more comfortable. But if the boss is in your office, it's easier for him to tell you to clean out your desk immediately and then take a powder, leaving you to deal with the issue—and the mess—by yourself.

> ### Don't Do It!
>
> When it comes to time, there are two types of people: larks and owls. Larks are chipper in the morning; owls are more alert later in the day. Don't try to hold an important conversation with an owl at 7 A.M. Try 11 A.M. or even 2 P.M. You'll get a better reception.

A conference room is neutral, but it's also where a lot of people get canned, so it won't feel safe. The lunchroom works. People do get fired over lunch, but not usually in their own building (they take you out for that).

When you plan for a conversation, particularly one that has the potential to be difficult or unpleasant, it's wise to consider the surroundings. Ambience matters.

So does timing. Don't schedule a critical conversation with someone who's in the middle of a major project (unless it's about the project itself), suffering from jet lag, leaving town in an hour, is recovering from illness, or has just received bad news. Would you want to talk then?

Small World, Isn't It?

To succeed in the global village, it's important to understand the conversation basics not only of our own country, but also those of other cultural groups. It's not enough to be able to speak another language (although it helps); one must also understand that various countries may share a language but not a culture.

For example, Spanish is the second most-spoken language in the world, but the cultures of Costa Rica, Cuba, and Chile are vastly different in spite of their common language. Culture is also based on geography, history, economics, politics, demographics, immigration patterns, and other factors. To be effective in conversing with people from other countries, it's important to be aware of the nuances of the particular culture from which they come.

The Benefits of the Basics

In an era of electronic communication, never underestimate the importance of face-to-face conversation. Clear conversation keeps many mistakes from happening and saves businesses both time and money.

Being able to speak effectively and listen attentively helps you ...

◆ **Build better, stronger professional and personal relationships.** People are drawn to those who are unfailingly warm, courteous, and accepting of ideas.

◆ **Stand out in a crowd.** Most people haven't given much attention to conversational skills. If you polish those skills, you'll differentiate yourself and be on the receiving end of opportunities that pass others by.

◆ **Be a leader.** Men and women who are powerful conversationalists are often perceived as leaders, and in fact, may become leaders more easily than those whose conversation is awkward.

Knowing how conversation works makes everyday communication easier and it also helps you prepare both to initiate and respond to those difficult conversations you can't avoid.

The Least You Need to Know

◆ Technology can encourage misunderstandings that only face-to-face conversations can clear up.

◆ Every conversation has three parts: a beginning, a middle, and an end.

◆ Conversation breaks down in the absence of trust.

◆ Conversation requires that you respect those with whom you're speaking, even if you vigorously disagree with their positions.

◆ The meaning of a conversation can be affected by when and where it is held.

◆ Conversation consists both of what's said and what isn't said.

Chapter 2

What You Don't Say

In This Chapter

- ◆ Personal space and conversation
- ◆ Talking and touching
- ◆ About eye contact
- ◆ Reading body language

What you say is important, but only a small portion of the meaning of any conversation is conveyed by the words. Most of the meaning is carried by your posture, gestures, facial expressions, pitch, volume, tone of voice, and more. This chapter gives some insights into how nonverbals can help or hinder conversation.

The Body Talks

Nonverbal communication, that is, everything that isn't spoken, makes up anywhere from 75 to 90 percent of total communication. Some conversations become difficult, not because of the content itself, but because of what your nonverbal signals may be telling the other person, or conversely, what nonverbal cues you're picking up from your conversational partner.

While the mouth is speaking, the whole body is usually in action through postural changes, movements, and gestures—and it's in these elements of the conversation that the most telling points may be made.

For example, let's say you're in your office when a new employee comes by to introduce herself. You may form an opinion of her in the twinkling of an eye, because even before she says anything, you've subconsciously noted that her posture is erect and confident; she holds your gaze for an appropriate amount of time; and comes close enough to shake hands, but doesn't invade your personal space. She stands quietly without fidgeting or toying with her hair or clothing. Her facial expression is pleasant, with a slight smile.

Before she has spoken a word, your overall opinion probably is positive because her nonverbal presentation is impressive.

On the other hand, another new employee, even one with skills superior to the first, may seem less remarkable because she slumps, twists her necklace, and gives you a dead-fish handshake. She'll have to work hard to gain your confidence because she appears not to have any of her own.

Keep Your Distance

There are a variety of aspects to nonverbal communication. One of the most important is the concept of personal space, or *proxemics*. In the United States, there are specific types of spatial boundaries we draw around ourselves, based on the type of conversation that's occurring. These limits include …

def•i•ni•tion

Proxemics refers to the amount of physical space people need to feel comfortable in communicating with one another.

- Intimate distance (6 to 18 inches), for whispering or hugging.
- Personal distance (1.5 to 4 feet) for conversations among close friends.
- Social distance (4 to 12 feet) for conversations among acquaintances who are not considered confidants or close personal friends.
- Public distance (more than 12 feet) for delivering speeches or presentations.

If you want to amuse yourself by watching personal space considerations in action, observe people in an elevator, subway, airport shuttle, or any other situation in which crowding occurs somewhat gradually. On the first floor or at the beginning of the ride, when there may be few people aboard, passengers stake out their personal space. In an elevator, they may back into the four corners, while on a bus they search for a seat next to one that is unoccupied. They are careful not to invade others' space even with their eyes. Although people may greet one another in a perfunctory way, there's not much eye contact or conversation. In an elevator, most people face forward and watch the floor indicator, while those in a vehicle may look out the window or concentrate on the back of the driver's head.

As more and more people fill the area, occupants begin to protect their personal space. They move as far away from one another as possible. And when they can't move any farther, they may stand or sit very straight, as if drawing inward will make them thinner and give them another inch of space. They often pull in their arms and place their hands on top of one another.

If they entered an elevator carrying a briefcase or tote bag at their sides, they move it to the center of the body and hold it with both hands directly in front of them at thigh level. In extreme cases, they may clasp it to their chest, placing both arms around it. It may look as if they're simply trying not to bump anyone with the case, but in fact it's more likely they're trying to create a zone of personal comfort. If they're seated, the briefcase may end up on their laps, behind their legs, or turned sideways directly in front of them, both to protect their own space and to avoid encroaching on another's.

The Culture of Space

A violation of personal space—a co-worker entering the sphere you reserve only for intimate friends, for example—can feel like an assault, and it can turn what should be an innocuous encounter into a difficult conversation. Before you dismiss another person as pushy and intrusive, however, remember that spatial issues are culturally conditioned.

In Mediterranean, Middle Eastern, and Latin cultures, the circle of personal space is smaller—sometimes much smaller. People sit and stand close to one another. If you're conversing with someone who's been conditioned this way, the invasion of space can be unnerving. You may step back to reestablish your comfort zone, and the other person may then step forward to restore the closeness he's used to. Before long, you're practically running around the desk, each of you trying to meet your need for appropriate space. It would be funny if it weren't so detrimental to understanding and to the business or personal relationship. You think he's aggressive, he thinks you're aloof, and neither one of you is right.

Don't Touch Me

Closely related to personal space is the issue of touch. Many of the cultures that believe in physical closeness during conversation also believe that it's okay and, in fact, desirable, to touch the conversational partner. The cultures that maintain more physical distance tend to have a "keep your hands to yourself" attitude.

Some cultures have a hands-off policy during business hours, but are quite touchy-feely with their families, friends, and business associates when they're away from the office. And they'll also knock you down to get on a subway or bus. Others believe in a lot of touching, but only among segregated groups: women may touch women and men may touch men, but no man should touch a woman and vice versa.

Touching can express sympathy, friendship, intimacy, or kinship, and in those instances, it's usually welcomed and reciprocal. In other situations, however, touching also can convey power and dominance, particularly if it would be considered improper or inappropriate for the one who is being touched to return the gesture.

Cultural or sexually based differences related to touch can cause misunderstandings and discomfort that can quickly overshadow the words that are being spoken and turn a pleasant chat into a difficult conversation.

> **Talking Points**
>
> Want to impress someone? Throw the word *haptics* or *oculesics* into your conversation. They're the scientific disciplines related to touch and eye contact.

Look Me in the Eye

How we use our eyes in conversation is an important consideration. In the United States, we place a high value on looking someone in the eye, or at least somewhere between the eyebrows and the chin. First of all, it's polite to look at other people while they're speaking. Scanning the room over their shoulders or glancing at your watch makes you appear discourteous and unfocused. The other person may be offended by your apparent lack of interest in what he or she has to say.

Once again, however, be aware that other cultures often don't share our viewpoint about appropriate eye gaze. Those from some Middle Eastern and Latin cultures may hold a gaze for such a long time the other person may start to feel anxious and uneasy.

> **Words to the Wise**
>
> While you should maintain eye contact most of the time, it's good to glance away occasionally. A protracted gaze into the eyes of another often is equated with romantic or sexual interest.

In many Asian and African cultures, however, averting the eyes is a sign of respect. People from these countries consider it rude to maintain eye contact for too long, and they may direct their gaze more toward the neck and throat rather than toward the eyes. Some cultures proscribe a woman's making eye contact with a man.

The Importance of Congruence

Congruence, that is, a match between the words we speak and nonverbal signals we send, helps conversational partners trust one another; a lack of congruence often leads to suspicion. Most people can sense when words and actions don't correspond, although they may not be able to verbalize the reason for their discomfort. They just feel that there's some sort of dissonance between what someone is saying and what they believe the person really means.

For example, if you say, "I'm not mad," but you make the statement through clenched teeth, it's pretty obvious you're not telling the truth. At that point, your conversational partner may begin to distrust everything you say and the conversation dives into a downward spiral.

Other signs are more subtle, however, and the ability to read another person's body language can help you understand what's really being communicated and allow you to address the issues. This skill may head off a difficult conversation altogether, but if you're already embroiled in such an exchange, translating the "silent language" may help you reconcile issues more quickly.

In the 1970s, writer Julius Fast popularized the term *body language* with his book of the same name. Many researchers have studied nonverbal communication in depth and have made it possible for laypeople to learn, at least to some degree, how to interpret the silent language of gestures, postures, facial expression, and eye movement. Being able to break the nonverbal code can be important in determining whether you can trust someone else or are sending signals that might confuse another person. The table below lists some common cues.

Body Language in Conversation

Body Part	Action	Usual Meaning
Eyes	Faster-than-normal blinking	Stress
	Dilated pupils	Positive feelings, interest in the other person

continues

continued

Body Language in Conversation

Body Part	Action	Usual Meaning
Eyes	Lowered brows	Disagreement, doubt, anger
	Raised brows	Surprise, disbelief
	Looking up and to the left or right	Thinking, considering, reflecting, remembering
Ears	Becoming red	Anger
Nose	Flaring nostrils	Anger
Mouth	Pursed lips	Disagreement
	Compressed lips	Disagreement, anger, annoyance, frustration. Can also be used to hold back tears or other expressions of strong emotion.
	Momentary protrusion of tip of tongue from between the lips	Disagreement, disliking, or displeasure
Face	Neutral face ("deadpan")	Desire to be left alone
Head	Tilted to one side	Openness, flirtation, submission
	Lifted back, with chin elevated	Superiority
Hands	Placing the fingertips of one hand against the fingertips of the other hand ("steepling").	Listening carefully, thinking, planning. When speaking, showing confidence.
	Hand behind the head, massaging neck	Negativity
	Palms up with fingers extended	Conciliation, welcome, harmony
	Palms down, with fingers extended	Confidence, dominance
Body	Leaning toward speaker	Interest
	Leaning away from speaker	Disagreement
Legs/feet	Pointed away from speaker	Desire to leave

An Inexact Science

Although social scientists and linguists have teased out the meaning of many gestures and postures, body language interpretation isn't flawless. For example, many people believe that when a person crosses his arms across his body, it invariably means that he is defensive or resistant to what he's hearing. That's one explanation, but there are several others that are equally valid:

- He is anxious and hugging himself to relieve stress.

- He is relaxed, comfortable, and confident.

- He is cold and trying to warm up.

A great deal of body language depends on context, but sometimes simply knowing what a gesture usually means can help defuse a conversation that has the potential to take an unpleasant turn.

Suppose, for example, you're talking with your spouse about buying a new car. You're very excited about a particular sports model. Although your spouse seems interested in what you're saying, you notice that at various times he purses his lips. When you see that gesture for the third time, you stop the conversation and say, "I'm getting a sense you have some reservations about this. Let's talk about them for a minute."

First of all, your spouse no doubt is surprised at your sensitivity and begins to share his or her concerns. "Well, we talked about starting a family, and I don't see this car as very practical if we do have a baby. There's no room for a car seat or any of the other equipment you have to carry when you travel with a child."

Bingo. A big, important issue is now on the table, all because you noticed a subtle change in your partner's face.

Or let's say you've asked your co-worker about the details of a project the two of you worked on six months ago. Rather than answer you immediately, she averts her eyes, looking upward and to the right.

> **Don't Do It!**
>
> Never use body language to give the impression you're listening to someone. It's actually easier to listen attentively than it is to pretend. If you don't have time to listen, say so.

You feel insulted. Is she impatient? Too busy for you? Why won't she look at you? Well, calm down. Averting her eyes allows her to block out distractions and concentrate on what you're asking. The upward, right-turning gaze often is associated with remembering. She's working hard on recalling all the specifics you've asked for. When she's collected her thoughts, she'll get back to looking at you.

It's best not to assume you know specifically what a particular gesture means. Instead, send up a trial balloon in the form of a neutral statement or question. "I think you're not too sure about this," or "Maybe this isn't quite the right time to discuss this," or "Shall I go on?" are effective ways to check your perception about what you think the other person is signaling, especially if some parts of the body appear to express interest and other parts are sending conflicting cues.

Talking with Your Hands

Gestures are universal, and various types of gestures serve various purposes. Gestures may …

- ◆ Stand in for a word itself. ("Thumbs up" to mean "okay" or "good job.")

- ◆ Illustrate concrete objects or abstract concepts. ("I caught a fish that was t-h-i-s big!" or using both hands to draw a circle in the air to illustrate inclusiveness.)

- ◆ Display emotion. (Covering your mouth while speaking to indicate, "I don't really want to say this.")

- ◆ Emphasize important points. (Stabbing the air.)

Although gestures are part of every culture's speech repertoire, similar gestures can have very different meanings in different countries. In some cultures, innocent American gestures can be either confusing or so insulting they bring conversation to an abrupt halt. Reviving the exchange may be more than difficult. It might be impossible.

Oops! That's Not What I Meant

Gesture	U.S. Meaning	Possible Meanings in Other Cultures
Circle with forefinger and thumb	A-OK	Sexual obscenity, money, zero, useless
Beckon with index finger	Come here	Sexual obscenity
V (with palm facing toward you)	Victory	"Put it where the sun don't shine"

Gesture	U.S. Meaning	Possible Meanings in Other Cultures
Thumbs up	Way to go!	Sexual obscenity
Nod head up and down	Yes	No
Index finger raised	One	Two
Pinky and index finger extended	"Hook 'em horns," Satan, "Rock on"	Your wife is unfaithful
Circling temple with index finger	Crazy	You have a phone call
Smile	Happiness	Happiness, embarrassment, anger, confusion
Feet up, with soles facing another person	Relaxation	Gross insult in many parts of the world because the feet are considered unclean

Before traveling to another country, it's wise to find out what gestures might get you into trouble so you don't unintentionally give offense.

How You Say What You Say

Another critical aspect of nonverbal communication is called *paralanguage*, which includes tone of voice, pitch, volume, intonation, and rate of speech. Take the simple phrase, "What do you want?" and place the accent on each word in turn.

- ◆ *What* do you what?

- ◆ What *do* you want?

- ◆ What do *you* want?

- ◆ What do you *want*?

Each sentence has a slightly different shade of meaning, based solely on what word is emphasized. Additional meaning is carried by tone of voice, as well as the rate and

def•i•ni•tion

In conversation, **paralanguage** refers to everything but the words themselves. It's sometimes referred to as *vocalics*. Nearly 40 percent of the meaning of conversation comes from the way ideas are expressed vocally.

volume of speech. Are the words delivered courteously or sarcastically? Are they spoken in haste as the speaker runs out the door? Is the speaker shouting angrily or speaking quietly? Every part of the vocal presentation matters to those on the receiving end of the message.

We make many assumptions about how we use our voices in conversation. For example:

◆ Those who speak rapidly often are viewed as more competent and interesting than those who speak in a more measured pace. But if the rate of speech is exceptionally fast, the speaker may be perceived as anxious.

◆ A low pitch often is equated with competence and high-pitched voices with timidity, tension, insecurity, and nervousness.

◆ Loud voices are associated both with competence and aggression, while soft-voiced people can be judged as polite but ineffectual.

◆ A breathy voice usually undermines the credibility of both male and female speakers.

◆ Listeners rate those who use considerable vocal variety as more exciting, interesting speakers than those who speak in a monotone.

Men and Women in Conversation

Men and women are different in their approach to nonverbal communication. They use their bodies, voices, and gestures differently.

For example, women smile more than men, and men interrupt those who smile more often than they do those who adopt more serious or deadpan expressions. Therefore, men frequently interrupt women, and even if they don't intend disrespect, the interruptions mean that women's contributions may get short shrift.

Also, from the time they are young boys, men take up more personal space than girls. Their arms and legs are often stretched out, while girls tend to draw their personal space boundaries more tightly. As a result, when girls grow up, they rarely intrude on another's comfort zone. But women's personal space is often unwittingly invaded by men who are used to claiming more area for themselves.

When it comes to eye contact, women are less likely to maintain a sustained gaze, while men often stare to achieve power or dominance. Men and women are both touchers, but often for different reasons.

None of these differences is intrinsically good or bad, but if misunderstood, the nonverbal actions of the two sexes can lead to negative opinions that in turn lead to unnecessarily difficult conversations.

The Least You Need to Know

- Words are often the least important part of a conversation.

- Personal space, touch, and eye contact are critical elements of any conversational exchange.

- Body language can be misinterpreted, which can lead to confusion about the message that's being sent.

- We often make assumptions about other people based on how they sound or move, rather than on the content of their conversation.

- Men and women sometimes have different styles of nonverbal communication.

3

The Importance of Listening

In This Chapter

- ◆ The powerful effects of listening
- ◆ How well do you listen?
- ◆ The listening skills you need
- ◆ The common listening errors to avoid

A Chinese proverb says, "To listen well is as powerful a means of influence as to talk well, and is as essential to all true conversation." In this chapter, we'll examine why listening is such an important skill, the reasons we don't listen well, and how we can become better, more effective listeners.

What Listening Does

Listening has all kinds of positive effects on conversation, and by listening carefully, you avoid misunderstandings that can turn a pleasant conversation into a difficult one.

Listening Builds Trust

Trust is essential to good conversation. And listening, more than any other single factor, creates trust. Listening defuses hot emotions, makes people feel valued, allows them to share ideas and thoughts without fear, and encourages them to make valuable contributions. Listening creates a zone of safety in which people can speak up—even to those who are more powerful—without worrying about retribution or humiliation.

For example, suppose a company is in danger of going into the red; executives are trying to squeeze waste and inefficiency out of every aspect of operations. Now suppose that an employee who works on the loading dock has a brilliant idea for managing inventory. His suggestion could save the company thousands of dollars every month.

If the organization has not cultivated a climate of thoughtful listening—if company officials believe that the only important conversations take place in the executive suite—the employee probably won't speak up for fear of being disregarded. An important perspective will be lost, along with a whole lot of money.

To create an atmosphere of trust, you have to listen respectfully to everyone you encounter and to welcome his or her ideas. Each person, from the humblest to the most exalted, has something to teach others; those who listen best, learn most.

Listening Builds Relationships

Years ago, when I worked in hospital marketing, a salesperson came to my office. After a few moments of small talk, he got down to business.

"I have a product that's going to help you with your nursing recruitment problem."

I replied that we didn't have a nursing recruitment problem. Occasionally we might have a retention problem, but we had no difficulty recruiting nurses.

"But everyone has trouble recruiting nurses," he replied.

"We don't," I repeated. "We have a very aggressive and successful recruitment process. Our only issue is retention in specific departments."

"But every hospital has a nursing shortage."

"That may be true elsewhere, but except for retaining nurses on our general medicine areas, we don't have any nursing concerns. We recruit very, very well."

"I don't understand it. Every other hospital I've visited really likes this recruitment tool. It works."

"I'm sure it does, but we don't have a recruitment problem," I said. "If you have any retention ideas, I'd be happy to hear them."

"I don't."

This was a frustrating exchange for both of us, and the frustration arose because he wasn't listening. He came to sell me something, not to find out what I needed. Three times I told him we had a retention issue, and I even shared what services were being affected by it, but he was dogged in his determination to solve the problem I didn't have rather than take an interest in the one I did.

Because he was focusing solely on his product, he lost the opportunity to forge a relationship with me and perhaps sell me something in the future.

Had he been listening, the conversation probably would have been very different. He might have said:

- ◆ "Retention isn't something I've heard a lot about. Why do you think you have that problem? Are the nurses going to other hospitals? Is it money or working conditions? Does it have to do with how they're treated by the medical staff?"

- ◆ "We don't have a retention product now, but you've pointed out that it's something we should think about. Obviously, if you can retain the nurses you have, you can save a lot of money. It's always cheaper to keep the staff you have than it is to hire and train new people all the time."

- ◆ "You know, the product I'm presenting really isn't going to work for you, but we do have a retention product in the works. Why don't we set up an appointment for later so I can show it to you when it's ready. If you'd like to serve as a test site for us, I'm sure I could offer it to you at a significant price break."

- ◆ "Can you share your recruitment process with me? I'd like to know how it works and if I see any way it could be made even stronger."

Talking Points
Listening is an effective way to build a network. As you listen to others, you may hear the name of a person who can help you achieve a goal or link you to someone else. If you're the one talking all the time, you miss the opportunity to learn what others know.

Questions and statements like those would have shown me that he was listening, trying to understand my unique situation, and thinking about my self-interest. The immediate sales result might have been the same—that is, no sale—but I would have kept his name in my contact information. If his company later developed a retention product, I would have listened and might have bought the program. As it was, I showed him the door, tossed his card in the round file, and went back to work.

Listening Saves Time and Money

When you don't listen with attention, you may miss important details, which can result in ...

♦ Shipping the wrong product.

♦ Making design errors.

♦ Quoting an inaccurate price.

♦ Missing an important meeting or showing up at the wrong time, in the wrong place, or on the wrong day.

♦ Misunderstanding a customer complaint.

♦ Replacing the wrong part.

All these mistakes cause false starts and force you to backtrack, clarify, redesign, apologize, and begin again. They're frustrating, annoying, embarrassing, costly—and they could have been avoided by listening more carefully.

def•i•ni•tion

Multitasking comes from the world of computers and means to run two programs simultaneously. In human terms, it means to attempt to do several tasks at the same time.

Often errors like this can be chalked up to *multitasking*.

How many times have you been talking with someone on the phone and heard him banging away on a computer keyboard? Did you feel you were receiving his full attention? If you try to multitask, do you find details slipping away? Do you have to reorient yourself to get back to the substance of the conversation?

Computers multitask effortlessly, moving seamlessly between programs. It's not that easy for people. With each task shift, time is lost as the brain puts the new tasks in place and reviews the procedures for accomplishing those tasks. The more complicated the task, the more time is required to make the shift. Each shift may take only a fraction of a second, but those tiny increments of time add up, and during each mini-second of inattention, you may miss a word, a number, or a nuance—and thus begin the chain of events that leads to a major mistake.

When it comes to conversation, multitasking is a bad idea. It draws focus from your conversational partners, which is bad manners, and makes it harder for you to concentrate on what they're saying, which is bad business. In this hurry-up world, multitasking may appear to be efficient, but in most cases it isn't. Listening is the key. Do it right and you don't have to do it over.

Are You Really a Good Listener?

Most of us think we listen very well, and most of us are wrong. The quiz below can help you determine where you fall on the continuum of good listening skills.

	Always	Usually	Sometimes	Never
I make eye contact with conversational partners.	❑	❑	❑	❑
I let the other person finish a line of thought before I chime in.	❑	❑	❑	❑
I refrain from completing other people's sentences for them.	❑	❑	❑	❑
I listen to the content of people's ideas rather than being concerned about how they present them.	❑	❑	❑	❑
I show I'm listening by nodding and maintaining an active posture.	❑	❑	❑	❑
I check for misunderstanding by paraphrasing what the other person said.	❑	❑	❑	❑
I try not to think about what I'm going to say while the other person is still speaking.	❑	❑	❑	❑

continues

continued

	Always	Usually	Sometimes	Never
I try to minimize distractions when I'm involved in a conversation.	❏	❏	❏	❏
Even if the subject is boring, I try to be interested in the person who's speaking.	❏	❏	❏	❏
I keep from judging ideas until I completely understand them.	❏	❏	❏	❏

If you answered three or more questions "Never," you need to learn how to listen better and more attentively.

The Big Five Listening Mistakes

Inattentiveness to what other people are saying is a conversation stopper, and most errors in listening can be grouped under the five headings below.

Rehearsing

Without question, the most common error in listening is not listening. Most of us hear only about 50 percent of what other people are saying, and 24 hours later, we may remember only half of that. The main reason we aren't listening is that we're figuring out what we're going to say in response.

If you find yourself mentally rehearsing your answer to what the other person is saying—while he's still saying it—you're not listening. While your brain is busily forming your rebuttal, you've checked out of the conversation. That can be embarrassing. "What were you saying?" is a pretty clear tip-off that you weren't paying attention to anyone but yourself.

Interrupting

Informal conversation over coffee generally includes some overlap, but "chiming in" is qualitatively different from deliberate interruption.

Interruptions are impolite because the interrupters are indicating that they're more important than the person who's speaking. People who are interrupting are people who aren't listening.

Interruptions sometimes do serve a purpose. You may be interrupted if …

- Others can't follow your train of thought and need clarification.

- They're excited about what you're saying and want to amplify your views.

- You're speaking too softly for them to hear.

- You're speaking so fast they can't keep up.

- You're drowning them in jargon they don't understand.

- You're monopolizing the conversation, and they're suffering from listener fatigue.

To forestall interruptions, speak as clearly and concisely as possible, and try not to be too offended if someone jumps into your conversational space without permission. Examine his or her motives.

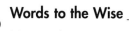

Words to the Wise

Use simple sentences to handle interrupters. "Please let me finish my thought," "I'll be happy to deal with your concerns when I've finished my entire presentation," or "I'd prefer not to be interrupted right now," solves the problem most of the time.

A subset of interrupting is finishing someone's sentences for him. Some people speak more slowly than others, or sometimes they pause to mentally search for the precise word they want to use. This is not a signal for someone else to rush in, supply the word, finish the sentence, and start adding her two cents' worth. That's disrespectful and shows that the interrupter is too impatient to listen until the speaker has completed a thought.

Perhaps even more disconcerting is the person who finishes the sentence *with* the speaker. You know these people. Nodding and smiling, they repeat, a nanosecond behind you, the last few words of your sentence. I believe this behavior is meant to show solidarity and agreement. It doesn't. What it does do is make you talk faster and faster in an attempt to evade the pursuer, or it shuts you down altogether. There's little you can do to correct Repeaters. They're usually unaware of what they're doing, and even if you point it out to them, they find it a nearly impossible habit to break.

Questioning

Questions are helpful conversational tools. A great question can clarify information, focus a discussion, illuminate the speaker's bias, and show the listener's interest in the topic.

The timing of questions is important. Questions should come at logical stopping points in the conversation, not in the middle of a sentence. If you wait until the speaker has come to the end of his thought, a question shows you've been listening and considering what's been said. If you question him too early, all it shows is that you've stopped listening and don't have the courtesy to wait for your turn in the conversation.

In addition, questions are often just statements in disguise. The questioner is not attempting to gain further information or greater understanding; she's trying to get another point of view on the table. Such questions are nothing more than run-ups to the questioner's taking over the conversation.

> **Words to the Wise**
>
> It's a good idea to make questions positive. "Do you think there's any way to reconcile the differences?" has a much different flavor from, "Don't you think your reasoning is flawed?" The second question says you're interested only in discrediting the speaker and showing off your own brilliance.

Run-up questions might include:

- "Have you thought this idea through, because I believe we should ... "

- "Do you really think anyone's going to listen to your plan? It won't work and here's why."

- "What do you think of the new compensation package? I think it's a loser."

Topping

Topping is using someone else's contribution as a springboard to show that what happened to you was worse, more dramatic and, in short, more interesting. If you have a cold, the Topper had pneumonia last month and almost died. If you've had a business success, the Topper recently brought her company back from the brink of ruin. Toppers listen only well enough to find a conversational opening that allows them to focus on themselves. They are often insecure people who need considerable attention from others to validate their own worth.

Dominating

Dominating is an unpleasant stew of all the previous errors. Dominators grab the floor and hold it interminably. They correct, judge, interrupt, top, and generally make life miserable for anyone in their conversational circle. Their mantra seems to be, "But enough about me. What do *you* think about me?" They need assertive handling or they will derail every conversation.

Be a Better Listener

If you ask most people to choose the best conversationalist they know, they'll usually pick the one who's the best listener. Good listeners serve critical functions: they keep discussion flowing, involve everyone, and note nonverbal cues. They may actually speak less than others, but because they have listened carefully, their contributions are on point and cogently presented.

Anyone can be a better listener because the ability to listen is not an inherited trait. It's a set of skills that can be learned and practiced.

Pay Attention

Paying attention means listening to the words and disregarding distractions such as the speaker's Minnie Mouse voice or her peculiar fashion sense. A good listener weighs the ideas and concepts rather than the style of presentation.

Those who are paying attention will also note nonverbal content. Are the speaker's ears getting red? Is he fidgety or calm? Is he making eye contact or talking to his shoes? All these unspoken messages are important; paying attention allows the listener to respond to all the meaning the speaker is conveying, both in words and in body language.

Concentrate

Have you ever heard someone say, "She makes you feel as if you're the only person in the world"? The person who can do that is the one who brings her full powers of concentration to the conversation. That ability engenders trust, loyalty, and relationship—and great conversation.

Unfortunately, in this time-pressured world, most of us don't concentrate well. As our minds wander to what we have to do next, we miss a great deal of what people are saying to us in the present moment. To enhance the quality of your conversation, switch off your cell phone and stop fiddling with your PDA. Quiet your mind and body and show genuine interest in the person in front of you.

Detach from Emotion

People who listen well can distance themselves from the emotion of the moment. If you're caught up in anger, fear, or even excitement, you might not hear what's really said; you might hear what you think someone said. You may focus on specific, loaded words or phrases and miss the context in which they were used. You hear what you expect to hear—and those expectations can be positive or negative.

Words to the Wise

If you want to increase your powers of concentration, learn to meditate. In meditation, you strengthen your ability to control your mind and improve your focus, not just when you're meditating, but also in your daily activities.

For example, suppose you're looking for a job. You're ready to apply for one when your spouse says, "It looks like your skills don't match up with the qualifications very well. It says you have to type fast and take transcription."

If you already feel like a failure because you don't have a job, you may decide that your spouse thinks you're a failure, too, and in that context, his or her reasonable, intelligent observation may feel very threatening. Your emotions take over. Instead of reflecting on what was said, you snap back, "So I'm not qualified for that? Do you think I'm qualified for anything? Maybe you'd just like me to sit in a chair for the rest of my life."

How do you think the rest of the conversation's going to go?

Alternatively, emotion can make you hear only the sunny side of a message. Children are very adept at this. "We'll go to the zoo Friday if I can get the day off" feels like a promise because they listened only to the first half of the sentence. The consequence can be floods of tears if you don't make yourself completely clear.

Detaching yourself from emotion is especially important in conversations you anticipate will be heated or unpleasant. Even though it may be difficult, remaining calm and being attentive to both content and context is often the key to keeping a situation from spinning out of control.

Active Listening: Pros and Cons

Experts have been touting the benefits of *active listening* since the 1960s, and the principles of the technique unquestionably contribute to clear conversation.

In brief, active listening means that people involved in conversation listen both to the words and to the feelings behind them. Those who listen actively ask questions, paraphrase, reflect feelings, and summarize to make sure that they understand everything the speaker says and means.

Active listening is powerful because it recognizes and acknowledges the importance of feelings. When it's done well, it removes many barriers to effective communication. Unfortunately, however, some people have reduced active listening simply to repeating everything the other person says.

def•i•ni•tion

Active listening is giving undivided attention to a speaker. It involves frequent checking for understanding so that miscommunication is held to a minimum.

However, paraphrasing, which is an important part of the process of active listening, is not simply parroting back the speaker's words. To paraphrase means to check your understanding by repeating the speaker's message in your own words. The speaker is then free to agree or to correct any inconsistencies between the two messages. Here's an example:

> Speaker: "I don't understand why we have to do a new marketing plan."
>
> Active listener: "It sounds as if you're not looking forward to the work we'll need to do to write a new one." (Reflecting feelings and paraphrasing)
>
> Speaker: "No, it's not the work. I just don't think we've given the old plan time to work." (Clarification)

This brief exchange has unearthed a wealth of information about the speaker's feelings, and both conversational partners understand one another. That doesn't always happen. Here's an example of so-called active listening that fails.

> Speaker: "I don't understand why we have to do a new marketing plan."

Don't Do It!

When active listening, don't say, "I hear you saying ..." It's a greatly overused phrase and some people are turned off the second they hear it. Try, "Do you mean ... ?" "Could you explain that another way?" "Have I understood you correctly?" or almost anything else.

Listener: "It sounds as if you don't understand why we have to do a new marketing plan."

Speaker: "Why are you telling me what I just said? I know what I said."

Now the speaker doesn't feel heard and the listener is insulted. It's not an auspicious way to begin a conversation. And if the repetition goes on and on, it drives everyone insane and is a great waste of time and energy. Although rephrasing can be very useful, you have to concern yourself with underlying feelings and not just the words themselves.

The Least You Need to Know

- Listening is the single most powerful aspect of communication and is essential for a trusting environment.

- Because of their poor listening skills, most people hear only about 50 percent of any conversation.

- Not listening carefully is a major reason for costly mistakes.

- To be an effective listener, stay in the present moment.

- Multitasking is the enemy of good listening.

Part 2

The Anatomy of Difficult Conversations

Here's where you learn about emotion and its place in making conversations difficult, how conversational snafus can throw a monkey wrench into cross-cultural understanding, and some questions to ask yourself if your conversations often are less pleasant than you'd like.

You'll also discover how healthy confrontation differs from conflict and how to use confrontation effectively.

"We're worried about your eating."

Chapter 4

Understanding Difficult Conversations

In This Chapter

- How emotions make conversation difficult
- Conversation and the fight or flight response
- The power of unmet expectations
- Two critical questions

A difficult conversation is any interchange with another person that makes you feel tense, edgy, nervous, angry, irritated, irked, humiliated, sad, or otherwise uncomfortable before, during, or after it occurs. In this chapter, you'll learn about how your emotional state can make conversations difficult—and what you can do to calm things down.

The #1 Emotion That Makes Conversation Difficult: Fear

No one escapes difficult conversations. At one time or another, we've all been involved in an unpleasant exchange with a friend, co-worker, family member, or even a stranger. Perhaps we've had to deal with an officemate's annoying personal habits or we've been disciplined by a supervisor. Maybe we've had to fire someone or we've been fired. In the personal arena, we might have had to confront a child's experimentation with alcohol or had a dispute with a neighbor.

Different people find different types of conversations trying. For some people, a telephone conversation with a bill collector is unnerving and stressful. Others couldn't care less about what a stranger thinks, but can be deeply hurt by a disturbing interlude with a friend, co-worker, or family member.

Some of us find the anticipation of a difficult conversation worse than the reality; for others, the conversation itself is painful. For a third group, the aftermath can linger for a long time, and for some unlucky folks, the entire experience is a disaster.

Although no one likes to be on the receiving end of a difficult conversation, most of us are more perturbed by having to initiate such an exchange. We face the process with a great deal of trepidation, and if we examine the reason for our uneasiness, we usually discover that the emotion we feel is fear.

Fear of Hurting Someone's Feelings (Or Being Hurt Ourselves)

Very few people in the world wake up in the morning and decide that this is a great day to be cruel. From childhood, we're admonished to be mindful of other people's feelings, and knowing we have to say something that may be painful to another makes us dread the encounter. Likewise, if we're aware that someone else's words will cut us, we'd prefer to skip out before it happens.

Fear of Not Being Liked

Most of us want other people to like us. Some people, however, take this desire to extremes. Their self-worth is largely tied up in others' opinions of them, and they will allow themselves to be walked on and taken advantage of to maintain others' good opinion. What's ironic, however, is that while others may like those they can manipulate, they usually don't respect them.

Fear of Losing an Important Relationship

Good relationships are precious. Damaging a close relationship feels bad enough; losing one may be unbearable, so we skate on the edges of the issues that bother us to keep from falling through the ice.

Fear of Being Wrong

Perhaps nothing is more embarrassing than confronting someone about an issue and discovering that our basic premise was flawed: our co-worker didn't say what was reported; the tree we've been trying to get our neighbor to trim turns out to be on our property; the pharmacist didn't make a mistake after all. Some folks are so afraid of making errors like this that they refuse to confront anyone, even if confrontation is long overdue.

Fear of Looking Stupid

A surprising number of people are caught in the grip of Imposter Syndrome, that is, persistent feelings of inadequacy even if they're performing at very high levels. A person suffering from Imposter Syndrome is plagued with low self-esteem, crippling self-doubt, and the feeling that he is faking his success and doesn't deserve it.

Such people may avoid a difficult conversation at all costs because they are afraid of a confrontation in which their inadequacies will be revealed. They are terrified they will be found out and will no longer be able to maintain a façade of competence.

> ### Talking Points
>
> In business, Imposter Syndrome is more commonly found among women and minorities, perhaps because they have fewer role models to reinforce their self-image.

How Scared Are You?

The amount of fear you might feel when beginning a difficult conversation is based on an interrelationship between the importance of the subject you need to discuss and the importance of your relationship with the other person. You might not be fearful about talking with a store clerk when returning a sweater, but very nervous when confronting a close co-worker about her unfortunate body odor. You could become agitated by discussing even a casual matter with your CEO. The Risk Matrix shows the potential risk you might feel in confronting or being confronted by another.

In this matrix, 3 represents the highest level of concern. If a number is followed by another in parentheses, it means that the first number represents the probable risk of fear, but that the situation has the potential to become more difficult. For example, discussing even a critical issue with someone you know slightly is usually low risk, but if you unintentionally push a "hot button," there's a possibility that the conversation could turn ugly.

The Risk Matrix

Issue	Relationships		
	Central	Important	Casual
Critical	3	2 (3)	1 (2)
Important	2 (3)	2	1
Insignificant	2	1 (2)	1

When you know you're facing a difficult conversation, plotting the amount of risk can help you reduce apprehension. Sometimes our nervousness about a conversation is out of proportion to the actual amount of risk.

Fear, Fight, and Flight

Why all this talk about fear? Because fear has a profound effect on conversation. When we are afraid, we feel threatened, and whether the threat is potentially lethal (we're about to get hit by a car) or only potentially uncomfortable (we have to talk to a friend or co-worker about an unpleasant subject), the body responds in the same way: it prepares us either to fight or to flee.

The feeling of being in danger unleashes a chain reaction of bodily changes. *Adrenaline* and other chemicals cascade into the system. The pupils of our eyes dilate so we can see better, even in the dark. Our hearts beat faster to get more blood to the large muscles we use either to escape or fight; circulation to nonessential organs is diminished.

def•i•ni•tion

Adrenaline is also called epinephrine. It is a hormone released into the bloodstream during times of physical or emotional stress.

The liver converts glycogen into sugar for quick energy. The sweat glands get busy to keep us cool in the heat of battle. Breathing speeds up to oxygenate the blood. The body brings its full wisdom to shield us from danger.

The fight or flight response is a life-saving mechanism that has come down to us from prehistory, and if we are in real peril, this primitive, hardwired reaction can often get us out of trouble. The kinds of threats we face today, however, are more likely to be assaults to the psyche rather than physical danger. Unfortunately, the body doesn't differentiate between psychic and physical danger. It gets us ready to defend ourselves one way or the other.

We live in a time-pressured, competitive, unpredictable environment that often engenders fear. Will the company merger cost us our jobs? And what will we do about health care if we don't have a job? Is the guy we just inadvertently cut off in traffic packing a gun? Will we ever have enough money to give our children a good education and retire when we want to? How do we balance the demands of job, children, and, increasingly, elder care?

This constant state of unease activates our fight-or-flight mechanism far too often. Our bodies are overloaded with stress chemicals that keep us hyper-alert and on edge. It shouldn't be surprising, then, that if a conversation feels threatening to us, we respond as we would to any other situation that offers some degree of risk. We are likely to fight, which causes all sorts of ill will, or flee, avoiding the conversation altogether. Avoidance may relieve the immediate threat, but running away keeps us from solving problems or repairing relationships.

Because we have at least a modicum more civility than our prehistoric ancestors, we probably aren't going to bop our irritating co-worker on the head with a club or dash frantically out of the coffee bar, upending other patrons in the process. However, we may do the oral equivalent, engaging in fight-or-flight behavior with words; many conversations that begin in fear end in anger or with someone backing away.

> **Talking Points**
>
> Sometimes called "acute stress response," the fight-or-flight reaction was first defined by Walter Cannon in 1929; it is the basis for many studies of stress and the field of stress medicine.

"Fight" Reactions

The "fight" end of the spectrum includes several possible responses to the danger of an unpleasant conversation.

Aggression

When we feel threatened, one of the most common fight reactions is to meet fire with fire—to go on the muscle and become aggressive. Aggression sounds like this:

"I'd like to speak with you about the mistakes in the sales report."

"Oh, yeah? Well, you'd better get the whole staff in here then, because if you think you're going to hang that around my neck, you've got another thing coming."

Although the best defense may be a good offense, there's not much hope for the rest of this conversation.

Aggression is often accompanied by an increase in volume, inappropriate language, and belittling of others. It makes life very uncomfortable for everyone within earshot and can turn any conversation into a difficult encounter. If aggression goes too far, it can become the basis for a hefty lawsuit.

Sarcasm

Sarcasm is a very common fight response. A sarcastic exchange might consist of words like these:

def•i•ni•tion

A **sarcastic** remark is one whose meaning is opposite from the words spoken. It's often accompanied by a snide tone of voice and an unpleasant facial expression. Although sarcasm can be very witty, it is anger-based and aggressive.

"What did you think of the department's work on the Annual Report?"

"Your editing was brilliant as always. Only four typos in the first six pages."

Although the purpose of sarcasm is to wound someone, it's often disguised as humor. If you react to the barb, you're often told, "Lighten up. It was only a joke." Sarcasm may bring conversation to an uncomfortable halt, and it can be very hard to get back on track.

Passive Aggression

Not as obvious as full-out nastiness, passive aggression is every bit as much a fight response. The passive aggressive person thwarts or obstructs others in achieving their goals, but does so indirectly by creating chaos, procrastinating, "forgetting," or otherwise leaving other people twisting in the wind. Like this:

"The program recommendations are due this afternoon and I don't have your pages. When will they be ready?"

"Oh, gosh, I forgot."

"Can you get them to me right after lunch? My head's on the chopping block if everything isn't complete by four o'clock."

"I'll try, but I'm in meetings most of the day. I think I can pull something together, but it may not be very complete. Just topline stuff."

"That won't be enough. The board is demanding a complete assessment, and you knew how important this was to all of us."

"Well, you should have reminded me."

Passive-aggressive people are good at undermining co-workers, but they often sabotage supervisors as well. For example, an administrative assistant despises one of the people she supports. There's an obvious, amusing, but very embarrassing error in a report she received from the person she dislikes. Her job is to distribute the report.

She sees the mistake and laughs about it, but doesn't call it to the attention of the writer. Instead she distributes the report as written.

When confronted, she says, "I was told to get the report out. I did. No one told me I was supposed to proofread it." She has attacked, but she hasn't left any fingerprints. That's top-shelf passive aggression.

"Flight" Reactions

The alternative to fighting is to go underground, to run away from a conversation that you think might be disagreeable.

Seething in Silence

Some people make a choice to avoid confrontation about issues that don't matter. They simply walk away from unnecessary altercations and disagreements. They give others the benefit of the doubt, don't hold grudges, and don't waste time seeking revenge.

Seethers are different. Although they may avoid confrontation by remaining silent, they stew and fret about it. They can't let go of what they perceive as slights and insults. They collect injustices and construct elaborate interior monologues about what they could have or should have said and what they will say in the future.

Seethers are like volcanoes. If they can vent a little steam now and then, they can keep the lid on, but if not, they eventually explode, spilling the pent-up ash of invective and insult on everyone in sight. It's not pretty.

Stifle, Edith

Stiflers aren't like Seethers. They avoid difficult conversations by staying quiet and keeping the peace. They often negate, deny, or tamp down their own feelings in an effort to maintain a serene atmosphere. Someday, they may explode like a Seether, but it's more likely they'll become depressed.

The Explosive Power of Unmet Expectations

Conversation sometimes becomes difficult because we have an unspoken expectation of the way other people should behave. When they deviate from our script for them, we may become defensive, judgmental, impatient, frustrated, and, finally, angry. Once our emotions are engaged, rational conversation may go right out the window.

For example, I once had an officemate who loved to listen to the opera all day. I don't happen to be a big opera fan (at least not in the office), and I asked her if she could keep the radio turned down. Earphones were out of the question because she fielded phone calls several hours a day. She responded very positively and did what I asked.

But what if she had said, "I have to keep it turned up or I miss a lot of the music." That response would have been unacceptable to me because I had to share the office and the constant music impeded my ability to work. At that point, the conversation would have become more difficult. I might have become irritated, because I had an expectation of what any conscientious, polite co-worker would do, and she was violating that expectation.

We have so many expectations of people: we expect our children will obey, spouses will be supportive, grandparents will want to be involved with their grandchildren, bosses will be reasonable, and service people will be interested in helping us solve problems. When those expectations go unmet, we may immediately make the jump from reason to emotion and turn a reasonable conversation into a rant.

Putting the Pin Back in the Grenade: Two Important Questions

If you find yourself at a flashpoint—a time when emotion threatens to hijack a conversation—you can turn down the flame by asking yourself a couple of important questions.

The First Important Question

The initial thing you should examine is this:

> What unmet expectation is causing me to feel this way?

A strategic marketing consultant was recently involved with a very young communications specialist on a project for a mutual client.

"On paper, [the young communications specialist] outranked me, and he was supercilious, rude, and very dismissive. Finally, we had a telephone conversation that threatened to go over the edge. He wanted to cut some corners that would have diminished the quality of the project and angered the client.

"I argued with him about it, but since he was the alpha dog on the project, he overruled me. My anger was out of proportion to the issue, so I asked myself why. There was the obvious quality problem, but the real trouble was that my expectations were out of line.

"I expected that he would behave like a seasoned professional, and he couldn't. He had about six months' experience in the real world. He didn't understand the first thing about client management or teamwork—or courtesy, for that matter.

"I also expected that he would defer to my experience and judgment. When I saw that wasn't going to happen, the first emotion I felt was consternation, followed rapidly by irritation and anger.

"Once I'd looked at my expectations, I saw that his behavior, while obnoxious, was somewhat understandable. I calmed down. I also realized we probably wouldn't work together again, and I made the conscious decision not to expend a lot of energy worrying about his behavior.

Words to the Wise

Although you may believe that emotions rise up by themselves, the fact is that before you feel an emotion, you have experienced a thought, even if the thought was so fleeting you weren't aware of it. How you think about a conversational exchange determines your emotional response to it.

"The project failed in exactly the way I told him it would. Although I'm ashamed to say it, I took a certain amount of satisfaction at the outcome."

There's more to the story, however. About six months later, the consultant received an e-mail from her former colleague, apologizing for his behavior. He'd had another project go down in flames and wondered if she could help him see where he was going wrong. "He was now eager for mentoring," she says. "I've decided to work with him a little bit, just to see what develops."

The Second Important Question

Once you've looked at your expectations, you need to answer the next question:

> What responsibility do I bear for this situation?

This is a toughie, because if we're in an unpleasant interchange with someone else, we like to believe we're in the right and the other person is wrong.

Suppose, for example, that a co-worker is in your face about a project you're both working on. He thinks you're shirking your part of the project, and he's really letting you have it, shouting and swearing. This isn't the first time he's behaved this way. It seems he's constantly incensed about something, and you're his target of choice. It may seem peculiar to ask yourself what responsibility you bear, but there are two sides to any conversation, and there's enough responsibility to go around.

In this case, you're being screamed at because you've allowed yourself to be screamed at in the past. Had you spoken up the first time it happened, you might have been able to effect a change. Now it will be difficult to do so because your co-worker believes his conduct is acceptable to you. You have to retrain him, and because you have permitted this behavior to persist, the training period may take quite a while.

> **Don't Do It!**
>
> Never tell another person, "You asked for it. You made me (get angry, behave badly, hit you)." Unless you are being physically threatened, no one else's behavior can compel you to do anything. If you got angry, behaved badly, or hit someone, the responsibility lies with you.

It has to start somewhere, however, and now is the time. There is no reason whatsoever for co-workers to scream at each other, no matter how upset they may be. Your next step is to put a stop to the behavior, and to use the appropriate words to do it.

> "Ron, I see that you're very upset. But when I'm screamed at, I can't concentrate on what the problem is. I just want to get away from the screaming. I'd like to know what's bothering you, but I can't know what you want me to do until you lower the volume."

If there's no useful response, you can become more assertive.

"I'd like to talk with you about this, Ron, but I've explained my feelings about being screamed at. I'm going back to my office (or to the lunchroom or anywhere he isn't), and I'll be happy to discuss this with you there when you feel calmer."

Who's in Control?

The two questions point out some important truths. We do not have control over what other people say. We do, however, have control over how we react.

Taking the time to put a rational thought between what someone says and your reaction to it can help keep a conversation from turning into a train wreck. It relieves pressure and gives you a moment to pause, reflect, consider your response, and put the conversation on a more positive track.

Words to the Wise _____

When a conversation has become contentious, use the person's name in your responses. Sometimes just hearing his name can bring someone who's out of control back to reality.

The Least You Need to Know

◆ When we feel we are in danger, we prepare to fight or flee.

◆ Difficult conversations can make us feel threatened and can result in fight-or-flight reactions.

◆ Many difficult conversations arise from holding unspoken assumptions about how other people will—or should—behave.

◆ Hot conversations can be cooled by inserting a thought between emotional exchanges.

Underneath It All: How Culture Can Make Conversation Difficult

In This Chapter

- How culture affects conversation
- The different ways in which time is used
- The differences between high-context and low-context cultures
- The importance of saving face
- Speaking effectively in different cultures

The world and the workplace are full of people of various ethnicities and cultures, and even if we're speaking the same language, cultural differences may lead to misunderstandings that have little or nothing to do with the words we say. Conversation can break down completely if we inadvertently insult one another by ignoring the cultural conventions in which the conversations occur.

In most of this book, you'll read about specific conversational strategies that work well in North America. In this chapter, however, you'll learn about how cultures of conversational partners can affect the way messages are sent and received. This understanding will make you more effective in managing conversation with every style of co-worker or friend.

What Makes a Culture?

Culture includes customs, attitudes, ideals, mores, beliefs, and values. Essentially, a culture represents what a group of people believes about the way the world works— or should work. Cultural beliefs are passed down from generation to generation, gaining strength from decades of repetition and reinforcement, and unless force is applied either internally or externally, a culture will roll merrily on, changing little, sometimes for centuries. Cultural traditions are transmitted orally, in writing, and by unspoken behaviors.

Cultures can be geographic (the cultures of Fiji, Finland, or France), interest-based (Mac vs. PC users), family-centered (the Hatfields and McCoys), ethnic (recent immigrant communities from a specific country), and industry or company related (general aviation or all employees of a specific aircraft manufacturing plant). Cultures can be very stable and enduring (a small Amish community) or ephemeral (guests at a wedding reception). And of course, there are cultures within cultures (rappers within the community of recording artists).

The cultures in which we find ourselves, however briefly, provide structure. They tell us what is expected of us in various situations. Although we may occasionally rebel against cultural expectations, in general we do what the culture dictates.

In today's multicultural world, interchanges between those of differing cultures offer opportunities for learning and understanding, but they are equally likely to be exercises in confusion. Some of the most common issues that create misunderstandings— even before we add the difficulties of language itself—include:

- Attitudes about time

- Social context

- The concept of "face"

If not handled appropriately, differences related to domestic or foreign cultures can cause misunderstandings, hurt feelings, animosity, hot conversations, and ruptured relationships, all of which can be prevented by being attentive to your surrounding culture.

Beat the Clock

Different cultural orientations toward time can be a major stumbling block in understanding one another. The quiz below will give you some insight into your perception of time.

The Time Style Inventory

	Agree				Disagree
I believe meetings should start and end on time.	1	2	3	4	5
I think that being late for a scheduled appointment is rude and disrespectful.	1	2	3	4	5
I believe in setting priorities to get work done.	1	2	3	4	5
I believe meetings work much better if there's a timed agenda.	1	2	3	4	5
I'd have trouble functioning if I lost my PDA.	1	2	3	4	5
I prefer to work on one thing at a time.	1	2	3	4	5
Time is money.	1	2	3	4	5
I use a to-do list and check things off as they are completed.	1	2	3	4	5
I believe that to keep people waiting is to spend a little of their lives.	1	2	3	4	5

If the majority of your answers are 4's and 5's, you are considered a polychronic person. Mostly 1's and 2's? You're monochronic.

I Can Only Be in One Place at One Time

Monochronic people experience time as tangible. They believe that time is linear and can be managed, divided, spent, saved, or squandered. They respect the reality and value of their own time and believe others' time is important, too; they are prompt for appointments and wouldn't consider missing a deadline.

If you're late for a meeting with a monochronic co-worker, expect that she'll be irritated—or gone. She took the meeting seriously enough to be on time; if she feels you blew her off by not showing up when you agreed to, she might not wait around wondering what happened to you. She'll move on to the next thing in her day planner.

Look, Ma! I'm Juggling!

Polychronic people have a totally different orientation to time, viewing it as fluid and infinite. They consider time a vast, indivisible ocean, not a collection of individual water droplets. Rather than believing that everyone should be on time for a meeting, polychronic folks tend to think that the meeting begins when everyone is present, whether that's two seconds or an hour after the stated time.

In their individual offices, polychronic people work on many projects at once, moving from one to the other and back again. They may appear disorganized but, in fact, they are often as efficient as their buttoned-down *monochronic* co-workers who complete projects one by one on a carefully orchestrated schedule.

def·i·ni·tion

Monochronism is a person's tendency to manage activities one at a time, in sequence and on a schedule, while **polychronism** means a preference for managing several activities at one time.

How Can You Be So Inconsiderate?

Arguments can flare up and clashes become ugly if differing attitudes toward time are construed as character flaws, such as laziness, or deliberate acts of discourtesy.

For example, a manager who comes from a polychronic background and supervises a group of monochronic employees may often be late to meetings with the group. It's likely that the employees don't understand their boss's time style, and after a while, they may become resentful of what they consider her rudeness and lack of regard for them. After all, they reason, if she doesn't respect their time, she doesn't respect them.

If the behavior continues, the boss may find herself subject to sullenness or sabotage. Efficiency plummets and effectiveness wanes, and if the issue is not confronted, she may never know why her leadership style isn't working.

To help mitigate the problem, you might set up a time to meet with the boss (realizing she'll probably keep you waiting) and explain why employees feel disgruntled. You could say:

> "I notice that when the group comes to a meeting at the time we've all agreed on, you often aren't there. Sometimes we wait as much as a half-hour, and we wonder if you've forgotten the meeting.

> "Because we have so much to do, all this waiting makes it seem as if you don't value our time. It feels disrespectful.

> "How about this? We set a time for the meeting, and if you aren't there within fifteen minutes, we are free to leave. Or maybe we could set a time and stay in our offices until you let us know you're ready. That way we can continue to work and still have the meeting without wasting a lot of time."

When the boss is from another country, steer clear of such statements as, "That's the way we do it in this country." That's demeaning, and demeaning the boss, even with the best of intentions, is a bad idea.

If the boss is a reasonable person, she may welcome your suggestions, but because the boss is the boss, she may also respond with the managerial equivalent of "tough cookies," and you'll have to find another way to deal with the problem.

Is the Whole World Late?

Entire countries and regions generally adopt one time style or the other. The United States, the United Kingdom, and most of western Europe are distinctly monochronic, while many parts of the Middle East, Africa, Asia, and Latin America are much more polychronic.

During a business appointment in the United States, participants usually concentrate on a specific topic. They may route their calls to voice mail and close their doors to interruptions. They often use the appointment to devise strategies for meeting deadlines.

In polychronic countries, however, an appointment may be only part of what the participants are doing at any one time. They may take and make calls during a meeting; deal with other, unrelated problems; or chat pleasantly and sometimes at length with those who happen to walk in through the always-open door. To polychronic folks, these activities are not distractions or interruptions; they are an integral part of daily life.

Talking Points
Experts agree that the most monochronic countries in the world are Germany and Switzerland. Many countries contend for the most polychronic.

Of course, if you're a typical hard-driving Western businessperson trying to accomplish a task within a rigid time frame, you may be intensely frustrated by having to deal with someone who believes that things will unfold naturally in their own sweet time.

Positive Communication: Dealing with Time Differences

You can't let your frustration get the better of you if you want to continue dealing effectively with your overseas peers. Watch your words and remember that:

◆ Their time sense is a difference, not a deficit. Both monochronic and polychronic styles are valid. Neither is superior in every case.

◆ You may have to adapt your goals. Perhaps you'll be able to carry out only a part of your mission during the time allotted. If the relationship with your counterpart is important, you have little choice but to learn to go with the flow.

No matter where you fall on the time spectrum, be aware that much of the world is at the opposite pole.

What's the Context?

Context refers to the environment in which communication happens. These environments can be *high-context* or *low-context*, depending on the degree to which speakers and listeners use factors other than the words themselves to convey the meaning of messages.

def•i•ni•tion

In **high-context** cultures, information often is transmitted nonverbally through looks and gestures that are universally understood by the members of the group. In **low-context** cultures, words are used to convey information. Although nonverbal communication occurs, the important facts are carefully stated.

The Context Is the Message

High-context and low-context cultures often misunderstand one another because they don't attach enough importance to the entire milieu in which the conversation occurs.

In a high-context climate:

- Communication tends to be understood quickly because members of the community have developed both oral and nonverbal shortcuts that are universally understood.

- Strong networks exist between and among groups.

- Long-term relationships are the norm.

- In-groups and out-groups are common, and it may be hard for members of out-groups to understand what's being said (or not said).

In low-context situations:

- Relationships may be shorter, sometimes lasting only the life of a particular transaction.

- Networks are looser and weaker.

- Communication must be more direct and precise because there is less commonality among group participants.

A task group is an example of a low-context environment. People who may know one another only slightly are brought together to solve a problem. They meet, talk, devise strategies, assign roles and responsibilities, provide for follow-up, and disband. No one expects the relationships to last for generations, and everyone is happy if the work is completed satisfactorily.

International Contexts

The United States is a low-context society. We believe in personal freedom and responsibility. The founders wrote an entire declaration about the necessity for independence. We admire rugged individualism and respect those who pull themselves up by their own bootstraps.

Don't Do It!

In international dealings, it is the height of presumption to enter a foreign country and expect those who live there to do everything your way. Don't trample over local customs and mores just because they're different from what you're used to.

Because of the importance of individual attainments and the fact that the United States has welcomed so many different cultures, our social bonds are relatively loose unless we face a threat from the outside. We are a live-and-let-live heterogeneous society. Although various ethnic subgroups may have a shared heritage, the country as a whole is a mixture of various cultures and customs.

We bridge our differences with words. We use a lot of them and we're direct in what we say. We assume that others understand us because we choose our words with care and back them up with memoranda, meeting notes, letters of agreement, and other types of documentation. The meaning of the communication is found in the words themselves. We rarely do business on a handshake.

In much of the rest of the world, however, families, clans, groups, and organizations take precedence over the individual. These cultures tend to be somewhat homogeneous, and because of their long shared history and understanding of nonverbal nuances, there's less need for members of the society to be precise in their oral communication.

It's like having an identical twin; the two of you often communicate without any words at all: a glance, a nod of the head, or a tiny smile may be all that's needed to convey a whole constellation of meanings. The words matter less than the context in which the words are set—the place, the time, or the speaker's tone of voice.

In these high-context cultures, relationships matter. The society usually values group, rather than individual achievement. Independent thought and action are rare; consensus is preferred. Conversely, members of low-context societies want to identify the top dog and deal with that person; they want loose ends tied up and details spelled out.

Unless we understand one another's dependence on context, cultural clashes are a given. In a meeting or appointment, low-context attendees can be very confused because they believe they aren't receiving the information they need to make good decisions. "They just sit around and look at each other. They shrug or lift their eyebrows and don't say anything. I don't have any idea what they really think."

On the other hand, those who are high-context wonder why their counterparts never shut up. As the frustrated low-context people push for an answer, the high-context participants may become annoyed because of the information overload. Conversation may become testy and unpleasant. But there are ways around contextual issues.

> **Words to the Wise**
>
> If a cultural misunderstanding has resulted in inconvenience, loss of money, or other negative consequence, steer clear of pejorative terms and ultimatums. Words such as "liar" and "crook" won't get you very far.

Positive Conversation: Dealing with Context

Acknowledging contextual differences is the first step toward understanding one another and working well with those in other cultures. If you're a low-context person thrown into a high-context environment, be sure to:

- ◆ Recognize the status of those in attendance, and show respect for every member of the group. Because of tight relationships, if you insult one member of the group, you risk insulting everyone.

- ◆ Realize that high-context cultures don't compartmentalize as much as low-context societies. Business and personal relationships are often intertwined, and much of the real work takes place away from the office, where relationships can be fostered more easily.

- ◆ Communicate directly, but always diplomatically.

- ◆ Expect that decisions may take longer than you'd like. Consensus-building is often slow going.

- ◆ Understand that cultural tradition may call for more structured, formal language than you're used to. For a high-context individual, cut-to-the-chase conversation may be considered impolite, while convoluted spoken courtesies are thought to enhance relationships.

On the other hand, if you're a member of a high-context group who is thrust into a low-context situation, remember that:

- In general, the language carries the meaning. Hidden inferences are less common in low-context conversation.

- The status of the speaker is not as important as what he or she has to say. The most junior member of the group may contribute and be listened to with respect.

- There will be less focus on relationships and more attention to the business at hand.

- Questions and forthright opinions are expected in order to highlight important points of discussion.

- Formal, indirect, and nuanced communication may be met with impatience, which may or may not be disguised.

Facing Facts

Most Westerners are cards-on-the-table, call-a-spade-a-spade people who place a high value on forthrightness. We aren't afraid of a good squabble, and we'll sometimes vociferously disagree with one another even if others are present to witness the contest. Vigorous debate and occasional confrontations are considered healthy.

In much of the rest of the world, however, such directness may be unsettling or even insulting. The concept of *face*—and *saving or losing face*—is important in many countries and cultures.

def•i•ni•tion

To have **face** is to enjoy high standing and prestige within a community. To **lose face** is to be disgraced and to have one's credibility called into question. To **save face** is to solve problems with as little conflict as possible.

In many societies, it would be a mortifying loss of face to tell you that something you want can't be done. In fact, in a few linguistic and cultural groups, the word "no" is consciously avoided. Out of courtesy, you might be told that something will be "very difficult" or "take a long time," which is tantamount to refusing your request, but unless you understand what these polite phrases mean, you may move ahead with your plans, unaware that your overseas partners cannot accomplish what you believe they have agreed to do.

If you find yourself in such a situation, it's critical that you not berate those who have caused you stress and annoyance. You may believe that they haven't been truthful, but they don't see it that way; if you castigate them, their loss of face is tremendous.

You may enjoy a short-term victory, but you will irreparably damage the relationship—and in many countries of the world, the relationship must be stable before business can be conducted. To allow others to save face and work more productively in the future, you need to:

- Concentrate on the issue, rather than on the error or failure.

- Discuss the matter privately. Don't increase their embarrassment by publicly pointing out their errors.

- Avoid placing blame, even if you know you're right.

- Try to give your counterparts a graceful way out without patronizing or demeaning them.

> **Talking Points**
>
> Although we often think of face as an Asian idea, nearly every negotiation seeks to give participants some of what they want; if no one walks away from the table empty-handed, everyone's dignity is preserved. That's saving face.

A Word About Accents

Never assume that a person who speaks with a pronounced accent is a recent immigrant. A colleague of mine once asked a co-worker, who spoke heavily accented English, where she came from. The co-worker was incensed. "Texas," she said, "and I'm the sixth generation from there. How long has your family been in this country? Not all of us come here illegally, you know." She stormed away, furious.

"I don't know why her accent was so prominent," my colleague said, "but it was, and I jumped to the wrong conclusion." An innocent question had become a difficult conversation, and it took a while for the two co-workers to fix the misunderstanding.

Overcoming Language Barriers

When words themselves become the issue, we need to take special care to prevent misunderstanding. If you can't understand another, listen as carefully as possible. Use the other person's gestures to give you clues about what he's trying to say. Don't make him nervous by rolling your eyes, sighing, looking at your watch, or showing other signs of impatience. He's doing the best he can. If you're at an impasse, say you're sorry and try to find someone else to help.

If you're the one others can't understand, don't raise your voice. Although your listeners may not know what you're saying, they can hear you just fine. Slow down, use gestures. Learn the phrase, "Do you speak English?" in many different languages, and if you're going to be in another country, try to learn at least some of the language. Americans who make an effort to muddle along in another's language make a better impression than those who arrogantly assume the rest of the world should speak English.

People of good will can overcome cultural barriers. Respect for others' customs and traditions is an important first step. You needn't abandon your own culture to appreciate another.

The Least You Need to Know

- How people behave is a reflection of their culture.
- Cultural differences can create difficult conversations.
- Traditional patterns of behavior are resistant to change.
- Don't view others' cultures as inferior to your own.
- Learn as much as possible about a culture before doing business there.

Chapter 6

When It's Gone Too Far: Positive Confrontation

In This Chapter

- Peaceful confrontation
- Honest confrontation and relationships
- Why I-messages work
- A three-step confrontation process
- Two sides of the same coin: confrontation and listening

Our lives include lots of other people, and unfortunately, many of those people do things that bug, irritate, and tick us off. Your officemate rifles your desk for supplies; your mother-in-law makes nasty, cutting remarks in front of your children; your friend drinks too much and insists on driving. You need to confront these people to put a stop to the irritating or even dangerous behavior, but you'd like to do it with the least possible damage to your relationships. This chapter provides some tips for doing that.

The Power of Confrontation

Confrontation is not a dirty word or something to be feared. Yet most of the time we'll twist ourselves into a pretzel to avoid a confrontation. We chatter to our office-mates about the behavior of a co-worker rather than ask him to modify it. We duck down the frozen food aisle rather than encounter the neighbor whose cat is trashing our garden. We empty our savings rather than tell our spouse that her extravagance is ruining the family's credit rating.

For example, Rae is responsible for fact checking a presentation you're giving. Her notes were supposed to be in your hands five business days before your presentation. It's now two days before the presentation, and she's given you nothing. You're in a panic and very distressed with her lack of performance. What do you do? Do you avoid confrontation with Rae while you whimper to officemates about your worries? Do you go behind her back, damaging her reputation by telling everyone she's unreliable? Do you find the data yourself because Rae is noted for her hot temper when she feels cornered?

We engage in tactics like these because we've bought in to a bunch of untruths about what a confrontation really is. A confrontation is not a barroom brawl or even a *conflict*. To *confront* means simply to look someone in the eye.

We often try to sidestep confrontation because we believe:

- It's negative and unpleasant.

- It destroys relationships.

- It stirs up trouble and results in conflict.

- It should be used only in a crisis.

None of these statements is true. Confrontation does not necessarily involve conflict. In fact, it often results in understanding and *compromise*. If approached with tact and goodwill, confrontation can be a positive step that clears the air, relieves pressure on a relationship, and keeps a crisis from occurring.

Relationships thrive in an atmosphere of truth and openness. Your conversational partner is not a mind reader; if you're cloaking your annoyance behind a curtain of niceness, he doesn't know you're irritated with him. He's going to continue his irk-some behavior, not because he wants to drive you up the wall, but because he doesn't know you're upset.

def•i•ni•tion

> To **confront** is to come face to face with; to meet or encounter. **Conflict** means fighting or disharmony. It occurs when at least two people have differing opinions about how to reach a specific goal and are unwilling to consider any approach but their own.
>
> To **compromise** is to settle a disagreement by incorporating parts of each person's position into the solution. Its root is the Latin word *compromissum*, which means *promise together*. In business, such a result is commonly called a win-win.

While confrontations should be as diplomatic as possible, a problem that doesn't get addressed and resolved may grow like an invasive vine. Tendrils of resentment start to creep into every area of the relationship. You avoid your friend, family member, or co-worker. Or you snipe at him. Or treat him with contempt and sarcasm. Now your counterpart knows you're mad at him, but he still doesn't know why.

Eventually, if you're pushed far enough, you may explode. This behavior not only ruins the relationship, but if the blow-up occurs at work, you also might find yourself the subject of a grievance or disciplinary action. Nonconfrontational, passive aggressive behavior often ends up in conflict; positive confrontation reduces the incidence of open warfare.

A good confrontation has some essential elements: timeliness, privacy, respect, and value for everyone.

Timeliness

You can't always wait to see if a situation takes care of itself. It usually won't. If Rae misses the deadline for giving you the data you need for your presentation, you must confront her the next morning, not wait for three days because you're worried about her reaction. You may discover that she's forgotten the assignment altogether or hasn't been able to find the source of one of your most important points. You need that information right away, not 10 minutes before you leave to make your speech. A face-to-face confrontation at the right time will bring issues to the surface in time to make corrections.

Privacy

No one wants to be taken to task, even gently, in front of other people. Find a quiet place where you won't be interrupted.

Respect

Don't expect others to respond positively if you don't respect their dignity and viewpoint, even if you disagree with it.

Value for Everyone

The result of a confrontation should be greater understanding, a more efficient work environment, or a more serene home life, all of which are beneficial to both participants.

Taking Off the Wrong Leg: The Necessity for Confrontation

Years ago, in what's euphemistically referred to as a therapeutic misadventure, a British physician amputated a patient's leg. Unfortunately for everyone, but especially the patient, it was the wrong leg. Of course, the other leg then had to be removed as well.

Two things were remarkable about the situation. First the patient quickly forgave the doctor. She was quoted as saying that he had saved many lives before this unfortunate incident, and she had no anger toward him. Second, and most glaring, was the fact that not one person in the operating room questioned the doctor. Was everyone asleep at the switch? Was the doctor's reputation so pristine that everyone believed he knew what he was doing, even if the chart said otherwise? Was the staff so cowed by his godlike status that they allowed a patient to be harmed rather than point out his mistake? What happened to the communication process?

The point of this story is that sometimes you must confront another person, no matter how anxious you may be about his or her reaction. You must not ride in a car with someone who's drunk—and you must tell her why. You must tell the high and mighty I-never-make-a-mistake CFO that you've found an error in his calculations before the Annual Report is published. You must tell your child you've found marijuana in her pillowcase and what the consequences are.

> **Words to the Wise**
>
> Confront someone only when the time is right and you are under control. Ask if the person has time to speak with you, and if not, when she might have a moment. You'll get nowhere if your counterpart is stressed, rushed, or anxious. In addition, if you're hotter than a pistol, you're going to say things you regret. Put your emotions on ice before you open your mouth.

Three Steps to Success

Confrontation is a necessary part of life at work and at home, and you want it to be productive, not degenerate into a donnybrook. Fortunately, there's a three-step process that makes confrontation, if not painless, at least more pleasant than it might otherwise be. Remember the simple phrase, "I see, I feel, I want." These *I-messages* keep the other person from feeling attacked.

def•i•ni•tion

An **I-message** is a nonaccusatory, non-judgmental method of telling another person that the two of you have a problem that requires attention.

Describing the Problem: I See

All your life, you've probably been told to put others first. When it comes to confrontation, however, turn the spotlight on yourself. Yes, you're trying to change another's behavior, but the way to do that is to show what effect it has on you.

The first step in the confrontation process is to say what you see. Emphasize the word "I," not "you." If you start out by saying, "You never did the fact checking you promised," your conversational partner probably will perceive your words as hostile; she'll defend herself and the battle is on. But you can say, "I'm worried that I still have a hole in my presentation. I'm particularly concerned about the statistics from the Department of Transportation. Were you able to get them or should I adjust that part of the presentation?" and invite discussion and defuse the other's defensiveness.

You don't actually have to say the words, "I see." You can use "I notice," "It seems to me," "I'm concerned that," or any other phrase that communicates your discomfort with the current situation.

Before you take the "I see" step, look beyond the immediate facts to discover what's really bothering you. Is there a bigger picture that needs to be addressed?

If your officemate is taking supplies from your desk, the problem probably is not just the supplies themselves (although that's annoying and inconvenient), but the invasion of personal space. If your mother-in-law is wretched to you

Talking Points

Many workplace conflicts are based in prejudice about another's sex, age, race, national origin, or looks. While it may be impossible to eliminate the prejudice, unacceptable behavior resulting from the prejudice must be confronted.

in front of your children, the issue is not only what she says, but your boundaries—what's off-limits where your kids are concerned. If your child is hiding drugs in her pillowcase, the problem is bigger than the drugs. It's her health, safety, and perhaps her life—and her betrayal of your trust. To make confrontation meaningful, identify the central issue.

Clarifying the Problem: I Feel

Once you've outlined the problem as you see it, the next step is to specify how the situation makes you feel. Once again, steer clear of the word "you." "You made me feel like an idiot," is guaranteed to stir up disagreement—and with reason. No one else is responsible for your feelings. You choose how you feel. Of course, it's not pleasant if someone shoots a nasty remark in your direction, but how you react to it is up to you.

Typical feeling statements might include, "When my desk has been opened, I feel as if my privacy has been violated, and sometimes I'm irritated that the supplies I'm looking for aren't there," or "When the children hear such negative things about me from their grandmother, I worry that they may feel it's all right for them to show me the same disrespect," or "When I found the marijuana in your pillowcase, I felt so overwhelmed and scared."

Solving the Problem: I Want

The feeling statements above are a bridge to a declaration of how you'd like the situation resolved. For example, you might say, "I'd appreciate it if you'd ask me for the supplies you need or get them from the storeroom rather than out of my desk," or "In the future, I'd prefer that you share your opinions about what I do directly with me rather than involving the children," or "Now I need to know the extent of your involvement with marijuana so we can get the help we need. I cannot allow you to do drugs."

> **Don't Do It!**
>
> Avoid going into a confrontation with negative expectations and a chip on your shoulder. Stay cool, look at the situation as a puzzle to be solved, listen, and expect the best. People will often live down—or up—to your expectations.

These three steps—I see, I feel, I want—buttressed by appropriate words and congruent body language, can go a long way toward keeping the atmosphere pleasant. You're neither tamping down what you need to say nor engaging in belligerent posturing. You develop a reputation for forthright honesty. That can only help you, both personally and professionally.

In the quiz below, see if you can choose the best response from the I See, I Feel, I Want options.

The Confrontation Menu

Choose one statement from each column to create the best confrontation strategy for the situation.

Your boss seems to be ignoring you in meetings, but you think you have valuable insights. What is the best way to confront him about it?

A I See	B I Feel	C I Want
1. I see you showing a lot of favoritism to Don in meetings. Does he have pictures of you with a stripper?	I'm concerned that we're about to make a major decision without considering everyone's opinion.	I want my opinion heard. It's different from Don's, and I'm not budging until someone listens to me.
2. It seems to me we didn't get every perspective on the table today.	I feel very worried that you're proceeding on the basis of one person's opinion.	Although Don has valuable insights, I'd like us to consider other options as well.
3. I notice you call on Don a great deal in every meeting.	I feel neglected and angry that you never ask what I think.	I recommend one more meeting because I'm sure there are people who aren't speaking up. They think the decision has been made already.

The best combination of answers is A2, B1, and C3. All the others are either too aggressive, too whiny, or focused on the boss rather than on the situation. The correct statements are respectful but not wimpy, and assertive but not overbearing. They show that the speaker is concerned about the business ramifications of the boss's behavior rather than petty self-interest. In addition, they don't make assumptions about the boss's motives, which the speaker cannot possibly know with certainty.

The Most Important Part: Listening

Now that you've put your position on the table, it's time to employ every listening skill you have to hear the other person's response. Be prepared for a variety of comebacks. Some people are receptive to confrontation, while others view the slightest hint of criticism as a call to arms. Some will appear to be hurt; others initially will get huffy but then settle down quickly in the interest of problem solving and harmony.

When you ask Rae for the results of her fact checking, she might respond:

♦ "You never asked me if I had time to get the work done. Like always. It never occurs to you that I work for three people. Jack wanted to have the sales report compiled, Lauren needed additions to the marketing plan, and you suddenly piled on the fact checking. It's your presentation. Why didn't you do it yourself?"

♦ "I'm sorry, but when Mr. Bigboss says to hop on something, his work takes precedence and you have to get in line. You'll get it when you get it."

♦ "I've done the fact checking, and everything you're saying is accurate. The D.O.T. statistics took longer to get, but your conclusions are fine. Go ahead and finish the presentation, and I'll have the paperwork to you this afternoon. I should have told you sooner. I'm sorry."

♦ "What!"

Every one of these responses (except the last one, and heaven help you if that's what you hear) contains a kernel of truth. You might have made the assignment with too little regard for Rae's schedule. Other priorities might have intervened. The paperwork might have taken longer than the assignment itself. If you had consulted with Rae first, you might have considered doing the work yourself. Although you're probably not crazy about the way Rae expresses herself, if you can maintain your composure and be attentive to what's behind the words, you can begin to strategize about the current problem and the issue that caused it.

Don't get bogged down in the overarching concern unless you have time to address it fully. Deal with what you need now and make plans to work on the hidden agenda later.

You might say, "Rae, I'm sorry if I've been insensitive to your workload. I never thought about how hard it must be to juggle assignments and be the total support staff for three people. When I get back from my presentation this week, let's sit down and figure out some ways to streamline schedules and keep this from happening again. Maybe it would be good if Jack and Lauren were involved, too.

"Right now, though, I need to know where we are with the presentation. It's two days away, and I'm really worried about whether everything I'm saying is accurate. My audience will pick apart every detail, so I need to be able to back myself up. How do you suggest we work together to get the project back on track?"

At this point, it's probable that Rae will have put aside her defensiveness, at least enough to discuss the situation rationally. You have heard and acknowledged her unhappiness and have indicated that you're going to try to work it out.

Remember to keep your word. When the presentation is behind you, get back to Rae as quickly as possible, thanking her for her help and making an appointment to have that important conversation with her.

Words to the Wise

In confrontation, avoid the word "why" in favor of the words "how" and "what." "Why are you reading my e-mail?" sounds less rational than, "I feel very uncomfortable when someone reads over my shoulder. What information do you need?"

Once you've resolved the issue, schedule a follow-up meeting to discover if things are going smoothly for both of you. Share your feelings and observations and listen to the other person's. There's no joy in a resolution that benefits only one of you; that just perpetuates a bad situation. Collaborate on new arrangements if the first stab at a solution doesn't work.

When Confrontation Goes Awry

It's nice to think that all confrontations come to a peaceful conclusion and everyone holds hands and sings "Kumbaya," but we all know that's unrealistic. Some people will blow up and become impossible and some people are impossible to begin with, so if your careful preparation goes up in smoke, remember to:

- **Stay calm.** You won't make any progress if you get into an escalating tit-for-tat exchange. Sit quietly, squarely facing the other person, and maintain eye contact. Give him enough time to vent, but don't let it go on endlessly.

- **Keep to the issue.** Don't respond if the other person brings up unrelated topics that he's been *gunnysacking* for just such an occasion. "I'd prefer that we deal with one issue at a time" is all you need to say.

def•i•ni•tion

Gunnysacking means storing up grievances rather than dealing with them at the time they arise. Spouses often engage in this behavior, referring to disagreements from years ago to buttress today's complaint. ("Your mother is rude to me, and you don't care. You didn't even give me flowers on our fifth anniversary.") You can get whiplash trying to follow the argument of an accomplished gunnysacker.

- ◆ **Call a halt.** "I think we've exhausted this discussion," or "Let's give this topic a rest for now," are the types of statements that work well.

- ◆ **Don't give up.** Try to set a time to discuss the issue again. "I'd like to revisit this when we feel we're ready to hear one another out." Don't give the other person the idea that you're easily intimidated by outbursts of temper or insults. Calling for a cooling-off period does not imply that the subject is closed.

Don't Do It!

Never confront someone in an e-mail or on the phone. It's the coward's way out and it doesn't work. There are too many opportunities for misunderstanding if the other person can't read your body language and pick up your nonverbal cues. It can also be the beginning of a bitter exchange that makes the situation worse, especially if your e-mail is forwarded to other colleagues to show how unreasonable you are.

It's Your Turn in the Barrel

You're not always the one intruded on. Sometimes you've overstepped your boundaries with another and he or she needs to confront you. If so:

- ◆ **Take responsibility for your actions.** Don't pass the buck and try to place the blame elsewhere. Acceptance of responsibility and, if necessary, an honest apology can disarm and conciliate the person who's confronting you.

- ◆ **Give reasons for what you did, but don't make excuses.** "I must have misunderstood the deadline," is a reason for lack of performance. "Well, John mumbles so much he obviously didn't make himself clear," is an excuse and a buck pass all in one.

◆ **Plan for future success.** Think through how you can get your needs met without offending the other person. Show a willingness to try different approaches to getting work done or solving a personal problem. Make sure there's adequate check-in and follow-up to iron out any remaining difficulties.

Don't Use a Flame Thrower on a Housefly

Every little incursion doesn't require a full-blown confrontation. Ask yourself what the issue is, if it's worth confronting, and what the outcome will be if it's never resolved. Some things just aren't important enough to bother with. Life is too short. Live and let live.

If you can't do that, think of confrontation as a ladder. The bottom rung is simply a request for change at a particular time in a specific situation. "Jack, this caller is very soft-spoken and I can't hear her. Could you not use your speakerphone right now? Thanks." There's no particular need to share your feelings about it. Just get it done.

When another's annoying behavior is more systemic, climb to the next rung of the ladder. Explain your reasoning and your feelings. "I notice that everyone in this section is listening to your phone calls on the speakerphone. I know you like the hands-free aspect of the speakerphone, but people are having trouble paying attention to their own calls. I'm nervous about that because I'm responsible for productivity in this unit. I want us to meet our quotas so we don't all look bad. What solution would you propose?"

If you're getting nowhere, go up another rung and be even more direct. "Jack, I've mentioned before that the speakerphone is impeding everyone's ability to work effectively, and that affects me in a number of ways, including my performance review. From now on, please use the headset instead. It allows you to move around, which I know is important to you, but it isn't as distracting to others, and that improves productivity."

If you're still not making progress, take down the ladder and walk away. Document the times and dates you've asked for a change—and precisely what you both said—and take your concerns to a supervisor or human resources. This is a last resort, however. Your aim is to change someone's behavior, not get him in trouble, however tempting that might seem at the time. Try to resolve difficulties at the lowest level and in the simplest way.

The Least You Need to Know

- ◆ Confrontation and conflict are different things.
- ◆ Confrontation is a healthy part of life on and off the job.
- ◆ Delayed confrontation often leads to hard feelings and damaged relationships.
- ◆ Confrontations come in all sizes, from simple requests for change to full-blown interventions.
- ◆ Confrontation skills can be learned and must be practiced.

Part 3

Difficult Conversations for Everyone

No matter how skilled or diplomatic you may be at conversation, there are some situations that are just plain tough to handle. How do you tell someone she has a body odor so offensive it would peel paint? How do you confront money issues, both at home and at work?

What do you say when you learn a co-worker has an illness that will have a great impact on his life? How do you avoid embarrassing gaffes and hurtful words when someone dies? And how do you deliver bad news with the least pain?

This part has examples—and answers.

"I need some eye contact here."

Chapter 7

Touchy, Touchy

In This Chapter

- ◆ Hygiene and other personal issues
- ◆ When to speak up and when to pass the buck
- ◆ Avoiding legal issues
- ◆ Is it really your business?
- ◆ Silence really may be golden

Some of the most difficult conversations involve intimate issues—everything from body odor to weight concerns to family planning. Sometimes you must speak up, sometimes you must maintain silence, and sometimes you find yourself in a gray area, unsure of what to do. This chapter gives you some pointers about what to say—or not to say—and when.

Handling Hygiene

Let's face it. People smell, some more than others. There are a variety of reasons for body odor or bad breath: bacteria that live in sweat or in the mouth; inadequate bathing or oral care; specific health problems, such as diabetes or thyroid disorders; consumption of large amounts of onion,

def•i•ni•tion

> When the body burns fat for fuel, it produces ketones, which build up and cause a condition called **ketosis**. Ketosis often produces breath that smells like nail polish remover.

garlic, or other aromatic foods; smoking; illness, such as a cold or sinus infection; medications of various types; or even incontinence. Lots of Americans smell funny because they're on very-low-carbohydrate diets, which can cause an unusual odor called *ketosis* **breath.**

Sometimes we just live with the odors. If our spouse or friend occasionally smells of onions or is a little gamey after a workout, we usually let it pass. In a business environment, however, a co-worker with a persistent and overwhelming odor often affects others' ability to work. They avoid the offender, who, apart from his unfortunate odor, may be a valuable member of the team. Avoidance isolates him unfairly, leads to the loss of his contributions, and decreases productivity. Customers also may be put off by his disagreeable smell.

At that point, a personal problem has become a corporate liability. It has to be dealt with. Nonetheless, people agonize over the way to tell a colleague that his aroma is, in fact, a stench. They avoid the confrontation because they are afraid the person may be hurt or angry. They worry about what's legal to say. What are the respective rights of the offensive co-worker and those who have to work with him?

What's the best way to bring up the subject? Send an anonymous e-mail? Leave a deodorant stick on the offender's desk while she's at lunch? Slip a note under the door? Take the co-worker out for drinks and tell her as a group?

Although anonymity may help you feel better, it won't have the same effect on the offender. She won't have anyone to talk with about the problem or the reasons for it because she won't know who sent the e-mail or left the note. She'll wonder if everyone is talking about her or trying to get rid of her, and she'll feel ill at ease in the workplace. The quality of her work may take a nosedive. There's no way around it. This has to be a face-to-face conversation—and it can't be a group. That's unfair.

Who Speaks?

If the problem is with a family member or close friend, you might be the best person to carry the message. At work, however, there can be repercussions, and if you think even tactful confrontation will be misperceived or cause greater problems, it's probably best to ask a supervisor or human resources representative to handle the conversation.

If you've decided on a do-it-yourself approach with a friend or relative, remember the steps of confrontation and apply them gently.

The Words You Use

You might start by admitting your own discomfort: "Fred, I need to talk with you about a personal issue and there's no way to make it easy for either one of us." You then move quickly to the issue, using the three-step confrontation technique you learned in Chapter 6.

1. Say what you see (or, in this case, smell): "I've noticed that you often have considerable body odor that you may not be aware of."

2. Say how it makes you feel: "I'm concerned because this is a new problem. I've never noticed it before. Sometimes an odor can indicate a physical problem, and I want to be sure there's nothing wrong."

3. Say what you want: "I hope you'll check it out and do something about it. Frankly, it's pretty unpleasant."

The responses to your little bombshell may vary. Fred may:

♦ Close down the conversation as quickly as possible because he's embarrassed. Expect this. No one wants to hang around for a detailed dissection of his offensiveness.

♦ Thank you for bringing it to his attention. This is the ideal outcome. Don't count on it.

♦ Tell you he's started taking garlic tablets (or some other medication) and had no idea it was bothering anyone else. He may say something like, "You know, it gave me an awful taste in my mouth, but I didn't know it went beyond my own body. I'll see what I can do to tone it down."

♦ Blow up and tell you to mind your own business. Still, you might notice a change for the better in spite of the initial resistance.

Potential Landmines

At work, the supervisor or human resources representative has to treat bodily concerns with even greater sensitivity because of possible legal hassles. Therefore, if you're the one to meet with the employee, there are some steps to take before you launch a confrontation.

First make sure the problem actually exists. Check it out yourself. If co-workers aren't getting along, they can find very inventive ways of making life tough for each other. It's important to deal with the right issue. Sniff around. If there's nothing to the complaint, get back to the person who lodged it; say you've investigated and found no reason to act.

> **Words to the Wise**
>
> Discussions of bodily issues demand privacy. Find a quiet place and close the door, or if the odor is so rank you can't do that, the two of you can take a walk. Allow enough time. Employees may be upset and need a few minutes to calm down before going back to work.

If your eyes start to sting when you step into the offender's cubicle, however, confront the issue gently and with diplomacy, making an appointment to see him privately. In your meeting, be positive and helpful. Explain that your conversation is confidential. Don't threaten him with loss of his job.

Make it clear that the hygiene issue has to be addressed because it is having a negative impact on the work environment. Tell him you'll be following up with him to see how things are going. You may have to follow up more than once, because people often clean up their act for a while only to regress to former habits within a few days or weeks.

The employee may ask you who ratted him out. You might respond that several people have mentioned it to you and that they are concerned, from both a personal and a business standpoint. Don't tell him who reported it, however, or say that everyone in the department is nauseated most of the day. It's your job to solve the problem, not to humiliate the person who has it or foment disagreements between co-workers.

It's crucial that you listen to the employee's reaction to what you say. If he responds that where he comes from people don't use deodorant or bathe every day and that Americans are obsessed with masking natural scents, do not engage in culture wars or denigrate his country of origin as backward or uncivilized. Simply explain that company standards require a specific level of hygiene to keep the workplace healthy and the environment pleasant for employees and customers. Offer suggestions about ways he can meet the hygiene directives.

> **Talking Points**
>
> Americans spend more than 1 billion dollars per year on deodorants and antiperspirants.

If he says eating ethnic foods or foods required as a religious practice cause his odor, you may have to step back a bit. You can't tell him not to eat his ethnic diet or practice his faith unless you want to get hit with a grievance or even a discrimination lawsuit. Focus on the issue and not the reason for it. Your response might be something like, "Let's see if we can design some ways to mitigate this situation," and brainstorm with the employee to do just that. Make sure he understands that this is a performance issue, not a personal attack on his ethnicity, religion, character, or culture.

The same cautions apply to health problems. If an employee has a medical condition that makes her odoriferous, talk about workarounds, not her illness. Employees have been known to throw the *Americans with Disabilities Act* into the mix, insisting that their body odor must be accommodated because it's the result of an illness.

You might request medical documentation, saying that you need to find out if her condition actually qualifies as a disability and requires accommodation. If it does, accommodation might range from moving her desk to providing a job that doesn't require interaction with customers.

def•i•ni•tion

The **Americans with Disabilities Act** covers businesses with more than 15 employees and states that reasonable accommodation must be made for employees with physical and mental disabilities so they can perform the essential duties of their jobs.

Other hygiene issues that need the same kind of delicate handling include filthy hair, unwashed hands (which are unquestionably a health hazard to co-workers), nose-picking, toenail clipping, flatulence—a whole gamut of personal habits that range from offensive to disgusting and are difficult to discuss. The key is discretion, a deft hand, empathy—and firmness.

Don't Do It!

Don't tell the employee what he or she must do to resolve the issue: "You have to take a bath every day" or "You must wash your hair every two days." Employees are adults and should be allowed to solve the problem their own way. If their solutions don't work, you'll have to deal with the issue again, but only as it affects productivity.

A Matter of Taste

Beyond matters of hygiene are issues of personal preference. Some people think tattoos are works of art; others find them a desecration of the body. Piercings can cause huge blow-ups, especially between parents and children (unless, of course, the parents also are pierced from their ears to their toes). Black fingernail polish and lipstick, purple or magenta hair, clothing that bares the midriff or rides too low on the buttocks—all are expressions of taste.

Because Americans believe in personal freedom, taste issues can be hard to confront. But company policies often dictate appropriate attire and appearance, and employers can enforce the rules, either tactfully or with a heavy hand.

Once again, address the issue in private, and see if you can find ways to compromise or at least make compliance more pleasant. You might say:

> "Sheena, I see you have a new eyebrow piercing, but during company hours, please remove the rings. They may become a safety hazard, and it's a violation of the dress code."

> "Paul, our company requires that your pants cover your underwear. We don't have a problem with the pants themselves, but we can't have you flashing your underwear in front of our customers. Please pull them up or use a belt when you're on the job."

There's not much need for the three-step confrontation when someone is outside the boundaries of company policy and needs to be informed. And not every weird affectation of dress or style requires intervention. That magenta hair, while it might not work on the sales floor, is probably not a liability on the loading dock. If it doesn't affect productivity or constitute a safety hazard, it may not be worth getting excited about.

Everyday Annoyances

Almost every office includes people who exhibit the full spectrum of irritating behaviors. Here are some folks you might recognize:

- ◆ The Whistler (or the Hummer) cannot be silent and subjects everyone to off-key renditions of "Hey, Jude" that may go on for hours.

- ◆ The Reader stands behind you and scans your e-mail or flips through your snail mail while he talks with you.

- ◆ The Gum Popper's enjoyment doesn't come from the taste; it comes from that satisfying crack that drives other people right out of their gourds.

◆ The E-Mailer forwards every joke, letter about an angel, urban legend, chain letter, motivational message, and *Dilbert* or *Maxine* cartoon. She never omits the former addresses, so your address book is clotted with the names of people you don't know. She does all this on company time.

◆ The Sick One prides himself on never missing a day of work, and his desk is littered with nasty used tissues. He groans a lot, too.

◆ The Coffee Room Pig takes the last cup of coffee, never makes a new pot, and leaves coffee rings and sugar all over the counters.

◆ The Shrieker's voice could cut glass. If she'd take it up just one more decibel, she could be heard only by dogs, and that would be a relief.

◆ The Baggage Handler brings every personal problem, no matter how minuscule, to work and buttonholes everyone with recitations of life's unfairness and difficulties.

Sometimes these problems can be solved without involving the other person. You can delete non-business-related messages from the E-Mailer or use earphones to drown out the Hummer, the Gum Popper, or the Shrieker. You can quickly bring up a screensaver when you hear the Reader's footsteps behind you.

> **Words to the Wise**
>
> Remember that habits can be deeply ingrained, and it usually takes at least a month to change one. If you've confronted a co-worker about something that annoys you, don't expect immediate change. Appreciate small steps—and say so.

If these solutions don't work or you prefer to address the issues in person, you can use the three-step method to confront these insensitive people. Once again, tell them what you see (or hear), what effect it has on you, and what you need to resolve the issue. Keep judgment and accusations to yourself; focus on the facts and see what can be worked out. If you're a peer, you could try something like:

> "Harry, you sound miserably sick, and frankly, I don't want what you have. I'd really appreciate it if you'd consider going home. We have so much to do, and if your illness sweeps through the office, it's going to put us in the hole. Is there anything I can do to help while you get some rest?"

If he says no, this is a health issue that can be reported to a supervisor.

For the Baggage Handler, you may say:

> "Charissa, it sounds as if you're really upset about something and need to talk. I don't like to put you off, but I have a huge project right now and the interruptions are breaking my concentration. How about lunch today or tomorrow? That way I can give you the attention you deserve."

Sometimes letting the Baggage Handler vent for a specific period of time is enough to calm her down for quite a while. You don't have to get involved or assume her burdens. You just have to listen for a few minutes—at your convenience, not hers. It's a small price to pay for peace, and your co-workers will nominate you for sainthood.

If her complaints are substantive, you might suggest that she make an appointment with human resources, where she can get real help.

The Coffee Pig's behavior is more concrete than being a whiner, and you can use a more direct approach. Try:

> "Ted, the coffee room is a mess. It's everyone's responsibility to leave it clean, but it isn't working, and we're getting bugs in there. We're setting up a schedule so everyone has a day to be in charge of making coffee and cleaning up the space. What day would you like?"

Peer pressure should whip him into shape quickly.

Of course, supervisors can deal with these problems quickly because they have greater power, but if you're the boss, remember that even the most annoying employee is a person first. Concentrate on the behavior and treat your employee with courtesy.

And Off the Job, Too

Touchy conversations may be more a feature of private life than they are of the business world. We often find ourselves in a quagmire with family and friends and don't know what to say when a ticklish situation arises.

Spousal Issues

For example, being in a position to comment on a friend's marriage has the potential for disaster. Suppose your friend's spouse is a louse. He treats her rudely, interrupts, criticizes her in front of others, yells and hollers, and generally is an all-round bad guy. It's painful for you to watch because you know how embarrassing it is for her. What should you say? It depends.

If she never brings it up, you probably should keep your mouth shut—unless you feel she's in danger. If you see bruises or observe depression, you have an obligation to speak, but with the understanding that you may do irreparable harm to your relationship.

If she mentions her frustration with her spouse's behavior, you can respond—carefully. Listen attentively to what she says; you can then reflect, paraphrase, empathize, and ask questions without offering unasked-for advice. Your objective is to get her to think about her situation. It's not your job to solve the problem. You might say something like:

- "It sounds as if that's very painful for you."
- "I can hear that you're upset."
- "That must have been mortifying."
- "What do you think you should do if it happens again?"
- "Why do you think he believes it's okay to speak to you that way?"

Steer clear of statements such as:

- "Why do you put up with that? Throw the bum out."
- "I wouldn't let my husband do that to me. What's the matter with you?"
- "Don't apologize for his behavior. He's the idiot, not you."

If the conversation hasn't been touchy before, these types of pronouncements may take you to a level of touchiness you never knew existed. Remember that nothing drives a couple together like outside criticism. You just called her husband a bum. Even though she's angry with him, she may feel she has to defend him, and suddenly you're on the outs with your friend. Perhaps permanently.

Crimes and Misdemeanors

People succumb to all sorts of temptations. They make mistakes, and sometimes those mistakes land them on the front page. John's wife is arrested for shoplifting. Kathleen's husband is charged with cooking his company's books. Corey's long-simmering affair is publicly revealed. Helen's picked up for drunk driving.

If, in spite of the circumstances, you value your friend and don't want to abandon him or her, you may find yourself on the horns of a dilemma. Obviously, you can't ignore the situation; you have to say something, so how do you make the conversation as painless as possible?

Until you're invited to comment on the situation, keep your communication focused on the friend, not on the circumstances that placed her in the middle of a public humiliation. Although you may want to say, "How could you be such a fool?" or "I'm furious that you thought you could get away with that!" you may have to eat your words if John's wife is exonerated; Kathleen's husband is found not guilty; Corey is a victim of mistaken identity; or Helen wasn't drunk, but sick.

In the United States, everyone is innocent until proven guilty. Zero in on the relationship and let the legal machinery grind toward a resolution.

Statements like these may be helpful:

♦ "I've been thinking about you. How are you doing?"

♦ "I know this is hard and I'm sad for you."

♦ "I read about your problem in the paper, and I wanted you to know you're in my thoughts."

Resist the temptation to ask a lot of prying questions. Show concern and compassion, not curiosity. If your friends want you to know the details, they'll tell you. And don't lecture. The damage is done and your self-righteousness won't make things any better.

The Most Personal Topics

Have you ever been asked:

♦ "Why don't you have children?"

♦ "Don't you think you should have another child? Only children are spoiled and lonesome."

♦ "Four children in this day and age? Haven't you heard of birth control?"

♦ "Why would you give up your career to be a stay-at-home mom? It's a waste of your brain."

♦ "Why don't you stay home and take care of your children?"

- "Why aren't you married? You're so good looking. Are you gay (or a lesbian)?"

- "You look great. Have you had work done?"

- "How much money do you make?"

- "Is your daughter adopted? She doesn't look like you."

- "You're so skinny I hate you. Are you anorexic?"

- "Why don't you lose about fifty pounds? You'd be really attractive then."

These conversational droppings are simply unacceptable from anyone, even Great Aunt Bertha at the family reunion. Being nosy about things that are clearly none of your business can bring conversation to a halt or make it contentious; the people who are subjected to such an inappropriate third degree often are shocked into silence or come out swinging.

> **Words to the Wise** _____
>
> Though you might consider a question inappropriate, remember that in some cultures, highly personal questions are considered signs of interest rather than invasions of privacy. Consider the context before you become upset.

The reason these questions are so insulting is that in most cases they aren't questions at all; they're judgments, and being judged makes people feel defensive and irritated. You're under no obligation to listen to unsolicited opinions about how you conduct your life.

You can choose to answer such gross invasions of your personal life in several ways. If you're fast on your feet, you can try snappy retorts. However that kind of response may take the conversation in a negative direction and end up prolonging the discussion rather than cutting the questioner off. It's better to maintain decorum but let the intruder know he or she is way out of line. You could say:

- "I'll forgive you for asking such a personal question if you'll forgive me for not answering it." Add a smile. That should do it. Then walk away. Ann Landers always recommended this phrase, and it certainly gets the job done.

- "Why would you ask me that?" Look perplexed, not angry. It gives questioners a moment to think about their own behavior.

- "Why are you interested in that?" Such a nice way to say none of your business.

- "That's a personal matter, don't you think?" Once again, a slight smile will disarm the questioner. You'll be so charming he won't notice you haven't answered.

You also can be brutally honest. "That question is very hurtful to me and I'd prefer not to answer it," is an acceptable response to an unacceptable query.

It's natural to be interested in other people's lives and why they make the decisions they do, but sometimes we have to live with ambiguity. Some boundaries should be maintained, and self-censorship is a valuable social skill. To avoid the fallout from an inappropriate question, remember that the best way to keep a difficult conversation from happening might be to remain silent.

The Least You Need to Know

- Intimate issues are among the most difficult to address.
- Mishandling personal issues can get you into legal trouble.
- Everyday annoyances must sometimes be confronted, but often can be ignored or worked around.
- Draw a firm line between what is and what is not your business.
- Ask yourself if what you are saying is what you'd want to hear from someone else.

Chapter **8**

Money Talks

In This Chapter

- ◆ Information is power
- ◆ Choosing the right time to talk
- ◆ Co-workers and money
- ◆ Collecting what people owe
- ◆ Money and marriage

Your mother always told you not to talk about money. You probably learned the lesson well, and that's why conversations about money can be very difficult. Besides being the cause of more marital discord than any other topic, money also can cause problems at work. In this chapter, you'll learn how to navigate the tempestuous seas of talking profitably about money.

The Raise You Want and the Raise You Get

It's probably not a big shock to discover that most people feel underpaid and due for a raise almost anytime. If you're not the top dog at your company—or the offspring of said dog—the road to that raise may be long and rocky.

Talking Points
Between 2004 and 2005, the CEOs of America's 500 biggest public companies received an aggregate pay raise of 54 percent. Between 2005 and 2006, the aggregate pay raise was 6 percent, with the 500 executives earning $5.4 billion. (Source: *Forbes* magazine, April 20, 2006)

Although we continue to hear of multi-million-dollar salaries and incentive packages for corporate executives, you probably don't fare as well in your salary negotiations. Pay raises for those who work in the majority of jobs in the majority of American businesses continue to hover at around 3.7 percent—and for some workers it's even less and hardly worth campaigning for.

It used to be that employers had a pot of money and once a year or so, everyone got equivalent raises. Those days are gone because someone figured out that the policy devalued those who performed and rewarded those who didn't. Now there are all types of pay plans based on achievement of specific goals or other measures of performance, and there is a growing tendency to offer bonuses and non-monetary rewards, such as hefty gift certificates, as part of the compensation package.

Some people argue vehemently that rewards are a powerful motivator. Others believe just as strongly that rewards are effective only over the short haul and actually discourage long-term effort and productivity. Whatever your viewpoint, compensation today is clearly more than money, and you have to be creative in what you ask for.

Making the Pitch

Whether you want cold, hard cash or some other benefit or perk, asking for more money—or the equivalent of more money—can be difficult. The one thing that makes your request less stressful and more likely to be successful is information. Before you enter the arena, you need to know what you want, whether your company can meet your demands, your value in the market, and how your work has affected the company's business position.

What You Want

If it's cash, have a figure or a percentage of increase in mind. If it's nonmonetary compensation, ask for more vacation, flextime, two days of telecommuting, or whatever you think is an appropriate reward for your contributions. You weaken your position if you waffle and look confused. Before you open your mouth, know exactly what you're going to ask for.

The Company's Financial Condition

Raises tend to lag behind the economy. Of course, pay increases are more likely in an economic upturn, but they won't exactly parallel that positive trend. When the cycle stabilizes, you're in a better position to ask for more money.

Realize, however, that even if the market is up and economic indicators favorable, your company may be going through hard times or getting ready to make a huge expenditure you don't know about yet. And if times are tough throughout your entire industry, shaking the money tree may be a losing proposition unless you're so valuable your boss cannot afford to lose you.

Your Market Value

The best time to address your worth is during the hiring process, but if you discover you undersold yourself when you accepted the position, you might be able to use that as a bargaining chip. On the other hand, not doing your homework at the time of hire is a mistake you might have to live with for quite a while. The company is not required to make up for your research errors.

Your Contributions to Success

If you've come to work and done your job, that's great, but if that's all you've done, your request for a raise probably will fall on deaf ears. Why should you receive more than others who also are performing adequately at the same type of job?

Have you outperformed expectations or created a successful extension of your company's product line? Those are all things you can cite as you make your case. Don't guess at these important data. Have accurate facts and figures and ask for monetary recognition of what you've done for the company.

Spend some time compiling your list of accomplishments and quantifying your contributions: numbers matter. For example:

- "I supervised the installation of the new barcode system in the warehouse. It allows packages to be routed onto the trucks in half the time previously required. Next year, that increase in efficiency will amount to about $22,000 in savings, and as orders increase, the amount saved will continue to rise."

- "I got rid of the persistent bug in our home financing software, and customer returns are down 98 percent."

- "I suggested that we replace the advertising campaign the agency wanted with a far less expensive public relations program. We received 26 mentions on local media and five articles in national trade magazines, and it cost $40,000 less than the advertising."

- "When the computer network failed, I provided a workaround that allowed everyone to continue working until the manufacturer's technicians could get here. That kept 75 people on the job for a full day, so there was no loss of productivity."

Nonquantifiable but valuable contributions might include:

- "When my co-worker came to work with a gun, I was the one who kept things calm until security could arrive."

- "By instituting some small and cost-free recognition programs, I've taken a demoralized staff and turned them into a much happier and more efficient group. Retention in my unit is up 80 percent, which has saved a lot of retraining dollars."

Don't be vague and don't be diffident about your accomplishments in behalf of your company. Without becoming obnoxious or arrogant, toot your own horn—and then ask for what you want.

Time Is of the Essence

In addition to having the pertinent performance information in hand, you'll need to be cautious about timing your request. Most companies give increases around the time of performance reviews, and between-review raises may be much harder to get.

Words to the Wise

During your salary discussion, stick to the subject. This is not the time to moan about the co-worker who doesn't pull her weight. If you whine, you may be asked why you want to stay with the company at all. And you won't get the raise.

It's not wise to ask for a raise within the first six months, unless you negotiated that condition when you were hired. If you've taken a new position, the first six months are usually spent learning the ropes. Even when you're well-prepared to carry out the tasks of the job, you still have to figure out the culture of the organization, master different procedures, and get to know a whole new staff. You may not make large contributions during this period of learning.

Personal timing is important as well. Don't approach your boss about a raise the day she comes back from maternity leave or he's just returned from a family funeral. If you blindside your supervisor, you'll likely be asked to come back later because he isn't ready for the discussion. That's bad. Gearing up for an important conversation takes energy, and if you have to start all over again at a later date, it's possible you'll lose some of your momentum.

Meeting Objections

Many bosses resist doling out an extra dime to anyone for any reason. You might hear that there is simply no money available for raises.

There are several ways you can respond:

- ◆ "Are there other types of monetary compensation you might offer?" Sometimes you can score a one-time bonus if you have a significant accomplishment to point to.

- ◆ "I thought that might be the case, so I'd like to discuss nonsalary monetary incentives. I have a very long commute every day. Perhaps you could provide a mileage allowance." In times of high gasoline prices, this can amount to quite a tidy sum. Or find some other financial reward that doesn't qualify as a salary increase.

You may be asked to hold on to your request until your next review period. If that's a month away, you might acquiesce because you're not hurting yourself much. If your next review is in eight months, however, that's probably unacceptable.

You might agree to the delay but ask to have your review moved up a few months. When there's a firm policy that links pay raises to reviews, moving the review date is about the only way to get the raise you want earlier rather than later. However you may be told the time of review is cast in concrete. That's an inconvenient truth that can put a crimp in your plans.

Sometimes the boss will say she'll give you an answer later. This response keeps you on edge because "later" is a pretty loosey-goosey time frame. Do all you can to pin down whether it means two weeks, two months, or two millennia.

Words to the Wise

Practice may not make perfect, but it does make better. Rehearse the salient points in your raise request so you feel confident about saying them out loud.

When Not to Speak

Suppose you inadvertently discover that someone else in the company is receiving more than you are for doing roughly the same job. You're hot. You want to storm into your supervisor's office and demand an immediate raise. This is unfair! You've worked for the company longer than she has. How dare they?

Resist the urge. Although you may be right about the unfairness of it all, you might also be wrong. The person who told you about the other person's salary may be in error; your counterpart may have more relevant experience or be handling more complex projects. She may be more productive than you are, or she may have some specialized skills that warrant more money. She may have negotiated a higher starting rate at the outset. Although seniority is important, it's only one criterion for establishing rates of pay. What a co-worker makes has no place in the discussion of your salary; what matters is your work and your desire to be compensated fairly.

> **Don't Do It!**
>
> If you threaten to quit if you don't get everything you ask for in a pay raise negotiation, be prepared to do it. And if you storm out in a huff, or even a snit, remember you've burned a bridge.

When the Answer Is Yes

Your supervisor may agree that a raise is warranted but not be able to give you the amount you think is fair. If you've been wise, you've asked for a little more than you expected to get, so either accept the raise gracefully or say it's not quite what you hoped for and try to negotiate the rest in other types of compensation.

It's possible that your boss will fall in line with your well-reasoned argument and say you deserve the raise, but he can't promise it that day. He may ask you to come back for further discussion. Don't leave without scheduling the meeting.

When the date is on the calendar, use the interim time to make additional contributions you can bring to the table in the next round of talks. Being put off may not necessarily be a bad thing. Though it could be an avoidance tactic, it's possible that your boss may have to get approval for the raise from someone farther up the chain.

Once you have your facts and timing down, enter into negotiations with a quiet assurance and a concern not only for yourself, but also for the company. Naked greed is unattractive and often isn't rewarded.

Nickels and Dimes: Paying Your Share

In many offices, there's a small fund set aside for birthdays, flowers for new parents or hospitalized co-workers, and other niceties. If everyone contributes, you do too. It's probable you'll also be asked to contribute to United Way at the level you can afford (or maybe a bit more).

In some offices, however, there's no policy about other fund-raising activities, and it may seem that every other day someone's asking you for money. Officemates want you to buy their daughter's Girl Scout cookies, and there are sales of all kinds to benefit other youth activities, such as band trips to the Rose Bowl. You'll be asked to sponsor co-workers on various walks for worthy charities. If you buy everything and accede to every request, you'll be shelling out plenty of your hard-earned money.

You don't want to insult your co-workers by refusing to participate in activities they think are important, but you're sick of being tapped every time you turn around. The best response is this one: "I'd like to help out, but I just can't do it right now."

It's wise occasionally to make a token contribution for a cause you really believe in. It makes you seem less stand-offish and more a part of the team.

> **Talking Points**
>
> Many companies have a "no solicitations" policy that alleviates the stress of refusing colleagues' charitable requests. If your company doesn't, it's worth considering.

Lunch Money and Car Pools

In every office, there's someone who forgets Shakespeare's advice: neither a borrower nor a lender be. Of course, you'll help out a co-worker who needs some coins for the vending machine or a buck or two for the parking meter, and you know they'd do the same for you. Those are one-time events and you're probably meticulous about paying each other back.

However, some folks take advantage if you let them. These are the co-workers who "forgot" to go to the bank or "inadvertently" left their wallet in their desk and now need you to pick up the lunch tab. Once or twice, maybe. Several times with no repayment? That's a moocher, and you'll have to be firm to stop the behavior.

This situation really doesn't demand a full-scale confrontation, although you can use that technique if you wish. But in this instance, you want the other person to know you've caught on and that the personal loan office is closed. You don't need to be accusatory, but you must be direct. Subtlety doesn't work with these folks. Try the following:

- "Do you have your wallet? I'm a little cash poor today, so I can't pay for anyone but me."

- "I'd love to go, but it's your turn to buy today."

The same type of upfront conversation is necessary for carpool deadbeats. You should have forestalled the problem by establishing payment policies at the outset, but if you didn't, you now can say, "I've been driving the carpool for a month, and I notice you haven't paid for gas. That feels unfair to me, because everyone else has paid at least once. I'd like you to pay for the next fill-up, and then I think all of us should work out a schedule. That way, we'll all know when it's our turn to pay and we can budget for it."

More Serious Than Mooching

If a co-worker approaches you frequently for loans and mentions that debt is overwhelming him, it may mean only that your officemate is a rotten money manager. However constant requests for loans and worry about debt can also be an indication of an alcohol, drug, or gambling problem. He needs your money to feed his addiction. If other behavior leads you to believe he has a problem, or if you hear that others in the office are also being tapped, be aware that giving him money enables his habit, and you'll probably never be repaid.

Whatever the reason, it's poor policy to get into a borrower-lender pattern with a co-worker. It changes the balance of the relationship and can result in anger and frustration if you aren't paid back promptly.

When approached, you can respond with:

- "I'm sorry. I've stopped lending to anyone but my family."

- "I wish I could help, but I have to pay my own bills."

- "No can do. Sorry."

You needn't make a long apology or deliver a lecture on fiscal prudence. Just say no.

Special Issues for the Self-Employed

When you choose personal freedom over a guaranteed paycheck as a self-employed person, you take a risk. You may be happier, but you also are often at the mercy of clients who don't pay or pay slowly. That plays havoc with the business. How do you get people to pay up?

Billing and Collection

Collecting what's owed you, especially if you run a small business, can be a headache, and the conversations surrounding collection are almost always unpleasant. You want to preserve the relationship, but you also have to keep your business running. In this case, you'll just have to deal with the uncomfortable emotions money may stir up because your livelihood depends on collecting what clients and customers owe you.

Start politely and never stray from being courteous. The more you yell and scream, the more others resist and delay, even if they know they owe you the money. Here are some techniques that work.

You begin by stating the obvious. "Your bill has gone more than 30 days (or 60 days or 90 days). Is there a problem with payment?"

You may hear a variety of answers, from feeble excuses about bookkeepers or mail service to justifications that make sense to immediate promises to pay. For example:

> "I wasn't satisfied with the work. I want you to do it over."

This is the classic response of a manipulator who's trying to get something for nothing. If he accepted your work product and voiced no dissatisfaction at the time—or within a reasonable period—he needs to cough up the dough.

Firmness will sometimes get results. "Jack, I'm very surprised. You initialed your acceptance of each step of the process, and never said you were unhappy with anything we were doing. Nonpayment puts me in a tough spot with my vendors. If you now need to have something redone, I'll do it, of course, but there must be a new contract for that work. The initial project must be paid for first."

No matter how bellicose he becomes, remain calm and keep repeating that the work must be paid for. Assure him that you understand his objections, but you expect to be paid. Empathize freely, but don't get suckered into doing new work for old money—or no money.

Other common excuses include:

◆ "Your bill was far more than I expected, and I can't pay the whole thing." Yes, she can, but maybe not all at once. Don't back off your fee. Offer a payment plan instead. You might build in a small penalty for the privilege of spreading the payment over a longer period, but that's a personal choice. You don't have to.

◆ "I have a lot of unexpected expenses, and I don't have the money." Once again, structure some sort of payment plan. His expenses should not be your problem; a payment plan can help both of you.

◆ "I'm not paying for it." You need to find out, specifically, what the client's reasons are for nonpayment and take appropriate steps. Sometimes even the most assertive communication or payment demand goes nowhere, and you have to determine whether you'll continue to chase the client, chalk it up as a bad deal, or turn the bill over to a collector. If the bill is not too large, small claims court may be a relatively inexpensive answer.

When You Can't Pay

Whether a debt is professional or personal, when you find you can't pay it, you must make contact with your creditor. In good faith, you must tell him what you're prepared to do.

> "Ralph, I'm embarrassed to have to tell you this. I have a real cash flow problem right now, and I can't pay the bill you sent, at least not in full. May I make partial payments for the next three months? I promise full payment in 90 days or sooner. My problem will have resolved itself by then. I'm going to pay the bill, but I need a little patience. Do you have any to spare? How would you like me to proceed?"

Most reasonable people and businesses will accept installments if the payments are made as agreed upon. Don't be late or miss one altogether, at least not without full explanation. The key to solving this kind of problem is an honest presentation of the facts and a willingness to work toward resolution. Don't cut and run because you're ashamed you can't pay. Silence breeds suspicion. Face up to the mess you're in, enlist the cooperation of the other person, and see what can be worked out.

Raising Your Rates Without Raising the Roof

If you're preparing to raise your professional or freelance rates, you're probably not going to inform your clients by calling each one of them personally. You'll notify them by letter, telling them:

- What the new rates will be.

- When the rate increase will go into effect (give them at least a couple of months' notice, so they can adjust budgets).

- That all contracts in force at the old rates will remain at those rates until completion (you may see an influx of business as clients scurry to take advantage of the old rates).

After clients receive your letter, there may be some serious convincing to do, and if you aren't prepared, the conversation may not go well. Although some clients may barely notice the increase, others may demand that you justify it.

If you've thought things through carefully, you're ready to trot out the reasons for the rate hike: economic conditions in your area of the country, increases in the price of materials, or upgrades you're going to make to ensure greater efficiency for the client. You can also mention that you've become an expert in their needs. Breaking in someone new will be more expensive than paying you a bit more.

There are myriad ways you can raise your rates, and during the conversation, show clients that the decision is not a whim, but is based on solid business considerations. Businesspeople tend to respond well to carefully researched arguments. If a client walks away because of a reasonable increase in rates, you'll probably pick up another one who believes that higher prices mean higher quality. When businesses are choosing vendors, *perceived value* can be a powerful force.

Words to the Wise

Raising rates is like asking for a pay increase, except that it's your clients who grant the request. Prepare as carefully as you would if you were approaching an in-house boss for a raise.

def•i•ni•tion

Perceived value is your client's subjective opinion of your worth and is often based on considerations, such as image, that have nothing to do with your actual service. It's the reason people often will pay more for a brand name, even if two products are nearly indistinguishable.

Money at Home

The #1 cause of marital disputes is money (the other topics rounding out the top three are sex and children). Money spats often have to do with one person's opinion that the spouse is a spendthrift, and the other partner's opinion that the spouse is a cheapskate. These viewpoints may be played out in arguments about the use of credit versus the value of saving, instant gratification versus waiting for larger rewards later, or conservative versus higher-risk investment. The only way out of the constant round of disagreements is to stop fighting and start conversing.

> ### Talking Points
>
> A study for *Smart Money* magazine concluded that more than 70 percent of married couples discuss money at least once a week, and 40 percent of both sexes admit to lying about how much something cost.

In arguments about money, as in most marital issues, the I-message (see Chapter 6) is essential to enhancing harmony. Becoming unglued and screaming, "You're spending us into the poorhouse!" while it may be true, is not the way to encourage a solution to the problem.

You're much more likely to engage your partner in conversation if you say, "When so many bills are piled up, I get anxious about paying them. The credit card debt really scares me because I've figured out how long it will take us to pay it off if we pay the minimums every month. How do you think we should tackle this?"

Presuming that you and your partner are a team, a statement like that may open the way to very meaningful conversation, and you may develop an immediate policy regarding the credit card debt. Maybe you'll decide to "ladder" the payments, paying off the one with the lowest balance first and using the money saved to add to the payment for the next highest balance until they're all paid off.

Perhaps you'll agree to live on cash only as you pay down the debt. Maybe you'll agree that the one who runs up the debt will be responsible for managing it. The key is to observe the behavior and comment on what effects it has on you, rather than to accuse the partner of being a fiscal nincompoop.

Money, like other marital issues, can divide and conquer couples, turning spouse against spouse. The only way to avoid division is to join forces against the problem itself rather than snipping at one another.

If money is being used as a source of power in a marriage ("I make it, I spend it, and you're not entitled to any opinion about it"), a counselor may be helpful in mediating money conversations.

The Least You Need to Know

♦ Money issues must be dealt with forthrightly.

♦ Keeping track of your contributions to your company makes asking for a raise much easier.

♦ If not addressed quickly, even nickel and dime issues can drive a wedge between co-workers.

♦ If you can't pay a debt in full, don't run away from it. Negotiate terms.

♦ Conversely, offer terms to those who are having trouble discharging an obligation to you.

♦ Attitudes about money are the major cause of marital discord, and compromises are often necessary to restore harmony.

Chapter 9

Talking About Medical Issues

In This Chapter

- ◆ Working Americans with serious diseases
- ◆ What and when to tell the boss
- ◆ Understanding chronic illness
- ◆ Helpful words and hurtful words
- ◆ How to speak with children about illness

At one time or another, every workplace and every family will be affected by serious or chronic illness, which is frightening and stressful both for those who are fighting the disease and those who work or live with them. People who become ill may not know what to say about their disease. They often worry about how to tell supervisors, co-workers, friends, or family members, especially children.

On the other hand, those who are told of the illness may not know how to respond and often are afraid they'll say something inappropriate. This chapter answers some important questions about the difficult conversations that may accompany illness.

Illness Is a Fact of Life

If you wonder if you'll ever have to deal with a co-worker's illness, the answer is yes. Hundreds of thousands of American workers are diagnosed with serious illnesses every year; because of advances in medicine, many diseases that were once rapidly fatal are becoming manageable conditions that allow people to continue working, sometimes with accommodations. Below are some of the illnesses you may encounter—or even face yourself.

Illness and the Workplace

Disease	New Cases Diagnosed Annually
Men	
Prostate Cancer	234,000
Testicular Cancer	9,000
Subtotal	243,000
Women	
Breast Cancer	214,000
Ovarian Cancer	20,000
Cervical Cancer	13,000
Subtotal	247,000
Both Sexes	
Heart Attacks	1,200,000
Diabetes	700,000
Congestive Heart Failure	400,000
Lung Cancer	170,000
Colon Cancer	135,000
Multiple Sclerosis	10,000
ALS (Lou Gehrig's Disease)	5,000
Subtotal	2,620,000
Total	**3,110,000**

In addition, arthritis affects nearly 20 percent of American adults and is second only to heart disease as a cause of workplace disability. Several thousand cases of other autoimmune conditions, such as lupus, scleroderma, and thyroid disorders, are diagnosed every year, and these illnesses can be painful, debilitating, and hard to manage. Respiratory diseases—emphysema, asthma, and others—affect millions of Americans. Add to that the 18,000,000 people who are treated for depression every year, and you'll see that workplace illness touches everyone.

The numbers in the table represent only the new cases diagnosed each year; they do not include people who may have been diagnosed years ago and are still contending with a particular disease.

To Tell or Not to Tell

If you have received a diagnosis of serious illness, the shock can be overwhelming. Learning that you have cancer, congestive heart failure, multiple sclerosis, or any other serious disease may wipe out your ability to think rationally for a little while.

Your immediate concerns are prognosis and treatment. Has your life span just been abruptly shortened or will you be dealing with a series of health issues over a long span of time? Will your condition remain relatively stable or will you have periods of illness interspersed with intervals of remission? What kinds of treatment will you need? Can you find the treatment locally or will you have to travel? Does treatment offer a cure or only alleviation of symptoms?

Once the initial panic has ebbed a bit, you have practical matters to deal with, including your job. The big question you must settle in your own mind is whether you tell your employer of your illness. Most people are very apprehensive about this conversation because they are afraid they will be fired, which will cost them their health insurance just when they need it most; demoted; or given make-work tasks. They also may worry about being shunned by co-workers.

The majority of people agree that, if you have a good relationship with your boss and co-workers, speaking up is better than remaining silent. By sharing the facts, you may have access to sources of help within the company.

Job Accommodation

Human resources representatives can spell out the provisions of the Americans with Disabilities Act. If you have a qualifying condition, they can start the ball rolling to make the necessary accommodations, which might include such things as adjusting your schedule, modifying your work space, or making preparations that allow you to work from home as necessary. Of course, many workplaces will make those changes without your having to resort to the ADA, just because they value your contribution.

Paperwork Assistance

Human resources can help you maintain your benefits and file necessary forms. Lifting the burden of paperwork can be a huge advantage when you're trying to work while managing your illness. Human resources professionals have considerable experience in dealing with the effects and aftereffects of illness as it relates to the workplace, and they can be very good people to have on your team.

Personal Relationships

Obviously, if you're in and out of the office for frequent doctors' appointments and often call in sick, your co-workers are going to wonder and worry. Even if you never miss a day of work, they might not understand why you're entitled to a shortened workday or allowed to work from home occasionally. If they don't know the reason for what they see as perks, they may become jealous—and jealousy often leads to rumors of favoritism and other negative consequences. Colleagues may turn on you at the time you most need their support.

Telling them what's going on can relieve their apprehension and convert jealousy to understanding. In many companies, co-workers have been extremely generous about sharing their sick leave or vacation time with a colleague in need. They often pitch in to see that large projects get done, and sometimes they even provide meals for the family. Keeping your illness close to the vest can deprive you—and them—of the benefits of friendship.

> **Words to the Wise**
>
> Five minutes after your diagnosis, you are the same person you were the five minutes before your diagnosis. Knowing you have an illness doesn't rob you of your skills, talents, and abilities, and you have the legal right to be protected from discrimination.

You needn't share anything immediately, especially if your illness will not result in any major near-term changes. When fatigue or medications begin to have an impact on your ability to perform to your previous standards, however, it's probably time to have a talk with your supervisor.

Telling the Boss

When it's time for the boss to know, speak directly to him rather than going through intermediaries such as your insurance company or physician. You have a unique opportunity to educate your supervisor, and nothing works better than face-to-face communication.

Call It by Name

Tell your boss the name of your disease and whatever you can about your treatment. Mention the effects that treatment will have on your appearance if it's likely you'll lose your hair or need a cane or wheelchair to get around, but skip the more personal details. Some people are squeamish about illness. Keep the conversation focused on how your illness will affect your ability to work. Tell your supervisor whether you will need extended sick leave for comprehensive treatment, occasional days off for doctor's appointments or dealing with the effects of medication, or that you expect to be able to work without interruption, at least for a while.

Provide Documentation

If you need any kind of accommodation to continue working, the company may require proof that you actually have what you say you have. A letter from your doctor should be all that's required, at least initially.

Prepare for the Reaction

Some bosses are naturally empathetic and will say the right thing immediately. If you cry, they might be moved to tears themselves. Others' style is all business, which can make you feel that they don't care. Although there may be some who truly are unfeeling trolls, most are simply stunned by what you've told them and may need a while to recover.

Sometimes, the closer you are to a boss, the harder it is for her to hear bad news. She may react with anger or frustration. Be assured she's not mad at you; she's mad at what's happened to you. It's heartening to realize that in most cases the boss's reaction will be one of support and understanding.

Spreading the Word

If you decide to tell your officemates of your diagnosis, do so in exactly the same way you tell the boss—simply and directly. They may be ignorant about your disease, and this is the time to explain exactly what you have, how it will affect you, and that they can't catch it. Once again, supply the information they need, but gloss over anything highly personal. All of you, including your supervisor, may need to strategize about the best way to deal with sporadic absences, fatigue, or complications of treatment.

Don't Do It!

Don't overtax yourself when you're ill. Tell co-workers what you need from them. Pull your weight when you can, and ask for help when you can't. Most people are understanding and will pitch in. Steer clear of those who won't.

Sometimes your colleagues have unspoken expectations about what your diagnosis means. They may be afraid you'll be dead in a week or that your illness will immediately make you a less useful member of the team. If you feel up to it, you might invite them to ask questions so you can dispel myths and bring them accurate information.

No matter how well you prepare them, some colleagues probably will avoid you. Don't waste a lot of time worrying about them; keep up relationships with those who offer encouragement and support.

Responding to Illness

If a colleague tells you she's ill, you may be at a loss about what to say. Take a moment to compose yourself rather than blurting out the first thought that takes up residence in your brain. Below are some tips to help you navigate those first conversations.

Don't Blame the Victim

Although many diseases are brought on or worsened by lifestyle choices, once a person is sick there is nothing whatever to be gained by saying, "I tried to get you to stop smoking, but you wouldn't listen, and now look what's happened." No matter how much you feel your colleague's habits contributed to her illness (she overate, didn't exercise, and was always stressed out), keep your judgments to yourself. Concentrate on her, not on you.

Don't Pry

You don't need to know every detail of the treatment plan or how she found out about her illness. It's not necessary for you to be privy to what the doctor told her about her prognosis. Those are personal matters that she may choose to talk about or not.

Don't Give Advice

Don't tell her to take up a macrobiotic diet or try alternative medicine. Don't direct her to websites and megavitamins. You are not her doctor; you're her co-worker and perhaps her friend, so restrict yourself to caring comments. You can share your opinions later—if and when she asks for them.

Don't Tell War Stories

It's not helpful to tell her about your family member who had the same illness and did so well—until he died. In what universe is that a useful observation?

Don't Say, "I Know How You Feel"

You don't know how she feels unless you have the illness yourself, your family situation is exactly the same, and you have been through, or are currently undergoing, the identical treatment.

Do Support the Patient's Choices

Let her maintain her faith in her doctors. Treatment regimens change rapidly, so what the doctor did for your aunt five years ago might no longer be appropriate. A comment such as, "I've never heard of something like that. Are you sure he knows what he's doing?" may create uncertainty she doesn't need.

Do Be Appropriate

While positive comments are good, don't be such a Pollyanna that you sweep the seriousness of the situation under the rug. "Buck up and don't worry about it" is pretty cold.

Follow her lead. If her doctor has given her a good prognosis and she feels hopeful, by all means reinforce her optimism with comments such as, "I'm sorry you have to deal with this now, but it's wonderful your doctor has such effective treatment available. I'm sure you're going to do well. What can I do to help you?"

If the outlook isn't quite so rosy and she's anxious and frightened, you don't have to be all gloom and doom, but acknowledge her feelings and be as empathetic as possible, with comments such as:

- "I'm so sorry you have to go through this."
- "I'm here to talk if you want to."
- "I've got your back when you need help."

You may have very real concerns that your colleague's illness will result in overwork and stress for you. These are issues to discuss with your supervisor, not with your co-worker. Piling on the guilt about the inconvenience her diagnosis brings to you isn't compassionate. This isn't about you.

Silence Speaks Louder Than Words

At diagnosis, throughout treatment, or when illness becomes chronic, sometimes the most valuable thing you can say is nothing. People who are ill often need a listening ear and a shoulder to cry on.

Many people are uncomfortable when talking with someone who has a serious illness. Because they are afraid, anxious, or ill-prepared, they may deny or trivialize what the person is trying to say. They don't allow any discussion of negative topics, and they may rush to fill silence with inconsequential small talk.

Being permitted to talk freely and frankly, without judgment, is a luxury many people dealing with illness never get. All you need to do to be helpful is to eliminate distractions, sit quietly, make eye contact, ask questions when it's appropriate, and let the person talk until she wants to stop. If she's upset, let her be upset. Hold her hand or give her a hug. That may be all she needs.

"You Look Fine to Me"

Millions of Americans live with *chronic* diseases such as Crohn's disease, fibromyalgia, post-polio syndrome, Lyme disease, irritable bowel syndrome, closed head injuries, and other conditions that may cause severe pain, fatigue, nausea, dizziness, weakness, or confusion. These conditions are called "invisible" diseases because those who have them often look quite well.

Friends and co-workers sometimes can't seem to make sense of the fact that someone can look healthy and feel rotten. Those with chronic conditions often have to deal not only with their illnesses, but also with those who believe the sufferers are lazy and self-indulgent. They are often subjected to advice such as:

def•i•ni•tion

Chronic means a health condition that lasts a long time, sometimes for life. The patient may have remissions and relapses, but the underlying condition doesn't go away.

- "Cheer up. Smile."

- "You'd feel better if you got more exercise."

- "Stop dwelling on every little symptom. You sound like a hypochondriac."

- "If you have to live with it, you may as well develop a positive attitude about it."

- "Just ignore it. You can't let it rule your life."

- "Throw away all those pills and live a healthier lifestyle."

Think about the last time you had a rip-roaring case of the flu or a raging intestinal virus. Now imagine it never went away. Would you want to cheer up, exercise, toss out your pain relievers, and develop a positive attitude? Although some people with chronic illness have only moderate limitations, others are in pain nearly all the time, and just getting through the day is a triumph.

Talking Points

Chronic conditions, rather than acute illnesses, are now the most common medical problems.

If you need to comment at all on a person's health, you might try something that acknowledges the truth of her condition, such as:

- "I'm sorry you don't feel well enough to go out. I'd love to see you. Would you like me to visit or would you rather just rest today?"

- "I'm proud of the way you handle all you have to deal with."

- "I thought I'd bring dinner over tonight. What sounds good?"

Should I Tell the Children?

Absolutely tell them, and do it as soon as you know the whole story. Children, even very young ones, can sense when something is amiss. They notice whispered conversations and worried looks. If you say everything is fine, you are teaching them to disbelieve the evidence of their own eyes and ears. They learn they can't trust you to tell them the truth, and that can have serious consequences down the road. When they know you're lying, what they imagine may be far worse than the facts.

How Much of the Truth Do They Need?

Children should be told as much as their age and maturity will allow them to understand.

Children younger than three probably will not catch on to the ramifications of serious illness, no matter how you present the facts. Kids this age are egocentric, and what's important to them is their own life and activities. Surround them with people who love them; enlist the help of other family members and friends to try to make the transition to necessary new routines as smooth as possible. The children may be frightened and have many questions they can't articulate yet, so be as calm and reassuring as you can be.

Words to the Wise

Children believe in magical thinking: I was mad at Grandma for not letting me have another cookie and now she's sick. It must be my fault. Reassure the child that illness is not his fault, your fault, or the fault of the person who is sick. Help them understand that illness is not a punishment.

Preschoolers and younger elementary school children are always full of questions: Why? Why not? Who? How? Answer every question simply and directly, but without a lot of embellishment or frightening details.

What Words Do You Use?

Tell the children the name of the illness you or another family member has: "Daddy has a disease called cancer. He has to have an operation to take the cancer out of his body, and after that he will take medicine to help him get better. The medicine may make him tired, and sometimes he won't feel well. But Daddy can get better, and you can't catch cancer from him."

If the child visits Daddy in the hospital, there probably will be an avalanche of questions, unless the child is frightened into speechlessness. Answer each question factually, and if you think the child has questions or fears she isn't putting into words, you can say, "You might be wondering why Daddy had that tube in his arm. It's called an IV and it carries water and medicines into his body to make him feel better. It doesn't hurt."

Because young children often don't censor what they say, questions may be blunt. "Is Daddy going to die?" Do not promise a cure. You might answer that the doctors and nurses are doing everything they can to help Daddy get well.

If you know that the course of the disease is inevitably fatal, you can say, "Daddy has a very serious illness, but doctors are making new discoveries every day. We hope Daddy will get better." If you are a religious family, you can pray with your children and encourage them to pray for Daddy when they feel anxious or frightened.

Talking with Older Children

Older children have often heard horror stories about various ailments or may have studied diseases at school. They want and need facts and information. You may give them more details about the illness and the course of treatment than you would share with a younger child. If they ask questions to which you don't have answers, it's perfectly all right to say, "I'm not sure, but I can ask the doctor for you."

Older kids can understand that a disease may be fatal, and careful preparation can make the end a little less traumatic. As one 12-year-old boy told his mother after his grandfather's funeral, "This was so hard, Mom, but it would have been much worse if it had been a shock. Thanks for always telling me the truth."

All children may react to a parent's or other family member's illness in ways that aren't attractive. They may have tantrums, be testy and annoyed all the time, or act out at home or in school. Keep the lines of communication open, talk and listen, and understand that much of their behavior may be a reaction to fear and helplessness.

Be sure to notify the child's teacher and school counselor of the situation at home. Let them know exactly what you've told the child and ask them to keep in touch with you if the child exhibits signs of stress or depression. Children may need a team of adults to help them deal with the emotions surrounding illness, and a sensitive teacher or counselor can be a great sounding board for them.

If you are not up to answering questions on a particular day, don't hesitate to call on family, friends, and professionals you know to be loving and sensitive. Keep the child away from anyone who suggests that illness is God's judgment or the patient's own fault. Many hospitals have excellent support groups for children whose parents have life-threatening illnesses. They are great places for children to verbalize their feelings and discuss issues that are important to them.

The conversations surrounding illness are often very difficult but, like any other conversation, they can be made easier with tact, kindness, and a concern for everyone involved.

The Least You Need to Know

- Millions of American employees contend with serious illnesses every day.

- If you fall victim to a serious illness, it's probably best not to keep it to yourself. Your boss and co-workers can't help you if they don't know you need help.

- When you hear a co-worker is ill, refrain from judging his prior behavior and say only what is empathetic and helpful.

- Chronic illness is often misunderstood because it may not show on the outside.

- Children should be told the truth about serious illness, and the amount and type of information they receive should be based on their age and maturity levels.

Chapter 10

Death and Grief

In This Chapter

- ◆ A death in the family
- ◆ When a co-worker dies
- ◆ Talking about faith and spirituality
- ◆ How to say the right thing
- ◆ Special issues with children

The United States is probably the most death-denying culture on earth. Indeed, to hear Americans talk about it, people don't die at all. They code, expire, pass, pass away, pass on, leave us, go on to larger life, or go to meet God. More crassly, they bite the dust, kick the bucket, croak, or cash in their chips.

Because of amazing steps forward in pharmaceuticals, medical technology, and treatment, we often harbor the belief that all diseases can be cured and life can go on forever. And if we don't die, we never have to talk about it.

Unfortunately, people do die—from old age, illness, accidents, homicide, and suicide. Death visits the very young, the very old, and every age in between. Critical conversations must be held to prepare for death and difficult conversations are part of the process of grief and loss. This chapter contains some ideas for dealing with these often intense interchanges.

What Do I Say Now?

There's no doubt that at some time you will be faced with a death in a co-worker's family. Even if you didn't know the relative or the circumstances of the death, you can't simply ignore the situation and carry on as if nothing has happened. You will need to say something appropriate.

If you don't know the co-worker well, your expression of sympathy can be simple: "I've heard of your loss and I'm so sorry," is never wrong. Neither is, "I'll be thinking of you and your family during this tough time."

In a smaller work setting, where you are close to your co-workers and may have met members of their families, you can venture into more personal comments:

> **Don't Do It!**
>
> In expressing your sympathy, don't make statements such as, "I just don't know what to say. I'm always so awkward in situations like this." Condolences are not about how you feel. Keep the focus on the right person.

- "I'm so sorry to hear about your mom. I had such fun meeting her at the company picnic and hearing about her days as a teacher. She told me about the students she'd taught when she was younger, and I thought it was fascinating."

- "What a shame about your dad. I wish I'd had the opportunity to meet him because you've always made him sound like such an interesting man."

- "I know how much you loved your sister and how much you will miss her. I'm sorry."

These types of expressions allow the survivor to build on what you say, share his memories of the one who has died, or simply acknowledge your kindness if he doesn't feel like talking further.

When a Co-Worker Is Dying

Often, people who discover they have a terminal illness quit work to spend their remaining time with loved ones, doing things they've put off. Some, however, particularly those who love their work and enjoy their colleagues, want to continue on the job as long as they can.

While they're at work, you don't have to tiptoe around or watch every word you say, and it isn't necessary to check on your co-worker every few minutes to make sure she's all right. If she's acting normally, treat her normally.

As time goes on, however, she may want to talk with you about projects she doesn't think she'll get to finish or how to handle specific clients when she's no longer around. Don't tell her, "Now, stop. I won't hear of it. You're going to be with us for a long time." You may think such a positive assertion will make her feel better, but it won't. Tying up loose ends can give her considerable comfort. Not allowing her to tell you what she needs to is frustrating for her and robs her of a sense of completion and peace. It's far better to say, "Of course. Let's get together this afternoon and you can go over everything you want me to know. I'll appreciate your help."

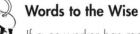

Words to the Wise

If a co-worker has received a terminal diagnosis but is still able and willing to work, don't treat her as someone who is dying, but as someone who is living. Welcome her ideas and contributions just as you did before you learned that her illness will take her life.

There may come a time, however, when the co-worker wants to talk about more than business. She may share how much she's enjoyed working with you or being your friend and want to say some goodbyes while she's still able to do so. Once again, don't hush her up. Let her speak and let her know what she has meant to you, too. Tell her you'll miss her. She may cry and so might you. So what? In this instance, tears in the workplace are appropriate.

When she's no longer able to work, visit her at home, at the hospital, or in a *hospice* facility. Let her lead the conversation. If she wants to talk about work, talk about work. If she wants to giggle about the things you've done together, laugh with her. Laughter is therapeutic for both of you.

Hold her hand if that's what she'd like. People who are dying often mention that people stop touching them. Taking her hand may be a very profound conversation. Reassure her if she's worried about her husband or children. Let her know that her friends and family will rally around them for support and comfort.

def•i•ni•tion

Hospice care is care provided in the home or in a facility for those who have a terminal diagnosis. Services include medical care, pain and symptom management, and supportive psychological and spiritual counseling for the patient and family.

Tread lightly when it comes to religion and spirituality unless she brings up faith issues. If you share the same beliefs, discussing them and perhaps praying together may bring a great measure of serenity, but if your views diverge, this is not the time to argue her into your version of religious faith or practice. Many people who do not attend religious services have profound spiritual lives in which they take comfort. Although you may be concerned about the state of her soul, a deathbed debate is not helpful to anyone.

When the Death Has Passed

Go to the funeral and share your memories, especially the happy ones, with the family. In some offices, co-workers put together a memory book in which each person writes remembrances of the one who has died. Some make a video to do the same thing. No matter how close families may be, they might not have a complete picture of their loved one's work life, and such a book or video can help them understand and see how their relative was viewed in another context.

The Office After the Death

The workplace feels strange after a colleague's death, and many co-workers will grieve for days, weeks, or even months. But work must go on. Tasks may be reassigned and a new person may have to be hired. Although it's natural to feel some resentment toward the person who replaces a much-loved officemate, it's not professional to show it. Avoid saying things such as:

- "You know, Tessa held your job for twelve years and she did it great. You've got some big shoes to fill. Good luck."

- "Why are you filing the orders that way? Tessa had a system all worked out and it worked just fine."

- "Tessa brought homemade muffins every Monday. I bet you don't even bake."

> **Words to the Wise**
>
> After the death of a co-worker, keep your eyes on those who are left. Although shock, grief, and impaired productivity are normal for a while, a colleague who is suffering intensely may need some outside help. If your company has an employee assistance program, you might ask your co-worker if she'd like to take advantage of the service.

That's not fair. It's not the new person's fault that Tessa died, and if she was as wonderful as everyone says, she'd want the team to rally around her successor. Don't criticize the new hire's every move and question her work style. Give her the respect every colleague deserves. Show her the ropes and help her adjust. She won't be Tessa, but she might be terrific.

If you're the person hired to fill a position vacated by a death, be sensitive to the feelings of the remaining staff. If they want to talk about the former co-worker, tell them you'd like to hear about her. Listen and encourage them to share their memories. But don't let those memories dictate how you do your work. You've been hired for your skills and you have the right to do your job your way.

Special Words for Special Circumstances

When confronted with death, people often say remarkably insensitive things. Before you attempt to offer comfort, consider what effect your words may have on those who are grieving. Think before putting your mouth in gear.

Death of a Spouse

On the list of life's stressful events, the death of a spouse ranks #1. If the marriage was long and happy, the surviving spouse may feel as if half of him has been torn away. If the marriage was of short duration, he may feel robbed, cheated, and angry. The proper words to say are things like:

- ◆ "I'm so sorry Jane is gone. It's wonderful that you had such a long and happy marriage, but I know how much you'll miss her. She was a lovely woman."

- ◆ "This is such a sad time. It seems wrong when someone dies so young. Shawna was such a vibrant person, and we're all going to miss her energy and spirit."

Yet rather than hearing comforting words, many survivors report the following kinds of comments as they face life alone:

- ◆ "At least she's not suffering anymore and you can be grateful for that."

It's true she's not suffering, but that's because she's dead—and what he's feeling at the moment probably isn't gratitude.

- ◆ "Jane would want you to marry again, and you've got a lot of money and a beautiful house and a great job. You'll have your pick of women."

Guess what? He's not looking for another wife right now. He's grieving the one he had for 30 years, and all his material goods are no substitute for the love he's lost.

- ◆ "You'll need someone to care for the kids, and there are lots of wonderful single women who'd consider you a catch. I bet you're married within the year."

If he needs a nanny, he can hire one. He doesn't have to marry her. And though it's true that many widowers, especially young ones, do remarry, putting a timetable on grief is crude and heartless.

Recently, a prominent physician died and his widow was faced with the ordeal of greeting hundreds of current and former patients over a three-day marathon of calling hours. Many came from miles away, and she felt it imperative to meet and talk with every one.

"Most people were so kind," she says. "They talked about what he had meant to them and what a difference he had made in their lives. They mentioned his compassion and how devoted he was to them, and all those things were very comforting.

"However, there was one woman who came up to me and went on and on about how she'd have to look for another doctor now and what a hardship that would be for her. She ended up by saying, 'What will I ever do without him?'

"I was exhausted by then, and I'm afraid I snapped. I looked her right in the eye and said, 'I ask myself the same question several times a day. The difference is you can find another doctor. He was my only husband.' And then I turned my back and walked away. I'm sorry I was rude, but can you imagine?"

Death of a Parent

At some time in our lives, most of us lose our parents. The fact that it's a normal part of life doesn't make it any easier. Becoming an orphan at any age is scary; our parents have always been the buffer, and now, suddenly, we're the older generation. Just as you would when comforting a spouse, mention your sorrow for those who are left. If you knew the parent, it's nice to comment on some aspect of his personality that was particularly outstanding or on a pleasant memory.

Death of a Child

Parents can experience no pain more intense than the loss of a child, and siblings are bereft, too. In frontier days, children died frequently from epidemics or accidents, and parents had big families because they expected that at least one of their children would not survive to adulthood. Today, with vaccinations, bike helmets, car seats, and every kind of safety device, we expect children to outlive their parents. Anything else feels like a violation of the natural order.

What parents need most in this circumstance is tender care, love, and to be surrounded by those who knew and loved the child. What's appropriate is something like the following:

♦ "My heart is breaking for you."

♦ "He was a beautiful child, and his time here was far too short."

♦ "We will miss her wonderful smile and her laughter."

Absolutely stay away from such sentiments as, "It was God's will," or "Everything happens for a reason."

First of all, this statement seeks to impose your spiritual understanding on parents at the worst moment of their lives. When they are ready (if ever) to place the death in a spiritual context, they'll do it, but right now the pain may be too fresh and raw.

In addition, rather than providing comfort, these sentiments invite parental anger and argument. What kind of God wills the death of a beautiful child who is the center of her parents' life? And what possible reason could there be for such grief and sorrow? If you want to bring a spiritual dimension to your condolences, it's enough to say you'll be praying for the child and her family.

Don't tell parents who have other children that they should be grateful for them. After a death, the other children are usually the only reason the bereaved parents even get up in the morning. They are grateful for them, but no matter how much they adore the remaining siblings, there's still an empty place in the family.

If the child who died was an only child, don't tell the parents they can have another. Maybe they can; maybe they can't, and children aren't interchangeable parts. One can never fill the void left by the death of the other and shouldn't be expected to. This is probably the most hurtful, inconsiderate thing you can say to grieving parents.

Words to the Wise

Remember that a miscarriage is the death of a much-anticipated child. The parents have thought about nurseries and names and may have shared the good news with family and friends. Don't say, "A miscarriage means there was something wrong with the baby." That's not always the case, and it doesn't make the parents any less sad.

When you are speaking to the siblings of the child who has died, acknowledge their pain and don't tell them they must be strong. That's not true. They're children, and they are frightened, worried, anxious, and confused. Could you be strong in those circumstances?

When Death Was Accidental

Accidental deaths are especially shocking for survivors. Perhaps they'd just had a disagreement with the deceased and their last words were harsh. And even if the relationship was solid and their memories are good, they didn't get to say good-bye, and that's a pain that may never heal.

Sometimes the survivors are angry, both at those who caused the death (such as a drunk driver) or even at the person who died (for cleaning the second-floor gutters on a rickety old ladder). They also may feel angry at themselves for not preventing the accident. In order not to feel so much anger, they may tamp down all their feelings and sink into depression.

> **Talking Points**
>
> The five leading causes of accidental death include motor vehicle accidents, falls, drowning, poisoning, and fire.

When you're speaking with the family, then, don't cause further pain by judging either the deceased or the family. It's far better to say, "What a tragedy. I'm terribly sorry," than to say, "Whatever possessed him to get into a car with someone who was so drunk? He should have taken the keys and called a cab." Of course he should have, but what good does it do to say that now?

When the Death Was a Suicide

Death by suicide leaves us at a loss as to what to say, and out of all the things we may choose, only a few are helpful. There is no need at all to mention the manner of death to the survivors, and if you don't know how their family member killed himself, you shouldn't ask. You needn't inquire into why they think he did it. He's gone. That's all you need to know. Tell the survivors how sorry you are. Share your pleasant memories of their loved one. Let them talk while you listen. Do not say:

- ◆ "Suicide is so selfish. They never think about those they leave behind. I don't know how you can forgive him for this." Most people who commit suicide are in such despair they can think of no other way out. Your assessment of the decision doesn't help anyone, so keep it to yourself.

♦ "He must have been insane. No one in his right mind would have done this." Telling survivors their relative was crazy isn't comforting. It may be what you believe, but you may not be right.

♦ "Most people who are going to commit suicide give some kinds of clues. Could you have missed something?" Don't even think about saying something like this. The family member is dead, and now it's the survivor's fault? If she isn't grief-stricken enough, now she gets to feel guilty, too.

♦ "Suicide is a sin." So is such an unfeeling, judgmental statement at a time of unspeakable grief.

> **Talking Points**
>
> Three times as many women as men attempt to take their lives, but four times as many men as women complete the act.

A survivor of suicide says, "The most helpful thing anyone said to me was, 'This is not your fault, and there was nothing you could have done to prevent it.' When I was blaming myself, I remembered that."

Speak Their Names

What survivors of any death need most is for their loved ones to be remembered, and yet once the funeral ceremonies are over, many people never mention the deceased again.

"I don't understand it," says the mother of a young man who took his life. "It's like he never existed. I think people are afraid that if they bring up his name and talk about him, it will somehow make me feel worse. What they don't understand is that I *can't* feel worse. Talking about him makes me feel better. I *want* to talk about him. Not just about his death, but about his life and what he meant to me."

To help any bereaved person, remember the person who died. If you know the deceased's birthday or their wedding anniversary, call or drop in and say, "I'm thinking about you today. And about Jack (or Lindsay)." Make a similar call on the anniversary of the death. As one man remembers, "My father was ill for a long time and then he died. A year later, a friend came over, hugged me, and said, 'How's it going for you today?' I was glad someone remembered. I talked about Dad a little bit and felt much better. That one person really lifted the burden of the day."

In the United States, we don't give people much time to grieve. They might get three days' bereavement leave and then be expected to hit the ground running at work.

We ask people to "get over it" quickly, not because it's best for them, but because it's more comfortable for us. A call, e-mail, or visit a few months after the death acknowledges the reality that people don't recover from a death in the blink of an eye, and that they are remembered and cared for.

Talking with Children About Death

Little children don't understand the permanence of death; they may ask the same questions over and over: "When is Mommy coming home?" "Why can't Grandpa come to my birthday party?" Even if the questions are very difficult for you to hear, try not to be impatient. Answer as simply as possible with the physical facts. "When a person dies, her body doesn't work any more. Her heart doesn't beat. Her lungs don't breathe. And her body doesn't see or hear or move."

Preschoolers often have very practical concerns. Who will get my lunch? Who will take me to school? Who will tell me a bedtime story? Explain that all those important tasks will be taken care of. Daddy will tell your bedtime story. Mrs. Johnson will take you to school, and the babysitter will fix your lunch. Routine is comforting to a child who will eventually confront the reality that a member of the family is missing and will not come back.

Talking with Older Children About Death

Older children, who have experienced the death of a pet or observed dead animals by the road, have more realistic notions about what death is, but they may still have questions about why someone died. Was the person bad? Did he do something wrong? Isn't death creepy?

Once again, it's best to lead with the facts. Everything dies, and it's not creepy. It's just a fact of life. Most people die from illness, old age, or accident, so you can say, "Grandma had a disease, and eventually there was nothing the doctors could do. Her body just wasn't strong enough to fight off her illness, and she died. We'll all miss her very much." Emphasize that Grandma's illness was very serious so the child won't believe that a cold or stomach virus will be fatal. You don't want her to be frightened every time someone in the family comes down with an inconsequential bug.

It's perfectly all right to cry in front of your child when discussing the death of a loved one. Children need to know that their parents are people, too, and that the end of life is sad.

Things Never, Never, Never to Say to a Child

◆ "Grandma went to sleep." The child may very well equate sleep with death and be afraid to go to bed or take a nap, and who can blame him? Grandma went to sleep and look what happened to her.

◆ "Grandpa went away." Now, there's a way to make a child nervous every time someone leaves the house. Will Mommy come home from the office? Will my brother come back from playing down the street? Did I do something bad that made Grandpa so mad he left? The idea is to reassure the child, not make him even more uncertain.

◆ "Mommy was such a good person, God took her to be with him." There are so many things wrong with this statement that it's hard to know where to begin. First of all, the child may reason that if God takes good people, she'd better misbehave so she gets to stay behind with Daddy and her brothers and sisters. Or alternatively, if she's very, very good, God might take her to visit Mommy.

A third possibility is that she'll conclude God is nasty to little girls, personally snatching their mothers away from them just because he can. None of these is a good outcome, so it's best not to plant the idea that goodness or lack of it has anything to do with death.

◆ "Now that Daddy's gone, you need to be the man of the family and take care of your mother." What a terrifying burden to place on a child! Daddy mowed the lawn and fixed the plumbing and sometimes he cooked the dinner. He went to work every day and earned money to pay bills. The child doesn't know how to do any of those things, and he may panic at the thought that he's now to assume these chores. In fact, the child's job is to go to school, do appropriate home chores, play with his friends, and grow up. It is the surviving parent's job to be the adult and care for the child.

The Least You Need to Know

◆ A co-worker's death can have profound effects on workplace relationships.

◆ Many people with life-threatening or chronic illness show up for work every day and are productive, useful workers.

- The main point of condolences is to comfort those who are bereaved, not to share your opinions or judgments about any aspect of the situation.

- Often the most useful thing you can do is listen.

- Children require special handling to help them cope with death.

Chapter 11

Delivering Bad News at Work

In This Chapter

- ◆ Is it bad news or is it just change?
- ◆ Eight steps to sharing bad news
- ◆ Telling the boss

Nobody likes to hear bad news, and too often recipients shoot the messenger. Surely being the bearer of bad tidings qualifies as a difficult conversation. In this chapter, you'll learn some ways to get the job done with the least amount of pain for everyone.

Is the News Really Bad?

Sometimes news is just news. It's factual, neutral information. But people generally perceive news as bad if it requires them to change some aspect of their life or work. They may become:

- ◆ Negative
- ◆ Resistant
- ◆ Apprehensive
- ◆ Angry
- ◆ Sad
- ◆ Resentful

These emotions are most prevalent if those involved have had no say in the decision-making process that has resulted in the change now facing them. They feel controlled, manipulated, and bitter. Some of the types of issues that might set off an emotional reaction include:

- A new reporting relationship

- A change in job responsibilities

- A consolidation or separation of departments

- Installation of new hardware or software

While all of these situations eventually may have positive consequences, at the moment they are introduced they can seem difficult or frightening. Managing the response to change is crucial to the successful implementation of the new realities. Whole companies have grown up around the concept of *change management*.

def•i•ni•tion

Change management means to direct organizational transformation in a way that minimizes resistance to change and to implement all aspects of the transition from one process to another.

Words to the Wise

When delivering bad news, do it eye to eye. Sit down with the other person. Don't stand over him or position yourself near the door. You want to be perceived as a caring colleague, not as someone who's ready to cut and run the moment the news is out of your mouth.

You can help defuse anxiety by listening fully to others' concerns and asking them for suggestions on how the change might be instituted with the least amount of disruption. Those who are most affected by a change often have valuable insights into issues others might not have considered. If you harness the cooperation of frontline personnel, they can help make the change go smoothly. If you ignore their wisdom, you are virtually guaranteed the opposite result.

Emphasize the positive aspects of the change, but be truthful. For example, "When we all get used to the new system, you'll be surprised at how it streamlines daily operations. The amount of data it generates is amazing and will help us be much more efficient. I think you'll be very happy with it. But it's a steep learning curve. I've seen it and used it and know you all will be able to master it, but it will take some time. I want you to know you can come to me any time you don't understand something. I'll be glad to help you out."

Keep the end result in the forefront of everyone's mind. As the change is taking place, it's your job to continue articulating the reasons for the change and the benefits to be gained.

When the News Really Is Bad

Life's only constant is change, and somewhere in America, people are receiving bad news every day. Companies close, throwing a small community into financial disarray. Operations are altered and entire divisions are moved overseas, costing hundreds of jobs at once. A beloved boss resigns to take a position in another state. A choice must be made to close a department or ask everyone who works there to take a 10 percent reduction in pay. Benefits are slashed. Pensions are abandoned. It's a nasty litany of harsh truths.

If you're the person who must deliver this life-changing news, the message must be clear, unequivocal, timely, and as compassionate as possible.

Rehearse

Bad news can alter the course of someone's career or life, so you can't be cavalier and offhand. Write down key points and practice what you have to say a couple of times. You don't want your presentation to sound canned, but you want to make sure you're accurate, candid, and compassionate. Think about what reactions you're likely to face and what you might say in response.

Spread the Word Quickly

In businesses large and small, there's little news that's really news. Rumors leak out in dribs and drabs, and once they hit the grapevine, they take on a life of their own. And as the story passes from person to person, it's often distorted, embellished, or transformed into something that has little relation to the facts. Everyone who hears it gets upset and you're faced with heavy damage control. The cure for the "grapevine effect" is accurate information as quickly as possible.

> **Talking Points**
>
> In 1982, seven people died after taking Extra-Strength Tylenol that had been laced with cyanide after the product left the factory. Johnson & Johnson's immediate response to the crisis and the company's candor are still the benchmarks by which "bad news" communications are judged.

Several years ago, a hospital was the subject of a negative news story. One minor point of the story was true; the rest was pure fabrication on the part of a disgruntled employee who had recently been fired. Only a few employees had seen the story on television, but those who did were full of questions. They were shocked and confused and didn't know how to respond to outsiders.

Upper management made the decision to deal with the issue head on. They obtained a copy of the news story from a video clip service and called several meetings during the day, evening, and night shifts so employees could view the clip. Employees also were given the facts to refute all the allegations. They were provided with information about the single story point that was accurate and how that situation would be handled. Management representatives answered every question employees raised during the meetings.

Within 24 hours, the entire staff knew everything there was to know and they were highly motivated to share the truth with anyone who asked. A story that could have had lasting repercussions instead served as a rallying point. There was no drop in productivity and no morale problem. Patient care continued as before and the media dropped the story entirely. The truth will set you free.

Be Clear

Today's business climate encourages the use of double speak and meaningless euphemisms. If you have to fire someone, "We have to let you go," is unambiguous. The employee is sure of what you mean. If you yammer on about involuntary attrition, deselection, negative retention, growing down the workforce surplus, or reducing the census, however, she may be very confused. Is she fired or not? Tell her what she needs to know. It's cruel to keep her guessing because you can't find it in you to spit out a simple declarative sentence.

Often the lack of clarity is an attempt to soften the blow, and occasionally a supervisor will resort to buzzwords because he's afraid of the employee's reaction. In fact, dancing around the issue just prolongs the agony and may result in a reaction far more negative than it would have if you'd been clear and concise in the first place.

Get to the Point

Much of the bad news that rains down falls on individual people, and it requires supervisors and managers to deal with situations one to one.

If you have unpleasant facts to deliver, don't waste time with idle chit chat and filler. Get to the bad news right away. When an employee is called to a supervisor's office, he's probably nervous, so you may as well end the suspense quickly, with words such as:

- ◆ "Shirley, I'm sorry to tell you that the copy for the annual report is unsatisfactory and you'll have to redo it by Friday."

- ◆ "Mike, your behavior at the employee recognition event reflected badly not only on you, but also on me and the department. Since this is not the first time you have exhibited inappropriate behavior, I'm filing a record of disciplinary action and placing you on probation."

- ◆ "Whitney, I'm afraid your request to go to part-time has been denied."

Stick to the Facts

Before you speak with your employee, marshal your facts. What were the business reasons for denying Whitney's request? What, specifically, was wrong with the annual report copy? Shirley can't fix it if you don't tell her what needs to be redone. What behavior was so egregious it requires a disciplinary action? Your employees will surely question you, so have your answers at the ready.

Be honest. If irrevocable decisions have been made, don't hold out hope that things might change. Don't be so sympathetic that you soften the message; get the person ready to face reality.

> **Don't Do It!**
> Unless there's a compelling reason, don't break bad news to employees on Friday. There's no sense in forcing them to fret and stew for 48 hours and arrive at work on Monday in a foul humor.

Watch Out for Strong Reactions

No one wants to hear that her department is being abolished or she has to make a choice between staying at her current job at a greatly reduced salary or relocating with her three children to East Overshoe, Nebraska, where she knows no one. Typical reactions include denial, and expressions of anger and frustration:

- ◆ "I've given ten years of my life to this company and you pull the rug out from under me like this?"

- ◆ "I'm sixty-four! Where am I supposed to find a job at my age?"

◆ "I know you have a responsibility to the shareholders, but what about your responsibility to your employees? Shareholders may own the company, but we *are* the company."

◆ "I don't believe it. I won't believe it. This isn't happening!"

Others may weep, yell, threaten suit, or swear at you. When they're losing their job anyway, they might not see the harm in burning a bridge.

Don't mirror the other's emotions. Remain calm. Sit quietly and do nothing unless you are in danger of bodily harm (and if you suspect you will be, make sure security is in the room or close by to intervene). Allow the other person to vent until she runs down. You'll make things worse by telling her to get a grip on herself.

> **Talking Points**
>
> New studies indicate that e-mail may be an effective tool for delivering bad news. It is an easy way to impart factual information accurately, and it reduces misunderstandings that might result from a badly structured face-to-face meeting. But don't use it to fire someone.

If the person appears to be particularly shocked or confused, assure yourself that the message has gotten through by asking a question or two:

◆ "Have I been clear in what I've said?"

◆ "You look very surprised at this news. Is there anything I can clarify for you?"

◆ "Do you have any questions for me at this point?"

Be Empathetic

It's not fair that you have to take the heat for the bad news, but when you're the only other person in the room, you're the only punching bag available. Even though you're uncomfortable and edgy yourself, do your best to show empathy and compassion. You needn't apologize for the decision that's been made nor should you waste your time trying to justify it, but you can soften the blow with such phrases as:

◆ "I know this is hard to hear."

◆ "I feel so bad about having to share this news."

◆ "It's a sad time."

◆ "I wish it weren't true, too."

When and if it's appropriate, point the employee to sources of help: unemployment compensation, outplacement assistance, or other resources.

End on an Upbeat Note

Sometimes there's just no way to put a good face on the news, and if you try, you can sound insincere and cold. If there's a promising nugget anywhere, promoting a positive attitude can sometimes change the atmosphere from gloom and doom to hope and possibility. You might say:

- ◆ "I know this merger is not what you expected and you were hoping for a promotion soon, but I'm sure that once the dust settles, your skills will position you for even greater responsibility."

- ◆ "Having your idea rejected was a blow, I'm sure, but the president took the time to write you a letter with suggestions on how to improve on the concept. He wouldn't have done that if he didn't think it had potential. Why don't you make the changes and try again?"

The reciprocal of this advice works, too. If you're the person who's been hit with bad news, give yourself time to hear, understand, and process what you've been told. Stay in the moment as much as possible. Remember that none of the consequences that might flood your mind have happened yet and it's possible they never will.

Then be attentive to the words you're saying to yourself. If you hear yourself saying that this is the worst thing that can possibly happen to you, it will be. But if you are able to tell yourself that there are two sides to everything and that maybe this is an opportunity in disguise, you will handle the news better. Sometimes it's a stretch to find anything positive or advantageous, but if you're able to, you'll right yourself much faster.

A former corporate vice president says, "I became very ill, and I kept trying to work. Finally my doctor said I had to quit or die. Although neither option was very attractive, dying was by far the less appealing option, so I quit a job I loved and opened a small consulting firm that allowed me to set my own hours and rest when I had to.

"As I recovered, I saw that the hiatus I had been forced into was the best thing that ever happened to me. I learned some new skills, and in two years, when I returned to corporate life, it was in an entirely different job. I went from finance to human resources, and I find it very satisfying. I learned from the experience that all but the most terrifying news—like a death in the family or some other tragedy—might have an upside and rather than worry unnecessarily, it's good to search for what that upside might be. This attitude helps me when I have to deliver bad news to an employee. I'm able to help them see possibilities."

Delivering Up: Telling the Boss Bad News

Your boss trumpets her open door policy, but you've observed that the door swings the other way if news isn't favorable. Now you have a dilemma. How do you deliver bad news and not have your head chopped off?

Qualify the News

Does what you're about to tell the boss rise to the level of something she needs to know about? The boss's responsibilities are to the entire department or company. Don't run to her with every petty squabble you have with a co-worker under the guise that it's interfering with productivity. Solve minor problems at a lower level, leaving the boss free to concentrate on issues that affect everyone.

Get There First

When you've made an error or your department hasn't met its goals, the boss needs to hear it directly from you, not from some third party whose primary interest is in taking over your job. And don't try to wiggle out with an e-mail. Critical messages demand face time. Do consider your boss's prime time. If he's a morning person, talk with him then. If he's better after lunch, schedule an afternoon meeting.

Prepare to Discuss the Details

Have facts, figures, and reasons (not excuses) prepared. "How could you have done this?" is one of the big questions you'll be facing. Be ready to explain fully. Lay out the whole situation and back yourself up with data. Don't give your best guess about what happened, instead be as accurate and precise as you can.

Take Responsibility

If the buck stops with you, it doesn't matter what happened down the chain.

A marketing director spent $17,000 printing a glossy brochure for a brand-new product offering. Right in the middle of the brochure was a typo set in a huge, brightly colored font. To her, it stood out like a beacon. Nonetheless, although every member of the communications staff had proofread the piece, no one else noticed the mistake.

There was a choice to be made in telling the boss about this situation: blame the employees or take the heat. The director chose the latter, saying, "I'm really sorry about this. This was on my watch. No one in the department caught the mistake, but I should have been more active in overseeing the project. I'm as responsible as anyone else."

The boss was stunned. He said, "Do you know how long it's been since someone stepped up and held himself accountable? Everyone seems to want to point the finger at someone else. What do you think we should do now?"

Certainly, this boss's reaction is not the norm. Most bosses are going to be angry, and you may be in for a rough half-hour or more. Although most supervisors aren't screamers, some are. If you know your boss is volatile, you know how to handle it. While he's hollering, remember that a mistake, even a serious one, doesn't make you a bad person. It makes you human.

 Words to the Wise

Sometimes bad news is good, and bosses should be attentive to those who bring them legitimate concerns about products or services. Naysayers often have important messages.

If the screamfest is protracted and degenerates into a personal attack, you have some options. You can sit still and take it, you can return the invective in kind and risk being fired, or you can get up and say, "I'm terribly sorry for this error, and I'd like to discuss how we might rectify it. I have some ideas in mind, but perhaps I should share them at a later time."

That's what's called playing guts ball, but it might turn down the volume. A mistake is no excuse for abuse, and if abuse is a feature of the boss's style, you might think long and hard about looking for someplace else to work.

Have a Plan

Before you deliver your bad news, think about ways to improve the situation. In the case above, the marketing director said, "I think I'd like to send the brochure to our ad agency with the request that they look for a mistake. I won't tell them what or where it is, but I will let them know there's a big error. If they have to hunt for it or think it's not a concern, maybe we can go ahead. It's contrary to what I'd normally do, but let's see if we can avoid the expense of reprinting."

It worked. The agency never found the error and the brochure went out, mistake and all. Beyond that, it was part of the entry for a national marketing award—and it won.

Not every mistake will have such a happy ending, but by being active in seeking solutions, you may be able to snatch victory from the jaws of defeat. Decide in advance what you might do to prevent the problem from occurring again, and make your solution part of your presentation.

Giving Bad News to a Group

As a rule, you'll break bad news to only one person at a time. There are occasions, however, when you'll need to inform a whole group about a negative event: the budget for their project has been eliminated, they missed their sales targets by a mile, or the marketing plan they designed didn't deliver the expected results.

If you share this news with one person at a time, by the time you get to the last employee on the list, the information already will have dribbled out, probably inaccurately. You need to include the entire group immediately.

Words to the Wise

When you're in charge of delivering bad news, such as a mass layoff, take care of yourself. Remember that you are only doing your job. You are not the problem nor did you cause the problem. It's easy to get caught up in emotionalism, but that's not helpful to anyone, including you.

Keep It Private

When there's been a terrible mistake, invite those who were involved in making it, not those who were affected by it. If you have to take people to the woodshed, they don't need onlookers.

Keep It Factual

Explain all the facts surrounding the unpleasant tidbit. Visual aids are sometimes helpful for those who learn best through their eyes, but don't get so involved in creating a slide show that you forget your message.

Keep It Impersonal

Separate what was done from who did it. A group meeting is no place to point fingers at individuals. If you need to deal with specific people, take them aside privately.

Keep It Positive (If You Can)

Maybe the marketing plan didn't deliver against its targets, but did anything positive come out of this embarrassing fiasco? Did you find out which groups were particularly resistant to the introduction of a new product? Which groups liked it? Was it the product itself people disliked or was it a matter of timing or message? What can be done to turn this failure into a win the next time?

Being positive is a fine characteristic, but if you have to announce that every person in the room will be out of a job in 30 days, don't try to put lipstick on a pig. This is just plain bad news and a rah-rah attitude is demeaning to those who are learning about their fate.

The Least You Need to Know

- ◆ Most change is perceived as bad news if those who hear it have not been involved in the decision.

- ◆ Delaying or prolonging bad news is more painful than delivering it quickly.

- ◆ Remember that you are not the cause of the bad news; you are only the carrier of the message.

- ◆ Be honest, factual, compassionate, and as positive as possible when the news is bad.

Part 4

Conversation and Productivity

Productivity is a critical measure of success, and positive communication makes workplaces, from factory floors to the executive suite, more productive. Difficult conversations, however, can hamper productivity and slow progress to a crawl.

And productivity isn't just a workplace issue. Some of the same problems may crop up in your personal life, as you deal with discipline, burnout, stress, and other problems at home.

This extensive part helps you handle the situations that can have a negative impact on productivity, from rudeness and gossip to issues surrounding customer service to bosses and co-workers from hell to substance abuse both on and off the job.

"Your job performance has been superb,
but there's been some talk around the office."

Chapter 12

How Rude!

In This Chapter

- The reasons for rudeness
- What's rude
- When you're unintentionally rude
- Dealing with rude co-workers
- It starts at the top

Look at any study of civility and courtesy for the last five years, and you'll find that most Americans believe rudeness has increased, both in the workplace and in the world at large. Rudeness and discourtesy can turn any conversation from pleasant to difficult, because it's not always what we say that makes a conversation difficult. It's often the way we say it.

In this chapter, you'll learn why rudeness is such a feature of daily life, how it affects productivity, what it costs, and how to confront it.

The Roots of Rudeness

On the way to work, you inadvertently cut someone off in traffic; he tailgates you for the next 10 miles, screaming and making obscene gestures. When you arrive at your office, your co-worker doesn't bother to respond

def•i•ni•tion

Civility is often defined as manners, but it's much more than formal etiquette. To be civil is to show respect and regard for the rights and feelings of others.

to your morning greeting. You go to a meeting and your boss singles you out for discipline in front of everyone. You're looking forward to lunch with a friend, but during the meal, she takes three cell phone calls and ignores you.

And that's just the morning. The afternoon doesn't get much better, and after work you slink home, defeated, deflated, and angry. Welcome to Rude New World.

According to *Aggravating Circumstances: A Status Report on Rudeness in America*, 88 percent of those surveyed witness rude behavior sometimes or often, 62 percent said rudeness and disrespect bother them—and 41 percent admitted engaging in the behavior.

Why is common courtesy no longer common? When did *civility* disappear—and why?

Overwork

Lean and mean (with emphasis on the mean) organizations try to squeeze every last drop of productivity out of every employee. Even part-time employees now find themselves working as much as 40 hours a week just to keep up with daily tasks. "Do more with less" means that fewer and fewer people are saddled with more and more work.

Days are routinely 12 hours long—or more—and instant availability by cell phone, PDA, and e-mail means that people often are unable to disconnect from work even when they're at home or on vacation. Too much too do. Too little time. Not enough sleep. When physical demands overwhelm us, we often become curt, distracted, and unpleasant. In short, rude.

Stress

Balancing work and family obligations is, for many working parents, a primary stressor. They often feel considerable guilt because they are torn between two conflicting priorities: their family's emotional needs and the work that supports the family's physical needs.

Constant change—mergers, acquisitions, restructuring—also engenders stress. In fact, a lack of control is one of the primary causes of stress in the American workplace. When people are unsure of what they'll have to adjust to tomorrow, they are uncertain and fearful, which can make them aggressive. If every officemate is a potential adversary in the fight to keep a job, nastiness is a common result.

Overcrowding

Many of us live in large cities, and cities often mean traffic congestion, long lines, pushing and shoving to enter and exit public transportation, and jostling and buffeting on the streets. "In your face" is often literal as people are crowded together in settings as disparate as airports and restaurants. Because most of us try to protect a small zone of personal space, these constant intrusions can make us feel uneasy and overly annoyed. We may "go off," reacting to even the most innocent remark or inadvertent bump with animosity.

> **Talking Points**
>
> Seventy-nine percent of Americans say that rudeness is a serious problem, and sixty-one percent say the problem has worsened in the last few years. (Source: *Aggravating Circumstances: A Status Report on Rudeness in America*)

Anonymity

Technology has given us a variety of ways to interact with people we know and those we don't. Although these interchanges with unknown people can be very productive, hiding behind a user name may encourage us to say things we might not if we were face to face with the other person. And we might regret it later.

Tunnel Vision

Most of us grew up believing that you should "do your own thing." In certain circumstances, doing your own thing is good advice, but it's rotten counsel if it means that you do whatever you feel like doing whenever you feel like doing it without regard for the effects of your actions on others. Too many of us have blinders on; we focus on what we want to the exclusion of others' rights to be treated with courtesy and respect. That's the definition—and height—of rudeness.

Media Representations

Do the media reflect the culture or create it? Whatever view you espouse, there's no doubt that rudeness is a staple of television programming. Talk shows feature participants showering one another with language so vile that only a few words can be aired. Entertainment programs are filled with put-down humor that insults and degrades—and the victim is usually a family member or co-worker. Even political debates end up as shouting matches in which everyone talks, no one listens, and discourtesy is nonpartisan. If impressionable people, especially young adults, take their cues from these programs, why is anyone mystified by the growth of rudeness in society as a whole?

The Face of Rudeness at Work

Overcrowded, overstressed, and overworked, a vast majority of Americans believe that they have been subjected to rudeness or outright bullying in the workplace. They say they have been:

◆ Belittled, demeaned, or reprimanded in front of workmates

◆ Insulted or yelled at by co-workers or supervisors

◆ Gossiped about

◆ Interrupted and/or disregarded when trying to make a point

◆ Given dirty looks or other signs of disrespect

Rudeness cuts across all segments of the workplace: peer to peer and manager to employee. Peer rudeness, while not much fun, usually doesn't result in long-term damage, but employees who confront their bosses about rudeness may face reprisals: being shut out of important discussion or decisions, denial of promotions, backbiting, slurs, or excessive discipline.

The Cost of Rudeness

You may believe that rudeness, though unpleasant, is largely a personal issue. It isn't. It's a serious productivity problem that costs American business millions of dollars every year. Employees who are subjected to continual rudeness, especially at the hands of their managers, become less committed to their jobs and their employers. In a comprehensive multi-year study, Christine Pearson, Ph.D., found that those who are subjected to rudeness …

◆ Waste company time worrying about how they are treated and trying to keep their distance from the person who's causing them trouble.

◆ Waste even more time by plotting how to get back at the person who has hurt them or by filing a series of grievances.

◆ Take more actual sick days related to stress ailments and call in sick when they aren't.

◆ Arrive late and leave early.

◆ Seek revenge by deliberately producing below their capabilities.

◆ Resign.

The cost in loss of productivity, turnover, and constantly retraining new employees is very high. Also businesses may face lawsuits if employees can prove that they were bullied so severely it caused physical or psychological problems. Even if the case is ultimately decided in favor of the company, the time and money required to defend the lawsuit may be burdensome. And if the employee wins, the financial drain can be substantial.

Talking Points
Some experts believe that casual dress policies have contributed to rudeness. They cite studies that show that a relaxed attitude toward dress is mirrored by a relaxed attitude toward manners.

In addition, business may dry up and blow away when customers are treated rudely or witness discourtesy between employees. Fully 60 to 70 percent of customers who are treated with disrespect vote with their feet by taking their business somewhere else. It's much cheaper to retain and expand current business than it is to create new business relationships, so losing several customers in a short time may cost a business more than it can afford.

Inadvertent Rudeness

In a survey conducted at the University of North Carolina, 89 percent of respondents said they believed rudeness of many types existed in the workplace. But only 1 percent of the same group said they ever indulged in rude behavior themselves.

Maybe they're right. Maybe they never scream or interrupt or are intentionally unkind. Other forms of rudeness, however, have become such a part of the business culture that those who indulge in them might not even consider them rude. But they are.

Do you ever do any of the following:

- Neglect to return phone calls?

- Notify only the successful candidate for a job and ignore the others who have interviewed?

- Have your assistant place a call and ask the other person to hold until you get on the phone?

- Swear in the office?

- Use a client or caller's first name before you have permission to do so?

- Call others by their first names while retaining your own title?

- Introduce people only by first name?

- Neglect to identify yourself when calling someone else?

- Forget to use "please" and "thank you"?

- Continue to work on papers or at your computer when someone is speaking to you?

Let's examine why these "business rude" behaviors are upsetting to people.

Neglecting to Return Phone Calls

You don't have to respond to unsolicited sales calls or cold-calling job seekers, but a business-related phone call should be returned promptly. Don't ever tell someone, "I'll call you back Thursday" and then not make the call. Even if you consider it a low-priority call, the other person may not, and to keep someone waiting all day for a call that never comes is inconsiderate.

The same goes for e-mail. If you're working with someone and he asks for information or an update, it's rude not to respond either with a return e-mail or a phone call.

Neglecting to Notify All Job Candidates

You needn't respond to every unsolicited resumé you receive (although it's polite to send a preprinted postcard or automatic e-mail that lets the job seeker know her materials went to the right place), but interviewees are in a different category. A job is not a small thing, and those you've interviewed may be on pins and needles, hoping they'll be selected.

Remember that you're dealing with people's lives. Have the kindness to notify all those who are waiting for word, not just the lucky person who got the job. To ignore the others tells them that they aren't important enough to bother with—and there's nothing more discourteous or disheartening than that.

Keeping People on Hold

How rude is this? Very. It's a clear signal to the person on the other end of the call that your time is much more valuable than his. It's a crude and boorish way of establishing a superior position. Many business leaders place their own calls. You can too.

Swearing

As someone who sometimes talks like a pirate, I admit that I was surprised when my assistant asked me to stop. Although I never directed my somewhat colorful language specifically at her, she objected to having to listen to it at all. I respected her for having the courage to tell me, and I toned it down.

With the "relaxed" language so prevalent in the rest of the culture, you might not be aware that impolite language is still offensive to many people. In fact, in some polls it tops the list of negative workplace behavior. Put a muzzle on it.

Addressing Others Improperly

You may use first names if you are peers, but if your clients or customers are older than you are or come from a culture in which formality is valued, ask if you may use their first names. And if you're using the other person's first name, don't flaunt your own title. "Susan, this is Dr. Smith calling," is pretty self-important. "Tom Smith" works just as well and isn't so condescending.

Introducing Others Improperly

A gracious introduction includes both first and last names and perhaps some identifying information about both people. In a business setting, the subordinate is introduced to the person higher in rank. "Ms. Lotsabucks, this is my administrative assistant, Sharon North. Sharon, this is Ms. Lotsabucks, the CFO. Sharon is new to my department, but she used to work for Mr. Bluster at Amalgamated Widget."

Neglecting to Identify Yourself on the Phone

Don't make the other person indulge in a guessing game about who's on the phone. Here is a typical frustrating example:

"Good morning. Quality Communications; this is Twila Tessmacher."

"Is Lex there?"

"May I ask who's calling?"

"Frank."

"Frank who?"

"Frank N. Stein."

"From?"

"Cleveland."

"Sir, may I have the name of the company?"

"Transylvania Trinkets."

That's a big waste of time, to say nothing about how vexing the cat and mouse game may be to both of you. The proper way to introduce yourself on the phone is to get all the pertinent information on the table right away. Once the person has announced herself, you respond, "Good morning, Ms. Tessmacher. This is Lois Lane at the *Daily Planet*. May I please speak with Lex Luthor?"

Forgetting to Use Your Manners

Remember when your parents called "please" and "thank you" the magic words? They still are. Use them liberally. "Get me the Robinson Report" doesn't sound nearly as pleasant as, "Chris, will you bring me the Robinson Report, please?" And when Sharon gives it to you, be sure to thank her. Yes, she's just doing her job, but courtesy is never wrong, and it's often the small things that employees appreciate most. Don't forget, an appreciative employee is one who stays on the job—and that saves both time and money.

Working While Others Are Speaking to You

If you're working and you receive a phone call or someone comes to your office door, have the courtesy to acknowledge her presence; stop what you're doing and give the

person your attention. If you can't—if you're
on deadline or in the midst of a project that
requires your full concentration—explain that
you're sorry, but you'll have to ask her to call
you back or drop in later. Don't just keep on
working as if she wasn't standing in front of
you. That's rude.

> **Talking Points**
>
> Although many Americans con-
> sider workplace incivility a greater
> problem than violence at work,
> many companies have policies
> that address only violent behavior.

How to Confront Rudeness

When you're bombarded by rude behavior, you may want to put a stop to it. The
steps are the same as in any other confrontation: "I See," "I Feel," "I Want."

Cool Off First

When you've been brushed off or pro-
voked, you may be tempted to be equally
provocative—to use sarcasm and bitterness
to make your point. It won't work and it
will make things worse. The idea is to put
an end to rudeness, not to further fan the
flames. Walk away with dignity, go to a
neutral corner, breathe, and prepare your
approach.

 Words to the Wise

During orientation for new
employees, management
should explain that civility is
an expectation and bullying is
expressly forbidden.

Speak Directly

Don't rely on hints or third-party messages delivered by others. Speak specifically to
the person who was rude to you and don't water down what you need to say. Couch
it in strong I-messages such as, "I have something I need to discuss with you," or "I
need to clear the air on an issue that's bothering me." Avoid such openings as "You
have a big problem with me," or "What do you have against me?" These types of
openings create defensiveness from the outset, and the conversation is doomed.

Concentrate on Effects

State your objections in terms of the effect the rudeness has on you. "Ross, when I'm
interrupted, I have to go back and start over to make my point. That wastes my time

and the time of everyone else in the meeting. I'd appreciate it if you'd let me finish what I'm saying. That way, everyone has a chance to hear the idea and comment on it."

Keep Above It

Some people can dish it out, but they can't take it. They may come back at you forcefully and maybe even abusively. Do not give up the advantage of professionalism. The minute you respond with equal vindictiveness, you've given away your power. If the other can goad you into blowing your cool, the battle's over and he's won. If you're getting nowhere, you can preserve your dignity by walking away and coming back at the issue another time and in another way.

Ask Questions

Suppose you've asked someone to stop making disparaging remarks about your height; you don't like to be called "Shrimp" or "Tiny." The perpetrator replies, "Oh, get over it. You're too sensitive."

You can respond, "Really? I don't think of myself that way. If I have that problem, I'd like to correct it, and maybe you can help me. Can you give me some examples of times you've seen me be oversensitive?"

If he has some examples, listen carefully. He may be right, but right or wrong, when he's finished speaking, you can then repeat your request that he not use the nicknames that offend you. "You know, you've shown me that I might take things a little too seriously, and I'll work on that, but whether I'm too sensitive or not, those nicknames bother me, and just out of consideration for my feelings, I'd appreciate it if you'd call me by my name instead."

If he can't dredge up any examples, ask him again to knock off the nicknames.

The Last Resort

Sometimes a colleague goes ballistic and is completely out of line. On those occasions, you can choose your reaction. You can wait or you can call her on it at the moment. Once again, though, if you think immediate action will make things even more untenable, you might want to wait.

When you're calm enough, ask to speak to her privately and tell her without hesitation that you will not tolerate that kind of rudeness and abuse ever again. Don't listen to excuses, explanations, or justifications. State your case clearly and leave the scene. After you've drawn your boundaries, you're well within your rights to seek a supervisor's help if it happens again. Be sure to document the entire incident.

When You're in the Wrong

If everyone is rude occasionally, everyone will at some point have the need to apologize. A heartfelt apology can keep a customer coming back, mend a friendship, and stop family squabbles quickly.

An apology consists of three parts: an acknowledgment of wrongdoing ("I took your idea and presented it as my own."), a sincere expression of regret ("I'm so sorry. It was very wrong of me to do that."), and a promise not to repeat the behavior ("I'll never do it again, and I hope you can forgive me."). An apology must be timely as well; it if comes too late, it's valueless.

Everything Rolls Downhill

Employers are waking up to the costs of incivility, and many are requiring employees to take courses in business etiquette. That's good as far as it goes, but creating a more civil workplace is more difficult than requiring people to learn how to leave voice mail, introduce people, and choose the right fork. Being courteous should not be seen as an add-on, but an integral part of every business interaction with both external and internal customers.

No matter how many "charm schools" you require of your employees, if you don't model courtesy yourself, don't expect to see it in those you supervise. Written policies about polite behavior mean nothing if your daily exchanges with your employees are humiliating and punitive. If you treat them shabbily, that's exactly how they'll treat one another and your customers.

As a manager, you're charged with making your team efficient and productive. You can't do that if employees are snipping at each other and throwing sand into the gears of your well-oiled machine. It's up to you to set the tone of courtesy and to promulgate policies that enhance respect among co-workers.

You may believe you have more important things to do than worry about everyone's feelings, but if you really want to burnish your reputation as a manager, there's nothing more important than creating an atmosphere in which people can work together peacefully and in harmony. When communication improves, everything improves:

work product, quality, effectiveness, absenteeism, and turnover. Those are significant bottom-line considerations, and if your team performs well, it reflects favorably on your management ability and positions you for advancement. Remember to:

♦ Request, not demand.

♦ Watch your tone. A sharp tone of voice and a clipped delivery can make you sound angry even if you aren't. Strive for a pleasant demeanor even if you're bothered, bewildered, or bored.

♦ Compliment good work. Reward exceptional effort with a handwritten note and public acknowledgment.

♦ Think of your team as "we," not "they."

♦ Share credit liberally.

♦ Draw up a code of civility and refer to it often. Create standards for answering the phone, dealing with upset customers, handling intra-office disagreements, and other challenges to courtesy.

♦ Require all team members to respect one another's dignity. Counsel those who need to be reminded, and root out those who can't or won't live up to your standards. You don't need bullies on your team.

The Least You Need to Know

♦ Every conversation that includes rudeness becomes difficult.

♦ Rudeness is an increasingly large cost to American business.

♦ Some people are intentionally unkind and hurtful, but many others are rude without being aware of it.

♦ You don't have to confront a bully, but sometimes calling one out stops the behavior.

♦ Courtesy—and discourtesy—begin at the top.

Chapter 13

Loose Lips Can Sink Your Ship

In This Chapter

- ◆ Why people gossip
- ◆ Surprising news about gossip
- ◆ Is it gossip if it's true?
- ◆ Gossip-stopping statements that work
- ◆ Protecting yourself from gossip

Office *gossip* is as common as paper clips. Maybe more so. There's informational gossip; personal gossip, which is usually innocuous; and speculative gossip, which may be very harmful, both to the person you gossip about and to you.

Informational gossip is business-related. "Did you hear that Gerry's resigned? His wife got a huge promotion and they're moving to Tampa. Sheila's going to take over his position." Personal gossip obviously is related to the off-the-job lives of those in the office. "Did you see Amy's engagement ring? It's beautiful."

And then there's speculative gossip, which can do serious damage to another's reputation and to yours as well: "Nice ring, but that wedding better come soon. Have you noticed she's been eating crackers at her desk?

I bet she's pregnant." This type of pernicious gossip can result in very difficult conversations between those who spread gossip and those who are the subject of it. In this chapter, we'll learn the pros and cons of gossip and its effect on productivity and relationships.

def•i•ni•tion

> **Gossip** derives from the Old English word for godparent. As time passed, the term came to mean a close friend, and because close friends tell secrets to one another, a gossip was one who told secrets or spread news and rumors. That's still the case today.

Why the Grapevine Twines

Grapevines are a feature of every business; such information sources can be useful or detrimental. They grow for several reasons, many of which are listed below.

Lack of Credible Information

Most companies do a poor job of communicating. Employees are often in the dark about changes in policy, promotions, and firings, or even events that are going to make the evening news. A lack of information can make people anxious, and when they become anxious they talk, trying to make sense of what they think might be going on—and how it will affect them.

Because others are in charge of the company's destiny (and thus the employees' futures as well), employees' talk often centers on other people's activities. The higher the level of anxiety, the more gossip is likely, and rumors can race through a company in hours if the majority of employees distrust management. When gossip takes over, it can be a huge barrier to productivity. Instead of concentrating on their jobs, people spend their time churning out rumors and indulging in what-ifs.

For example, let's put two pieces of information together and see how they add up.

> **Talking Points**
>
> A survey conducted by ISR, a research and consulting firm, indicates that more than 60 percent of American workers get the majority of information about their company from "water cooler" conversations.

- Greg, a department manager, is taking a lot of long lunches these days, and he doesn't offer any explanation for it.

- Greg was always a casual dresser; now he's wearing suits at least a couple of times a week, usually on the days he's going to lunch outside the building.

Hmm. Greg's dressing more professionally and going out to lunch. The rumor mill begins to grind and before you know it, Greg's interviewing for a job with another company. People begin to speculate about when Greg will be leaving and who will be taking over his job.

The gossip reaches Greg's boss, who now wonders if Greg is a short-timer and whether she should look for a replacement for him. Greg's future with the company may hang in the balance, all because of idle gossip. And Greg doesn't even know it.

The truth? Greg's wife suggested he spruce up his image, and those long lunches are meetings of a search committee to find a new director for a community organization he belongs to. How boring. It's not nearly as exciting as the titillating gossip that's been flying around the office.

The best way for employers to keep speculation at a minimum is to open up every channel of communication. Newsletters, blast e-mails, an active intranet, and employee meetings help to keep people informed. Even the best communication won't stop all gossip, but it may reduce speculation to a manageable level.

One company, which has employees in its facility 24 hours a day, schedules quarterly "round-the-clock" meetings. Executives, including the president, come to each meeting to bring news of significant changes or initiatives, and after their presentations, employees are welcome to ask any question they wish. "I've heard ..." is a frequent preamble to the questions, and having top management available to refute or confirm rumors is reassuring to those in attendance. Employees also are impressed that the executives come to every meeting, even the one at midnight.

In Greg's case, transparency about his activities might have helped tone down the gossip. Just a word to his assistant about his community involvement would have scotched the rumors and saved everyone a lot of time and energy.

In addition to maintaining good communication with employees, employers should cultivate an atmosphere in which cooperation and respect for one another are corporate values. When employees are pitted against one another in dog-eat-dog competition, gossip flourishes; if cooperation is valued, gossip tends to decrease.

Not Enough to Do

In a time of downsizing and consolidation, it may seem hard to believe that some people don't have enough work to fill the time they're in the office, but it's a fact. Bored and idle, they watch what's going on around them and comment on it. Sometimes it's funny, but sometimes it's brutal. A good manager will be alert to those who seem to have time on their hands and assign additional duties if necessary.

A Desire for Relationship

An office in which everyone comes in, does his or her job, and goes home is a pretty sterile place. No one feels connected to anyone else. The chitchat we engage in with our officemates is what makes coming to work more palatable. By sharing bits of our lives, we show that we trust our co-workers with information about ourselves. They reciprocate by telling us about themselves. We begin to create a social network that serves a variety of useful purposes: friendship, cooperation, and looking out for one another.

Sometimes we use our knowledge about others to create a bridge to a third party. By dishing up a tidbit about someone who isn't present, we solidify our relationship with the person who is. "Did you know that Hector's brother is very sick? That's why Hector's been leaving early. He's been going to the hospice every afternoon."

When gossip becomes backbiting, however, relationships may be damaged. If you tell me something cruel about another co-worker, I might wonder what you're saying about me to others—and I might begin to avoid you. So while certain types of gossip can build relationships, snipping and spitefulness can destroy them.

A Need for Importance

Some people have a desire to be important, and when they're privy to things other people don't know, it makes them feel special. Many times, these folks are warm, charming people whose personalities invite confidences; workmates feel comfortable talking with them and sharing the intimate details of their lives.

How the "good gossips" treat co-workers' confidences determines how long they'll continue to receive information. If they share only nonconfidential details, they may be at the top of the heap for a long time. But once they break a confidence to gain a momentary surge of self-importance or betray one employee to gain an advantage with another, their reign as gossip-in-chief is probably over.

A Hunger for Power

A fair number of employees, usually those with very weak self-esteem, see the workplace as a vast competitive arena. They seem to believe that success is like a pie; if others succeed, there's less pie for them. Therefore, the only way to get ahead is to make sure no one else gets a bite. They work hard to eliminate competition, and they do it in the most ruthless way possible.

They plant rumors, exaggerate, bend the truth, or lie outright. They are especially vicious in spreading gossip about someone whose life appears to be better than their own. If you've recently been promoted, enjoyed a vacation, had one of your children accepted at a prestigious university, or you're well-liked within your company, you're a target for this type of gossip monger.

Because they are often indiscriminate in choosing their targets or rash in what they say, nasty gossips sometimes get their moment in the spotlight just before they're unceremoniously escorted to the door. You can almost hear the applause.

Upsides: The Uses of Gossip

Gossip is a universal human activity and not always a bad thing. Sometimes gossip is simply chat that helps define how you should act in a specific workplace.

Good Behavior

Suppose a new employee hears, "Poor Ellen. She sent a memo to someone in operations without Maggie's approval, and Maggie went nuts." Clearly, Maggie controls department communication, and woe to the person who doesn't know that. That's valuable information for the new hire, and she learned it through talk about a third person. The gossip was factual, not judgmental, and sent a clear message.

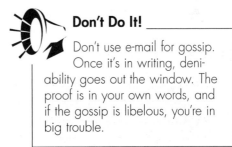

Don't Do It!

Don't use e-mail for gossip. Once it's in writing, deniability goes out the window. The proof is in your own words, and if the gossip is libelous, you're in big trouble.

"Behavioral" gossip doesn't have to be conveyed in words. A new staff member once took a seat at a meeting, not knowing that's where the meeting leader always sat. He looked at a co-worker, who shook her head almost imperceptibly. Of course he moved, saving himself embarrassment when the leader arrived. That nonverbal shake of the head was fine gossip: the leader sits in that chair, he's possessive about it, and you shouldn't usurp that position.

Honesty

According to some researchers, the grapevine can keep people honest. In a workplace in which people feel a great sense of interconnectedness, they are less likely to be dishonest. When the office staff feels like family, information flows freely. Staff members share information with one another throughout the day, so those who break the rules are less likely to get away with it. Their workmates will know about it, comment on it, and perhaps take what they learn to supervisors. Those in the workplace community know that the behavior of one member reflects on the group and will use information to rein in those who are running counter to the culture.

How Leadership Can Use Gossip

It's an exercise in futility to forbid gossip in the workplace. Wherever people gather, there will be gossip of one kind or another. Good managers should monitor the scuttlebutt to take the temperature of workplace morale. If you know what's bothering people, you can take steps to stop rumors and correct misconceptions. You also know if the gossip has gone beyond acceptable bounds and includes personal attacks or character assassination. You need to do all you can to stamp out that type of virus before it infects your whole department.

Savvy managers also know how to use the grapevine to their own advantage. A former communications director says, "I once heard that my nickname around the organization was 'Killer.' I was devastated because I think of myself as a pretty nurturing person, and my staff thought so, too. Coincidentally, however, a couple of people who did some projects for me were fired soon afterward. The blabbermouths in the company decided that I was responsible for those job losses. I wasn't, and I used the grapevine from my office to the rest of the company to set the record straight.

"It was easy. I just told a person with a record for sharing good information that I'd heard the rumor about myself, and I was hurt by it. I gave her the real scoop and she got it on the wire that afternoon. The trouble died down almost overnight."

You can use gossip to make certain that your team's good work gets talked about or to position a staffer for promotion. People tend to believe what they overhear, so by talking positively about the employee in places where your words will be overheard and repeated, you can start good buzz about a deserving employee. When upper management begins to hear positive things about a staffer through informal channels, they'll sometimes watch that person more closely to see what all the chatter is about.

Downsides: How Gossip Hurts

When office gossip veers from information-sharing to take-no-prisoners whispering campaigns, you have a problem on your hands. Productivity may dive as team members chew over all the details of the latest rumors directed at their co-workers. People choose up sides, flaming e-mails begin to circulate, conversations turn cold, or co-workers stop talking to each other altogether. Before long, very little work is being done. This is the type of gossip you should sidestep at all costs.

You Might Be Wrong

Very often, the juiciest gossip bears only the faintest resemblance to the truth. There might be a factual nugget buried in the avalanche of words, but constant retelling and embellishment may have obscured the facts. And of course, there's always the possibility that the whole story is fabricated. If you pass it on and find out later that you've been duped, you feel stupid and you've hurt another person. If that person decides to extract revenge, you're caught in a pointless, ugly exchange that could drag on for months.

You're Not Being Paid for It

When you're spending your time talking about your co-workers, you're not working, and the paycheck you receive is for doing your job. Monitor yourself, and if you find yourself spending an inordinate amount of time in water cooler conversations about others in your organization, get back to work.

You're Not Being Professional

Your gossipy tendencies may peg you as a lightweight who can't be trusted. Managers might decide you're not a candidate for promotion or greater responsibility because you spend so much time dishing the dirt about your co-workers you hardly have time to get your work done.

def•i•ni•tion

> A **hostile work environment** exists when employees can't do their jobs without feeling harassed or threatened. Vicious gossip can contribute to such an environment, especially if the employee feels that the gossip is related to sexual identity, race, ethnic origin, or any other protected civil right.

Additionally, if they can trace a deleterious rumor back to you, you may be subject to discipline or even firing, and if the gossip is serious enough, your company may be faced with liability issues. Gossip that runs rampant and is directed only at certain people can contribute to a *hostile work environment*, and you know what that means. Don't jeopardize your career because you can't keep your tongue from wagging.

Some companies have instituted antigossip policies; others depend on managers to handle things on a case-by-case basis. As a manager, you cannot allow gossip that demeans or damages another person. You should fire employees who persist in the destructive behavior after they've been counseled to knock it off.

Is It Gossip? How to Tell

Because most of us trade information so many times a day, it may be difficult to tease out what's appropriate and what isn't. A couple of simple questions can bring everything into perspective.

Is It Conjecture?

Facts are information, but conjecture is usually gossip.

For example, "Jeff's been put in charge of writing the strategic planning document" is information. "I think he got the job because he's dating the vice president's daughter" is an assumption and has no place in the conversation.

When you're talking about another person, be on the lookout for phrases such as, "It seems to me," "I wonder if," or "I bet." These can be lead-ins to conjecture and negative gossip. Stick to the facts.

What Is the Reason for Sharing It?

What is the motivation that causes someone to offer up personal (usually negative) information about another person? If you don't know why someone is feeding you a tasty morsel of gossip, you can always ask. "Why are you telling me this?" can be an immediate conversation stopper and might (but probably won't) cause the other person to question her reasons for blabbing.

Question your own motives as well. When you're tempted to pass something along, ask yourself why. Remember that you don't get any taller by making someone else kneel down. Debasing a colleague doesn't elevate your status among your co-workers; they're too busy worrying about when you'll get around to stabbing them in the back.

Gossipers engage in negative talk because …

♦ They are jealous of another's good fortune in which they did not share.

♦ They dislike the other person, with or without cause.

♦ They want to discredit the other to gain an advantage, such as a promotion that can go only to one.

♦ They don't know any better.

♦ They're just plain nasty, bitter people.

Words to the Wise

Did you succumb to temptation and say something you shouldn't have about a co-worker? If confronted about it, don't duck. Swallow your pride, make a true apology, and learn from your mistake.

Is It Helpful?

Sometimes gossip may revolve around an illness, death, or accident in a co-worker's family. If you're telling the news because you're setting up meals for the family or gathering signatures for a get-well card, you're on the side of the angels. But if you're sharing grisly details that are no one's business, think about it. Your motives are suspect.

Would You Be Ashamed If You Were Quoted?

My grandfather used to say, "Don't say anything you wouldn't want to see on the first page of the newspaper." I'd update that to include writing anything you wouldn't want to see on the company home page. Gossip has a way of getting back to those who are the subjects of the talk. If you'd feel bad about what you said later, don't say it now.

How to Gossip-Proof Yourself

No matter how careful you are, you may at some point be the target of gossip. If you want to minimize the chances that you'll be in the cross hairs, here are some tips:

- **Don't confide in people at work.** You don't have to be a sphinx. It's okay if co-workers know your husband's name and occupation, but they don't have to know you were separated for a while last year. You can mention your children, but it's not necessary to share that your older son might need to go to rehab soon.

  Be upbeat, positive, and make sure that what you talk about can't come back to haunt you later. If you have a serious concern that might affect your work, HR people might be able to offer concrete help—and they're paid to be discreet.

- **Don't talk about your co-workers at all unless what you say is positive.** No one can use positive comments against you.

- **Watch out for open-plan offices.** Acoustics in these arrangements can be tricky, and what you tell someone quietly and in confidence may be overheard by many others.

- **Don't spread gossip yourself.** Let toxic words fall into the Well of Silence. Good information will continue to flow your way because you've proven yourself trustworthy.

Stopping Gossip Cold

Gossip-stopping strategies can be difficult if being popular is important to you. Those who refuse to participate in bashing others often become targets themselves. ("He thinks he's so much better than we are!" "She's so snooty.") Grin and bear it because those who are interested in doing their jobs well will be only too happy to join with you in stamping out this wretched habit.

When confronted with spiteful gossip about another, you can fall back on the three-step approach to confrontation (see Chapter 6). "I hear you saying all these things about Brad (I see), and it makes me very uncomfortable because he isn't here to give us his side of the story (I feel). I'd like to stop talking about this now (I want)."

Some people won't respond to this gentle approach. You can then try something such as:

- ♦ "Really? That's interesting. I'll be sure to tell Brad you're concerned about him."

- ♦ "I know that what you're saying isn't accurate, and I think you should stop spreading that rumor."

- ♦ "I think you should discuss this with Brad and not with me."

- ♦ "How would you feel if Brad said the same thing about you?"

- ♦ "I doubt that you'd say this to Brad's face, so why would you say it behind his back?"

That ought to do it, but be prepared for some backlash.

When the Gossip Is About You

Someday an officemate may tell you that you're the subject of malicious gossip. Your best defense is a strong offense. Thank the person who brought it to your attention, because she took a risk by doing so. Then ask who the source was. Once you know, go to that person and be direct. Do not accuse. Just seek information.

> "Emmy, there's a rumor going around that I'm sleeping with Kevin. It's not true and it's very damaging both to me and to Kevin. Do you know anything about where this story started?"

Emmy may be so shocked at your directness that she gives up her source immediately. On the other hand, she may be ashamed that she participated in the gossip and say she doesn't have a clue what you're talking about.

Keep tracking it down. Realize that you may be in for some rough conversations, as people try to distance themselves from what they've done.

Stay calm and focused on your mission. Don't get dragged into side issues that have the potential to blow up into major altercations. As you seek the truth, you may find out that the initial remark was nothing like the rumor that's grown up. You might hear, "I said that I saw you and Kevin in the hardware store last Saturday and it looked like you were having a good time, but I never said you were sleeping together."

That's all you need to know. Be polite and controlled, but demand immediate action. "Please go to the people you spoke with and tell them you don't appreciate being mis-quoted and I don't appreciate being lied about. I know you didn't mean to hurt me, but by talking about me that way to people who like to gossip, you did, and it's only fair that you help me clean up the mess. You've hurt me and Kevin, and of course, Kevin's wife."

If you know with certainty who started the rumor that's causing you grief, go directly to that person and state in the strongest terms that you want such gossip about you to stop. Should that tactic not be successful, don't hesitate to involve your supervisor.

The most uncomfortable situation is to be the subject of unsavory gossip that happens to be true. As it begins to swirl around you, you may be tempted to pick up your marbles and find another place to work. Be aware, however, that the gossip will follow you. If you decide to stay where you are, then maintain your composure, do your work, and ride it out. You can't go back to fix the cause of the gossip, so keep your head up and remain above it all. Don't comment. Don't take the bait. When others find they can't rattle you, they'll search for another topic and you'll be yesterday's news. Dignity is a powerful antidote to gossip.

The Least You Need to Know

- Information sharing is good, but gossip is usually harmful.

- Gossip arises when people don't have enough information about issues that affect them or they don't have enough work to keep them occupied.

- Gossip wastes time and money and can have a profound effect on productivity.

- Participate in the life of your workplace, but shun personal gossip.

- Unchecked malicious gossip can result in legal problems for you and your company.

Chapter 14

Performance Reviews

In This Chapter

- ◆ Are performance reviews necessary?
- ◆ Common errors at review time
- ◆ The uses of feedback
- ◆ Why feedback works
- ◆ Handling the negative performance review

If a difficult conversation is one that makes you jittery, has a significant bearing on your future, and contains the potential for serious disagreement, then the annual performance review must be the poster child for these exchanges. Usually tied to salary increases, performance reviews are something both managers and employees dislike, for various reasons. In this chapter, you'll learn how to handle conversations about performance if you're the manager and how to react if you're the employee.

A Big Waste of Time?

Although most companies continue to perform annual reviews, there's a growing body of opinion that says they're a relatively useless activity, because the problems with them outweigh the benefits.

Lack of Frequency

Decades ago, when business moved more slowly and employees were expected to perform only one set of tasks, a once-a-year review might have been enough. Today, business moves at the speed of sound, and one employee may be responsible for a variety of functions. It's virtually impossible for a manager to keep an eye on everyone and remember how each employee performed over a 12-month period, even with the most careful notes.

A performance issue that arises in March should be discussed in March, not the next February. That's just too far away to be effective.

Differences in Style

Remember those professors who were "easy A's"? There are some supervisors like that. They give inflated performance scores just to keep people from being upset or to make themselves look more productive. At the other end of the spectrum, however, are those who give everybody a D because that's the way they perceive the world. Neither rating is fair, at least in most cases.

Personal Opinion

Some bosses let their feelings about an employee get in the way of a fair appraisal. Perhaps the employee looks exactly like the supervisor's Aunt Millie and he can't stand his Aunt Millie. If the manager isn't aware of his bias, the employee could receive a lower appraisal than she should.

Of course, the opposite is true as well. Bosses tend to favor and give higher marks to those who are most like them.

Specific Errors

Evaluators can be so impressed with one aspect of an employee's performance, such as an ability to close initial sales, that they bump up the scores in other dimensions as well, even though there could be room for significant improvement in these areas. This inflated appraisal is termed the *halo effect*. The opposite is called the *pitchfork effect*.

Some managers place too much emphasis on recent performance (*recency error*). For example, if an employee has just done an outstanding job on a project but has been a lackluster performer the rest of the year, the appraisal might be unnaturally rosy. On the other hand, suppose an otherwise superior employee has had a run of less-than-stellar work in the previous month. His performance could be rated lower than it should be.

The *central tendency error* means that the boss is uncomfortable with either "excellent" or "poor" ratings and usually ranks all employees as "average."

def•i•ni•tion

The **halo effect** is the tendency to judge all of a person's characteristics as outstanding because one of them is. The **pitchfork effect** is the tendency to rate an employee negatively in all areas because of lack of performance in one.

Recency error gives too much consideration to recent events in assessing performance. **Central tendency error** is bunching the majority of employees into a middle category for purposes of evaluation.

Using Feedback Effectively

With all the potential pitfalls surrounding evaluations, is there any hope for a review that's fair, balanced, and truthful? Yes. And the name of the game is *feedback*.

Of course, any employee evaluation includes feedback, but good feedback comes at regular intervals—sometimes as often as weekly, and maybe even daily during particularly critical initiatives. A strong feedback system helps employees know right away whether they're making good decisions and acting appropriately in every situation.

The point of feedback is to get employees to think and reflect on what they're doing right and wrong—and the reasons for their successes and failures.

Feedback should be:

def•i•ni•tion

Feedback is the sharing of observations about an employee's performance—both what she did and how she did it—and how it stacks up against what is expected of her.

- ◆ Immediate
- ◆ Specific
- ◆ Constructive
- ◆ Positive
- ◆ Focused on Behavior

Immediate

Yesterday morning you watched one of your staff do a presentation that caused everyone in the room to experience spontaneous narcolepsy. Within a couple of hours, you call your employee and say, "Do you have some time for me this afternoon? I'd like to discuss the presentation this morning. Are you up for some feedback?" He's going to get the feedback one way or another, but asking if he's ready to hear it is courteous. Maybe he'd like to recover a bit and do the feedback session the next day.

Although you can delay a day or so for his comfort, you'll want to intervene while the incident is still fresh in his mind. It will help him shift his focus from his embarrassing failure to the ways he can prevent such an outcome the next time. It's not fair to let him drift along for six months and then slam his presentation skills during his evaluation. Those six months could be filled with learning. If you don't give him any direction, how does he know what to fix?

Imagine a football coach who sees his quarterback consistently making the same error. He doesn't wait until the last game of the season to mention it. The two of them work together every day to eliminate the problem. One of the chief tasks of management is developing employees' skills, and coaching them is a daily occupation. If their performance isn't improving, then you aren't doing your job.

Specific

At three o'clock the day after the presentation, your team member is in your office, tense and nervous. You say, "Wow, yesterday morning stunk to high heaven. You've got to do something about your presentation skills or you're never going to get anywhere."

That's not effective feedback. And the other side of the coin—"Terrific presentation!"—isn't helpful either. One is critical and the other is puffery, but both are judgmental, and neither invites reflection or growth. People who receive negative comments feel stressed and anxious, while those who receive positive remarks may be confused because they don't know what they did right or how to repeat the behavior.

Feedback doesn't evaluate. It describes and gives the employee information he can use in assessing why he did or didn't succeed.

> "Bob, the research you did for your presentation was very detailed. I don't think there was a detail you didn't cover. You had great facts and solid information, but it got lost in the mechanics of your presentation. What do you think caused it to go off the track?"

Beginning with something positive and asking the employee for his viewpoint on the situation are essential to the success of feedback. If you lecture rather than collaborate, your staffer can become resentful or silent, both of which make a potentially useful conversation very difficult; and if you concentrate only on the negative, you open the door to argumentative responses and sulkiness.

In this case, though, you've begun correctly and invited collaboration. Bob might say, "You're right about the research. I worked like a dog on that thing. Maybe I didn't practice enough. The report certainly didn't get the reaction I expected."

Now it's time for you to chime in with what you observed. "What I saw was that you stood in front of the group and read your slides. I think that's because, as you say, you weren't prepared. You used your slides as your script, and that's an ineffective way to present. Also, there were too many slides and they were hard to read because there was too much information on each one.

"I noticed another problem as well. You didn't seem to know how to work the equipment. You spent a lot of trouble fumbling around trying to get everything to sync up, and when it didn't, your frustration detracted from your professionalism.

"So the areas you need to work on are practice, equipment, and slide preparation. Does that seem right to you?"

You and your employee have now come to an understanding of his specific shortcomings. You're ready to move on to the next step, which is to devise a plan for improvement.

Constructive

Good feedback doesn't set the employee adrift with vague indications of what needs to be done. It gives him some concrete steps he can take to make his performance better. For example, "Sometime in the next few days, I'd like you to work with our audiovisual group to get more familiar with the equipment. Schedule the conference room and have Chris show you where everything is and how to use it. Within the month, you can demonstrate it to me so I know you're on track.

"I'd like you to read a couple of books or do some online research on effective slide presentations. Then, this month, take two or three of the slides you used for this morning's presentation and revamp them. We'll meet and you can explain to me how you improved them.

"Also, in the next few months, it might be good for you to get involved in an organization like Toastmasters, so you're more comfortable speaking before a group. I know you're going to be called on to speak again. Let's make it a priority for you to improve this aspect of your job. This is training the company will pay for.

"And once again, great job on the research. That was really impressive."

This action plan includes follow-up, which is necessary to check for progress. If the employee is able to demonstrate mastery of the things you've asked for, that's a skill upgrade that should be noted in the next review.

Positive

Do the best you can to sandwich bad news between a couple of things you can compliment; hearing something positive makes it easier for the listener to absorb the critique. Don't go overboard on the good stuff, though, just because you don't want to hurt someone's feelings. The point of feedback is improvement.

Applaud mistakes. Those who enjoy nothing but success may not be learning anything, but a person who is making mistakes is moving out of his comfort zone and trying to grow. In time, a person who works his way out from under a mistake may be far more valuable to the company than one who never colors outside the lines.

> **Don't Do It!**
>
> When reviewing performance, stay away from phrases such as "You always …" or "You never …." Sweeping generalizations are usually inaccurate. Describe only the instances of behavior you've witnessed and how often you've observed them.

Immediate, specific feedback helps pinpoint trouble spots, but it reinforces good habits as well. "Jenny, I liked the way you approached that customer who was looking for the Atomic Roboman 4000. I noticed that you didn't just point and tell her it was on Aisle 3; you walked her down to the electronic toy section and showed her exactly where to find it. You were friendly and helpful. Great customer service!"

That kind of detailed feedback lets Jenny know exactly what behavior her boss values. Chances are she'll continue delivering exceptional service to other customers.

Focused on Behavior

"You just can't keep quiet, can you? Did it ever occur to you there are times when it's not appropriate to run your mouth?"

That's feedback all right, but it's a cold, vindictive, personal attack, and that's not good. Zero in on what she did, not who she is, and tie her behavior to self-interest.

"Stella, I noticed that you were passing notes and giggling during the president's presentation. That was inappropriate. People who are speaking, and especially the president of this company, deserve our full attention. I hope that in the future you'll be more courteous because it reflects badly not only on you, but also on the whole department. I'll need to see you showing more maturity before I can recommend you for promotion."

The Benefits of Frequent Feedback

Feedback takes advantage of what educators call the *teachable moment*: that is, a time when someone is primed to learn from an experience, either good or bad. It's an opportunity to explore why something occurred and to figure out how to replicate it or prevent it from happening again.

The teachable moment may be a time of great growth and change—an "aha" experience—and if you miss teachable moments by relegating your observations to a formal once-a-year or even once-a-quarter evaluation session, you may rob your team of opportunities to develop and mature.

def•i•ni•tion

The **teachable moment** is the time when the learner is most responsive to understanding something new.

Assistance and feedback must be continually available if you want to see measurable growth, not just at appraisal time, but day by day, week by week, and month by month.

If your company still does annual reviews, frequent feedback makes them far less stressful because they are, in fact, actual reviews of what employees already know about their strengths and weaknesses. What they hear is not a surprise because you've been guiding them toward better performance every day. They'll never feel that you've sandbagged or ambushed them.

Words to the Wise

If you have scheduled a performance review with an employee, don't cancel or delay it. Employees, especially those whose review is linked to compensation, want to have their reviews on time so they can plan for their financial futures. It's not fair to keep them on edge by delaying the review. In addition, not holding the meetings tells employees that they aren't a priority in your organization.

def•i•ni•tion

Intrinsic motivation arises from within people themselves. They work for the joy of work because the tasks are meaningful to them, both vocationally and emotionally. It is the opposite of extrinsic motivation, which occurs when people work for an external reward such as a paycheck or a promotion.

Because the tension of the review is relieved, you and your employee are far more able to concentrate on the company's plans for the period before the next evaluation, whether that's three, six, or twelve months from now.

You can spend the review time building greater rapport and communication with your staff member, clarifying her strengths as well as areas that need some attention, and charting personal development goals that are linked to department objectives.

While a standard-brand performance appraisal may demotivate, employees who spend quality time with a supervisor often say that those exchanges are among the most motivating aspects of their jobs. And since *intrinsic motivation* fuels performance, that's what you need to strive for.

Responding to Your Review

The most helpful thing you can do to ensure that you respond adequately to your review is to prepare for it. If there hasn't been enough feedback between you and your supervisor (and in many places there isn't), you need to be ready to demonstrate what you've done that's been good for the company.

Because many reviews are tied to compensation, if you want more than the standard cost-of-living adjustment, you need to have examples of why you're worth it. Far in advance of your review, and in fact, almost from your first day on the job, you should be keeping a log of achievements that are above and beyond what's on your job description. You're not asking for a raise per se, but you're setting the stage by explaining how your activities have benefited the company.

The Negative Review

There are always a few bad apples in every barrel, but most employees work hard and try to advance the company's goals. They show up for work on time, spend little time gossiping, and rarely abuse company policies. They have a sincere interest in learning, growing, and succeeding. For these people, a negative review can be devastating, and often a bad review is as much a function of poor management as it is a reflection on the employee's own efforts. The main reason a review can become contentious is because there's a significant divergence between the employee's assessment of his work and the reviewer's perspective on it. That difference of opinion may come about because the employee doesn't know precisely what management wants.

Goals may be ill-conceived, change may be too rapid, or communication may be virtually nonexistent. When employees are unclear about what their supervisors expect, they may miss critical deadlines, do slipshod work, or not understand when a project is headed for disaster. At review time, they end up taking the fall for what are essentially management errors.

Years ago, I heard a tape of singer Don McLean performing a song called "Babylon" in concert. After I'd listened to it several times, I realized it was one of the best examples of coaching and feedback I'd ever heard.

It's an audience participation song; McLean began by playing the song a couple of times so the audience could learn the tune. Then he led the audience in singing the song. At that point, he described the meaning of the song and the group sang it again.

Only then did he say that he was going to divide them into three groups and have them sing the song as a round. McLean sang with the first group as they began the round; while they continued, he brought in the second group, singing the beginning of the song with them so they knew when to start. He repeated that action with the third group. And then he told them to "just keep singing."

After a few more repetitions, he stopped singing entirely, but he played loudly enough and with a heavy enough beat that it was almost impossible for the audience to get lost. They never sang without his participation in one way or another, but he stopped overtly leading them.

Toward the end of the song, he indicated that one group was to stop singing, then the next, and finally the third.

In this experience, McLean demonstrated exactly what a great manager should do. He set clear expectations, shared the goals, taught the steps, gave a progressively greater challenge, kept the team on track, and, with the instrumentation, let the "employees" know how they were doing while they were in the midst of performing.

By the volume of the applause, it was easy to see that the audience thought the song had gone well. The constant feedback had made success possible. It will do it for you and your team, too.

Getting Slammed: What to Say, What to Do

A smart reviewer will concentrate on only one or two areas that need improvement. She won't harangue you for an hour with every nit-picky thing you've done wrong for the last year. Even if the supervisor sticks to big issues, though, it's hard to hear negative things about your performance and you may be tempted to respond angrily. That won't help the process.

When your review is going badly, here are some things to remember:

- **Do stay cool.** A review is about how you perform your job; it's not about you personally.

- **Do be honest with yourself.** Step away from your feeling of being judged and ask yourself if there's a grain of truth in what you're hearing about your performance.

- **Do ask lots of specific questions.** Don't let a reviewer get away with a blanket statement about some aspect of your work. You can't fix what you don't understand. Say, "When you say my reports are substandard, do you mean that there's not enough research or that that they need more editing?"

- **Do give reasons for sub-par performance, but don't offer excuses or blame others.** "I'm not sure you remember, Donna, but last October, I had pneumonia. Even though I missed only a week of work, my return to full strength was much slower than I thought it would be. I shouldn't have taken on the Robinson proposal. It was too big a job at that time. There's no question there was a dip in my performance then, but I think it's back to its previous level, don't you?"

- **Do ask for time to think things through.** If you feel besieged and don't think you can be objective in your responses, ask if you can take a day or so to reflect on what's been said. Continue the conversation when you're calmer.

- **Do respond in writing.** If you think the assessment is unfair—and they often are—ask for a copy of the review and write a careful, reasoned (not flaming) rebuttal. Discuss the document with your supervisor before asking that it be added to your review and kept in your personnel file. Don't make general statements about the injustices in the review. Back up any disagreements with concrete examples for which you have proof. If you have any reason to believe that your document will be "lost," take a copy of the review and your response to human resources yourself.

◆ **Don't be rude or combative.** Calling your supervisor an idiot doesn't win points. You can say, "I'm surprised to hear that I'm not careful enough in citing my sources. After I presented my last report to the committee, you wrote me this note saying how impressed you were with the strength of the references. Can you help me understand how I can do this better?"

◆ **Don't sulk, pout, or whine.** Be a professional, not a baby. Disagree if you feel there's an error, but do so calmly and rationally.

When the Employee Is Unhappy

Supervisors generally aren't any more enthusiastic about performance reviews than employees are, and one of the things they dread most is the employee who comes unhinged because her review isn't perfect. When you're in the supervisory position:

◆ Let the employee speak and listen carefully to what she has to say.

◆ Upgrade the assessment if the employee can give you compelling evidence that you've made an error in your rating. On the other hand, be ready to provide examples that support your position if necessary.

◆ Acknowledge the employee's feelings, even if you stand by your opinion of her performance. "I know it's hard for you to hear these things, and I don't like saying them either."

You want to avoid demotivation, and one of the ways to do that is to show true regard and respect for the employee's emotions. Even if a review is negative, it doesn't need to be unkind. Delivery can be everything.

The Least You Need to Know

◆ Although most supervisors and employees don't like annual performance reviews, they're still a fact of life in many companies.

◆ Performance reviews can be subject to many sorts of inequities, most of them based in human error.

◆ Continual feedback is a more effective way of managing and summarizing employees' performance.

◆ To be effective, feedback must be immediate and specific, as well as constructive and positive.

◆ Many mistakes for which employees are blamed are really management errors.

◆ The performance review should be a collaborative venture, in which both sides listen to one and respect one another.

Chapter 15

Discipline, Dismissal, or Departure

In This Chapter

- ◆ The truth about discipline
- ◆ The importance of empathy in discipline
- ◆ Announcing your departure
- ◆ Clues that you're about to be fired

"Parting is such sweet sorrow," Shakespeare said. He was right, in a way. But sometimes parting is mostly sweet, especially if you're leaving a job to go to something better—and even more especially if you're offloading a wretched boss or a bunch of unpleasant co-workers. On the other hand, parting can be very sad if you're being involuntarily separated from a job you like and workmates you're fond of. However you go, uprooting yourself is unsettling.

The conversations that surround separation, including those related to discipline, can be difficult because your emotions are engaged. This chapter gives you some pointers about the termination process from both sides and how to handle the words that may precede or accompany this issue.

Understanding Discipline

Discipline gets a really bad rap because the word has become corrupted. In the beginning, "to discipline" did not mean "to punish." It derives from the same root as the word "disciple," which roughly translates to learning and being taught. So to discipline someone was to teach him—to serve as an exemplar so he'd be inclined to become a disciple and follow your example.

Therefore, discipline has a great deal to do with the authenticity of the teacher. Whether you're dealing with a two-year-old's tantrum or an employee's out-of-line treatment of a customer, you won't get far if you don't practice what you preach. The foundation of all discipline is day-by-day modeling of the behavior you want to see.

def•i•ni•tion

Discipline means to train by instruction or practice. It can involve punishment, but it doesn't • have to. Its purpose is to bring about specific types of desirable behavior.

In the business context, however, discipline usually means reprimand or correction. An employee has done something wrong—his performance is substandard, he's broken a rule, or he's been engaged in some sort of misconduct—and you have to step in. You must let him know where he crossed the line and what the consequences are. Your aim is not to humiliate him, but to modify his behavior and teach him how to manage the situation if similar circumstances arise again.

Talking Points

You probably know the 80/20 sales rule: 80 percent of your sales come from 20 percent of your customers. The same rule applies to employee issues. It's likely that 80 percent of your disciplinary procedures involve no more than 20 percent of your employees.

To be effective, discipline must be:

- Consistent
- Timely
- Private
- Complete

Consistent

You can't reprimand one employee for behavior you tolerate in another. Discipline should be used for policy infractions the employee knows about and understands.

"Sam, I heard you shouting at José. Our policy is to work out disagreements respectfully. If you can't do that, you can ask me for help. But screaming at a co-worker isn't appropriate."

As I mentioned in Chapter 14, employees sometimes don't know what's expected of them. Before you begin a disciplinary process, you have to ascertain that the employee understands company policies and procedures. It's not appropriate to discipline someone for ignorance. Fill Sam in and see if his behavior improves.

Timely

Too often, managers let the first instance of a disciplinary issue ride, hoping to avoid conflict and a potentially difficult conversation. The problem with that approach is that the employee probably will do the same thing again—perhaps repeatedly—and then you must have the "habitual offender" conversation, which is much more difficult than an initial heads-up would have been.

Nip bad behavior in the bud. A first offense doesn't need a full-scale dressing down. A reminder is usually sufficient.

"Mary, I think you might have forgotten the smoking rule. Smoking is allowed only on the back patio, not at the front entrance. We don't want customers to have to enter the building through a smoking area."

If you overlooked the behavior the first time it happened, you might hear:

"You let me do it before. Why are you all bent out of shape about it now?"

That's a legitimate though somewhat insolent question. You can acknowledge your error, but make sure Mary understands that from now on, smoking is unacceptable.

"It was a mistake for me not to tell you right away, so this is just a reminder. Please obey the smoking policy, which restricts smoking to the patio at the rear of the building."

Private

There's no need to bring other people into the disciplinary process. If two employees are equally involved in an altercation, you might choose to interview them together, but unless others are directly affected by the issue, keep it between you and the person being disciplined.

Complete

If you say there will be consequences for a particular action, you have to impose them. "Mary, I asked you not to smoke in front of the building because it offended our customers. I've seen you smoking there twice since I told you what the policy is. Please consider this a first warning. If you continue to break the rule, I'll have to write a note to go into your file." Then do it. Discipline without follow-up is just a bunch of words.

What Do You Want?

Disciplinary conversations are often difficult because manager and employee are approaching a problem from different perspectives. The manager may feel the employee is shiftless and irresponsible, while the employee believes the manager is rigid and rule-bound. The employee wants the manager to understand the factors that have an impact on her performance, and the manager wants the employee to understand that policies and procedures should be followed.

Empathy can be useful in bridging the gap. Listening carefully to the issues that affect behavior can make a disciplinary meeting less contentious and make the employee more willing to move down the path you want her to go.

Here's how to use empathy effectively:

You: "Sally, I've noticed that you're late for every project meeting. I like to have the meetings start when they're supposed to, and when I have to stop and catch you up, it slows the meeting down and it's discourteous to those who arrived on time. Your participation in these meetings is critical. How do you think we should resolve this issue?" (Statement of desired results)

Sally: "Project meetings are on Tuesday, and I have a problem on Tuesdays. My mom was diagnosed with cancer last month, and she has chemotherapy every Tuesday. I use my lunch hour to take her, but sometimes they're running a little behind. By the time I take my mother home and get back here, I'm late for our meeting." (Mitigating circumstances)

You: "I'm so sorry. I didn't know your mother was ill. That's a big load you're carrying: working and taking care of your mom." (Empathy)

Sally: "Yes, it is. I'd like to do what you want, but I think you're demanding way too much. I can't be in two places at once and missing a few minutes of a meeting to help my mother is a no-brainer for me. What do you want me to do—let her go by herself?" (Potential Flash Point #1)

You: "This seems like a very stressful situation for you to be in" (Empathy). "Is there anyone who could help you on Tuesdays?" (Asking for change)

Sally: "No. I don't have any family here and all my neighbors work. If you want me to be here on time, you're going to have to move the meeting." (Potential Flash Point #2)

You: "It's tough to have this responsibility all by yourself" (Empathy). "The problem is that we originally picked Tuesday afternoon because that was the only day everyone could be in the office after lunch."

Sally: "The chemotherapy lasts six months. Maybe you could excuse me from the meetings until it's over."

You: "I wish I could, but your participation is essential."

Sally: "Well, I guess I'm stuck then, and you'll have to write me up every time I'm late. There's nothing I can do about it." (Potential Flash Point #3)

You: "I can see you're really feeling trapped with all these different demands on your time" (Empathy). "How about this? I'll talk with human resources and see if there's any kind of transportation service that could pick up your mom and take her home after her treatments. Would that work for you?"

Sally: "It might. I don't like coming in late any more than you do. I want to take her to her treatment, though. I don't use company time to do that."

You: "Sure. That's what I'd want to do, too, if I were in your shoes" (Empathy). I know it makes her feel better to have you there. I'll call HR this afternoon and see what we can work out."

This conversation was at times tense and held the potential to become explosive, but each time Sally became sarcastic or defensive, the manager dealt with underlying causes rather than current behavior. The supervisor's empathy for Sally's situation kept things under control, even when she was insisting that Sally be on time for the meetings. Empathy is a powerful tool for cooling down a hot-conversation-in-the-making.

You will still need to follow up to see that Sally is making the meetings. If she isn't, another interview and more problem solving are in order.

Jumping or Being Pushed: Leaving the Job

No relationship lasts forever, and sometimes a separation is the best thing you can do for yourself and your employer. You might jump ship because …

- ◆ Your salary has topped out or is inadequate, with no chance for additional pay. You can't make your expenses with what you're taking home.

- ◆ You've outgrown the job, there's no chance for advancement, and you're bored stiff.

- ◆ You're trapped behind a manager who isn't rising.

- ◆ Your boss is too difficult to work with.

- ◆ You're very good at your job and your current supervisor blocks every opportunity that would take you away from him.

- ◆ The atmosphere is so toxic and unpleasant that your health is suffering.

- ◆ You've been offered a better opportunity somewhere else.

How to Say "I Quit"

Once you've made the decision, it's best to let your boss know as quickly as possible. If your employee handbook stipulates how much notice you must give, abide by that. Otherwise, the standard is two weeks.

Don't Do It!

Never take leaving as an opportunity to tell off that co-worker you despise. Word gets around, and if someone in a position to help you hears that you're a pop-off, you've sacrificed some future good will for the momentary thrill of letting off steam. That's not a good trade.

Explain to your boss only that you're moving on to another opportunity. Don't discuss the pay raise, perks, and benefits you'll be getting at the new job; that sounds like the opening shot of a negotiation ploy and might give the employer the idea that you'll stay if he sweetens the pot. If you've already accepted a new position, that kind of negotiation is unfair to both your current and new employers.

Be gracious. Tell your boss how much you appreciate all you've learned and how she has helped you grow.

Even if your current situation has been primarily negative, you can usually find one or two nice things to say about some aspect of your time with the company. Drag them out and deliver them with sincerity.

Be prepared for a negative response. Many bosses like to see their employees succeed and move on to greater responsibilities. I once told my very young staff that if they were with me in five years, I hadn't done my job.

Other supervisors, however, get testy about losing people because they know that it means more work for them. They have to interview, whittle down, check references, hire someone, and break him in. All that activity takes time away from the supervisor's other duties and it costs the company money. That makes managers grouchy, and they may take it out on you. Don't rise to the bait. Leave with a smile on your face.

Telling the Team

You tell your co-workers about your decision in the same way you tell your boss: quickly and with few details.

> "I've taken a job with General Amalgamated and I'll be leaving in two weeks. I'm looking forward to the challenges of the new job, but I'm going to miss you all."

The reasons you're leaving are personal; you don't have to share them with anyone.

Words to the Wise

If you're still on the job when your replacement is hired, keep your thoughts about your former boss and co-workers to yourself, especially if your views are negative. Tell him only what he needs to know to do his job well. Let him enter his new workplace in a positive frame of mind. Just because you didn't find it rewarding doesn't mean he won't.

Being Pushed: How to See It Coming

Getting fired can be devastating, especially if it's a shock. But unless your firing is part of an unexpected company-wide restructuring, there are usually some hints that you're going to be asked to walk the plank.

The biggest hint is that you're being excluded from important meetings and decisions that affect how you do your job. When this happens, don't delay in confronting the issues with your supervisor.

> You: "Barry, I'm concerned that I haven't been invited to the last three strategic planning meetings. I feel I have something to contribute and wonder why I'm not asked to be there anymore."

> Barry: "This is hard for me to say, but we didn't feel you were bringing anything new to the table. Your skills aren't high level enough."

> You: "What would you recommend to get me to the level you need? Are there some seminars or training I could take? I'm interested in improving my skills so I can advance."

> Barry: "I can't think of anything."

The last response is the critical one. If your boss valued you, he'd try to help you build your skills and position yourself for advancement. He isn't doing that. The bell is tolling. Take the hint. Find a new job before it's your neck on the chopping block.

Other clues include:

- A pattern of substandard reviews.

- Progressively harsh disciplinary procedures, starting with oral warnings and ending with performance improvement plans, probation, or suspension.

- Minimal salary increases, unless that's all anyone gets.

- Disregard for your suggestions and ideas.

- A distribution of your duties to others.

It's time to move on.

If you don't jump quickly enough, and your supervisor says you're being let go, watch what you say.

Don't lash out in the termination meeting. You'll be tempted to, but hold your tongue. There is nothing good to be gained from erupting in fury. You don't want to be escorted from the building by security because you're out of control.

Don't ask for your boss to reconsider. The decision has been made or the meeting wouldn't have been held. Begging is embarrassing to everyone in the room, including you.

When the meeting is over, don't badmouth anyone at your former company (except at home to your partner—and tell that person to be discreet). When you spew venom about former colleagues, listeners may come to believe you deserved to be fired. Class tells. Keep your head up and maintain your composure.

"I'm Afraid We Have No Choice"

People who have to fire others suffer, too. It's hard to take a livelihood away from another person. But if you have to do it, remember to be both honest and kind. Explain the reasons for termination fully, whether those reasons are a company-wide firing or a single performance issue. Keep in mind that you can state the reasons for termination without rubbing an employee's nose in it. "We've worked with you a long time, and I think you've tried, too, but we've come to the conclusion that this just isn't a good fit. This is your last day with us."

Although you'll want to be as empathetic as possible, it's not necessary for you to apologize, nor should you voice a bunch of meaningless platitudes. "Chin up" remarks are insulting to someone who's just been given a body blow.

If you're firing an employee immediately for a gross violation of company policy—a physical attack on another employee, intolerable insubordination, or theft, to name just a few—you must act decisively, but also with as much compassion as you can muster.

If the employee is not dangerous to others, explain why the firing is essential; take back all company property, including identification and keys; and, if possible, allow the employee to clean out his work space—under supervision. If the employee is dangerous, however, you must protect others, and it might be necessary to involve security or even law enforcement.

> **Don't Do It!**
>
> While compassion is important, don't go so far as to say something like, "I'll do everything I can to help you." The employee will expect you to honor that pledge, and if you don't, there could be legal repercussions. If you are willing to write a letter of reference (or you even have one prepared), you can say so, but don't make open-ended offers of aid.

Of course, in these circumstances, rumors will fly, and you must exercise caution in what you say. The message should be clear, unequivocal, and brief. "As of today, Hank is no longer with the company." No matter what he did, to say more is to risk legal action.

The Least You Need to Know

◆ Discipline should not be viewed as punishment, but as a collaborative attempt to modify behavior.

◆ Discipline should be consistent for every employee, not applied more harshly to some than to others.

◆ Even if you've been unhappy at your job, don't burn bridges when you leave.

◆ Firing is rarely a surprise; it takes time to build a case, so be aware of clues that you're under scrutiny.

Chapter 16

The Price of Workplace Disputes

In This Chapter

- ◆ The costs of conflict
- ◆ Why disagreements can be good
- ◆ Why conflict grows
- ◆ Managing conflict

Take any group of diverse people of disparate ages and backgrounds, put them into a closed environment eight hours a day, add stress, deadlines, and unclear communication, and you have the recipe for conflict. In fact, you can almost guarantee that at one time or another two—or several—employees are going to clash, and you'll either be part of it or have to manage it. In this chapter, you'll get some ideas about how to do that.

A Disagreement or a Fight?

Disagreement is not a bad thing. Constructive disagreement focusing on issues can result in better products and services and innovative solutions to problems. Disagreement forces examination of ideas, options, and decisions. In fact, if there's no disagreement in your office or company, it's likely that there's not much innovation or creativity either.

Useful disagreement includes:

◆ Discussion around clearly defined expectations.

◆ Reasoned support for a position.

◆ Respect for boundaries.

Discussion Around Clearly Defined Expectations

"In this meeting, I would like us to come to agreement on the direction our marketing communications will take for the next two years. We have the input from our consultants, and now I want to see how we will enact those recommendations and change the style and message. I want to hear every viewpoint, so fire away." This expectation anticipates differences of opinion and lively dialogue.

> **Talking Points**
>
> Most estimates indicate that at least 25 percent of a manager's time is spent dealing with workplace conflicts.

Other expectations might include that each person's viewpoint must be heard, that all group members are required to participate in the discussion, and that no one is permitted to interrupt another.

Reasoned Support for a Position

Although it's important to listen to staff members who have intuitive feelings about the direction of a project, data are also important. Those who are arguing and disagreeing should be able to say why they are not in accord, and they should have facts and reasons to back up their opinions.

Respect for Boundaries

Although disagreements should be honest, frank, and candid, there is no reason whatsoever for arguments to become personal attacks or sniping about age, gender, sexual orientation, race, or any other factor not germane to the discussion. Those who indulge in it should be cut off immediately by other members of the group; if they won't put an end to such language, the leader should.

Conflict differs from healthy disagreement because it usually focuses on personalities. "I disagree with this design" is a far different statement from, "Where did you ever get the idea you could design something?"

Conflict drains employees' energy and desire to contribute. It costs enormous amounts of money as absenteeism and turnover rise; healthcare costs go up as employees seek treatment for stress-related illnesses. Employees spend more time getting even with each other than they do working.

A former manager of a division of a city government says, "My staff was so dysfunctional that they spent far more time filing grievances against one another than they did serving the public. When I tried to get to the bottom of disputes, I received anonymous threatening notes or found dead fish in my locker. Once I even got a dead rat.

"How much work do you suppose gets done in an atmosphere like that? I'll tell you how much. Next to none. I finally had to get out. I couldn't take it anymore. The entire department should have been swept clean and reconstituted, but there was too much legal protection for incompetence built into the system."

Other companies report secret meetings that generate hard feelings and vituperative e-mail wars in which everyone including the office dog gets copied. All these maneuverings are distasteful and counterproductive.

Factors that increase conflict include:

- **Differences in work ethic.** Some people come to work to be productive; others do the least amount of work possible to collect their salaries. Differing perspectives on pace and quality of work and responsibility to the company can lead to personal disputes.

- **Lack of understanding of other cultures.** Employees can start a conflict by making a thoughtless remark or observation that hurts the feelings of a co-worker of a different national origin, religion, or race. With increased immigration, ethnic conflicts that grew up centuries ago in other countries may find their way into today's American workplace.

- **Speed of change.** Some organizations are constantly in a state of flux. Employees barely absorb one set of changes before another comes along. The more change, the greater the likelihood of conflict as people struggle to figure out roles and responsibilities.

- **Balance of power.** A fair number of people can't deal with the fact that a boss has more clout than they do, and some bosses love to wield power inappropriately.

◆ **Uncertainty.** Businesses don't exist in a vacuum, and what happens in the outside world affects what happens in the office. A large-event planner says, "After 9/11, my business lost $250,000 in a week. Travel stopped. Meetings stopped. Events stopped for months. I was lucky. I didn't have the overhead of some of my competitors. They were underwater immediately, and the stress led to some huge internal battles in which people got fired. Several of those companies are now out of business because they couldn't get past the conflict stage and into problem solving. It was brutal."

Why People Fight

Office fights can blow up around issues that are related to the day-to-day workings of the company, but sometimes they have more to do with differences between people than work issues.

Moving Up

One of the interesting causes of conflict relates to a particular type of change: a promotion. Many new managers report that previous peers, perhaps because of jealousy, become very hard to deal with. They report that some of their former co-workers resent the new relationship. The former peers show their displeasure by ignoring requests, being disrespectful, and gossiping that the new manager has become "high and mighty." You have to deal with the situation quickly before you lose control of your team, and the conversation will probably be uncomfortable.

These people will usually be a minority of your work group. People who were your good friends before will remain your friends, and they will understand that your relationship has to change. While you can still be cordial and friendly to your former workmates, you can't be buddies and confidants because that's no longer appropriate. You can't go out for drinks after work with only one member of your team. You can't share your feelings about one team member with others in the group.

Most former peers will support you in your new role. They'll get down to work and make you look good by performing well. You'll have to take the other employees aside and see if you can get to the root of their problems. This conversation may be unpleasant, but if you're a manager, you have to act like one.

You: "Bill, I've noticed that you seem to be uncomfortable reporting to someone you used to work with as a peer. Is that right?"

Bill: "I don't have a problem. You have a problem. You're pretty high on yourself ever since this promotion. And frankly, I don't know why you got it. I was as qualified as you were." (Bill has just told you, rudely, what the problem is. He's upset about being passed over.)

You: "That may be true, but for whatever reason, the promotion went to me, and I'd like to develop a good working relationship with you. How do you think we could make this situation better?"

Bill: "You could listen more and talk less. Just because you're a manager now doesn't mean you're the only one with good ideas." (Bill is being disrespectful. He may be telling the truth, but this could also be a smokescreen.)

You: "I didn't know that my listening skills were a problem. If they are, I'd like to work on it. Can you give me some specifics about a time when I didn't listen?" (Good! You've stayed focused on the issue and avoided getting sidetracked by his attitude.)

Bill: "Not really. It's just something I noticed." (The fact that he can't say when you've engaged in the behavior proves it's a smokescreen.)

You: "I appreciate your telling me this, and I'll try to be aware of it, but my problem is that yesterday during the staff meeting, you read a book instead of paying attention to the rest of us. I need your support and participation if we're to meet our goals. Your contributions were valuable before and they're still valuable. For instance, what do you think we should do about the timing of the marketing report?"

Bill: "I think we should get it out by September 1."

You: "I agree. Can I count on your help?"

Bill: "Maybe. I'll give it a try."

You've done a good job of helping Bill get past his annoyance. You've engaged him, asked his opinion, and affirmed his value. What he does next is up to him. If he gets himself together, then the problem is solved; if he continues to treat you shabbily, you may have to begin a *progressive discipline* process until his behavior improves—or let him go if it doesn't.

def•i•ni•tion

Progressive discipline is a step-by-step process for correcting rules violations. The first step is usually an informal warning. If behavior doesn't change, harsher penalties are imposed one by one. The last step is firing.

Examples on paper, such as this one, always work out. In the real world, you may have to confront Bill's attitude several times. The thing to remember is that he's hurt and resentful. If his emotions continue to impede the team's progress, his employment is at risk, and you have to be strong enough to lay it on the line.

And you can't have favorites, either. Make no mistake about it. Your former work-mates will be watching closely to what happens if you have to discipline a close friend. If you let discipline slide out of consideration for your friendship, you erode your credibility with the others you supervise.

Personality Conflicts

While it's a fact that certain people just don't like each other and seem to have personalities that don't mix, very often what's perceived as a personality conflict is really a difference in work style.

In any office, you'll find what I like to call Party Animals and Loners, Left-Brainers and Right-Brainers, Sages and Detail Demons, Doers and Thinkers, and Altruists and Mechanics—and when they work together, confusion and misunderstanding are common.

Who's Who in the Office

Who You Are	What You Like
Party Animals	Brainstorming, collaboration, conversation
Loners	Time alone to think things through; a place to get away
Left Brainers	Explicit directions, good logistics, timelines
Right Brainers	"Build the rocket while I fly it," surprises, flexible deadlines
Sages	Leaps of faith, fantasy, and games
Detail Demons	Practicality, real-world thinking
Thinkers	Spontaneity, white space in the calendar, working right up to deadline to get the best product
Doers	Order, schedules, finishing ahead of the deadline
Altruists	Consideration of others' feelings, open-mindedness
Mechanics	Fairness to others, pragmatism

When a Party Animal finds himself in a nest of Loners, he's going to be looking for someone to talk to; he may end up bothering those who are more comfortable thinking and working alone. Mechanics often don't understand Altruists' concern with people's feelings. ("For Pete's sake, it doesn't matter how everybody feels about it! We have to make a decision that works for us.")

Left-Brainers don't get why Right-Brainers can't manage a deadline. Thinkers and Doers argue because the Thinker can't make up his mind, while the Doer may rush to action too fast. Sages, who believe in hunches, drive Detail Demons right up the wall.

And of course, every person combines many traits, so a right-brained, socially-minded Thinker will almost certainly cross swords with a left-brained, fact-oriented Doer. Whether these differences result in disputes and arguments is dependent on how insightful the employees are about the reasons for their differences.

I once resigned from a job and helped select my successor. Before I left, he and I led a staff retreat, in which we prepared our team for his leadership style, which was the polar opposite of mine. I was usually in my office, he was usually out; while I was concerned with staff cohesion, he was more interested in individual performance. I was a Doer, moving things along quickly. He was a Thinker, more interested in generating multiple solutions to various problems, so the resolution of issues took longer.

We worked with the staff to bring them to an understanding that my style was neither right nor wrong; it was simply different from his, and that they would do better as a team if they were aware of the differences before I left. The transition went very well, and the very productive group I'd developed remained committed and continued to turn out first-rate work.

Age Issues

The workplace today contains employees of different ages, and with those ages come differing attitudes about almost everything related to work. These differences are a function of how the world has changed from generation to generation. For instance, it's easy for someone who frequently deals with text to see which employees had difficulty making the jump from the typewriter to the computer. The typewriter people still put two spaces between sentences, even when their text is written on a computer. They have one foot in each camp. And that's just one tiny example.

Older workers, especially Baby Boomers who are nearing retirement, tend to be loyal to the company, do their jobs well, and not expect a whole lot of handholding or discussion. They've paid their dues and they expect others to do the same. They're comfortable with hierarchies, because that's what they know, and they may be resistant to change.

Talking Points

Baby Boomers were born between 1946 and 1964. Generation Xers were born between 1961 and 1981, and Generation Y was born between 1977 and 1995. There's overlap between generations, and older members of one generation may have more in common with the previous one than they do with the younger members of their generation.

Younger workers—the Gen X crowd—may go from job to job or even from career to career. They are loyal to their life plan, rather than to a corporation. They expect more guidance, feedback, and opportunities for networking. They are comfortable with a "web" style of management rather than a hierarchy, and they aren't intimidated by their managers or even the CEO. They expect change, go with the flow, and aren't impressed with rules that seem to have little relevance.

The youngest workers—Generation Y—are technologically sophisticated, like challenge, and want to be listened to. Many of them seek much more meaning from their work than did previous generations. They have life plans, but they also have fall-back positions where "I can be happy and at peace with myself if I don't succeed in achieving my real dream."

A university staff member says, "I frequently need to reach students, but it's very difficult. They have a university phone number and e-mail address, but they don't use them. They use another cell phone—sometimes a couple—and they have multiple e-mail accounts, some of which they check and some they don't. It's paradoxical in a way; they're wired to everything and yet hard to reach. When I told one of them I'd been trying to get hold of him, he said, 'Why didn't you just text me?' I was too embarrassed to tell him I didn't know how."

Older workers may see young colleagues as flighty and needy ("Honestly, he wants feedback if he blows his nose—and he can't spell 'cat'"), while young employees may see older ones as dinosaurs who are slow and inefficient ("Speed it up, Grandma! Multi-tasking is the name of the game!").

Possibly the biggest difference between the generations has to do with the willingness to work excessively long hours. Except for driven young entrepreneurs who routinely put in 140-hour weeks and for whom work is pleasure, younger workers are determined to spend time with their families and develop other aspects of their lives. They call it life balance, while many older workers view it as clock-watching and slackerism.

The life balance issue may show up in differences about money and office time. The youngest employees may be, at least for a time, less motivated by high salaries (especially if they are savvy money managers), and they sometimes question why they have to come to the office at all. Telecommuting may make more sense to them, while the older workers believe there's considerable value in the face-to-face contact provided by being in the office as a group.

Because the workplace is increasingly multigenerational, it's not unusual for a 55-year-old to report to a 35-year-old, and if the situation is reversed, it's common for the 35-year-old to question the older boss's decisions.

Although there's potential for generational arguments to arise, many observers say there's less of this kind of conflict in the workplace than might be expected. In many companies, younger employees are learning from the experience of those who've been around for a while, and older employees are leaning on the technological expertise of the young.

It's Not Always Personal

Age. Differences of opinion. Change. All of them contain the seeds of discord, but divisive disputes can be tempered if possible combatants realize that a disagreement may arise because of differences in world view rather than because of personal dislike. People are often too quick to take things personally and to come out swinging if someone disagrees with them.

Take a beat and examine what the other person said. If he called you a creep, that's a personal attack that needs to be dealt with, but if he simply pointed out some flaws in your argument or has a different perspective on an issue, that's information you can use. There's no need to get your back-up. Sometimes the best help comes from the most unexpected source. You just have to be willing to open your ears and listen.

> **Don't Do It!**
>
> Never decide that you know *why* someone said or did something. The only thing you know for certain is *what* he did. When you begin to attribute reasons and motives to his behavior, you open the door to even greater disagreement.

Solving Your Own Problems

If you're embroiled in a conflict with a co-worker, it's not always necessary to ask someone else to mediate. You might be able to do it yourselves. Begin by approaching your co-worker and saying, "It seems that you and I are frequently at odds and it's affecting how well we work together. Do you think we should sit down and try to hash it out? I'd like to get it behind us because it's causing a lot of tension."

Should the co-worker deny the problem or become abusive about your attempt to resolve the issue, you'll have to bring in a third party. Otherwise, here are some things you might do and say.

Get Agreement on What the Problem Is

> You: "Mandy, I think this problem began the day we had the meeting with Jack. You seemed to be angry with me after that meeting and it hasn't gotten better. Was there something that happened at that meeting that caused this rift between us?"

> Mandy: "You're kidding, right? I started sharing my ideas for the new advertising program, and you basically told me they were stupid. In front of Jack."

The issue is now on the table. You've both identified the meeting with Jack as the day the problem began, although you may have different perspectives on what was said or not said.

Check for Clarity

> You: "If I understand you correctly, I embarrassed you by belittling your ideas in front of Jack. It that right?"

> Mandy: "Darn straight."

That's clear.

Work Together on Solutions

> You: "I have a hard time seeing your point of view on this because I don't think I belittle people, but if I hurt you, especially publicly, I apologize."

You have not agreed with Mandy's position, but you have affirmed that her perception is valid for her. You may completely disagree with her characterization of you, but it's her truth, and you have to accept it.

Mandy: "It's possible you weren't as rude as I think you were, but it seemed to me you were putting me down so you could get your views across and get credit for them at my expense."

You: "Is there anything I need to do to heal this situation so we can work together the way we used to? If I disagree with you, how would you like me to handle it?"

Mandy may have all sorts of options in mind—don't speak up in meetings until I've made all my points; build on what I say rather than tearing it down, even if you disagree with me; don't humiliate me—and you can agree to one or even all. And be aware that a disagreement that is mended often leads to a relationship that is stronger than if there had never been a rift at all.

Office conflict probably cannot be avoided, but it doesn't have to tear the workplace apart.

The Least You Need to Know

- Conflict wastes managers' time and companies' money.

- Factors outside the company, such as the economy, can cause stress and disagreements within the company.

- Work style differences are common and often cause conflict.

- Newly promoted managers have to be sensitive to the feelings of former co-workers, but they must also take command of their departments.

- Courtesy and listening form the basis of all workplace problem resolutions.

Chapter 17

Good Boss, Bad Boss

In This Chapter

♦ Examining your perspective

♦ The worst bosses

♦ Working with bad bosses

♦ Why silence doesn't work

♦ The what-ifs of confrontation

Bosses come in all sizes, shapes, colors, and nationalities. Some of them have pleasing personalities and some of them don't. Some are competent and some aren't. Some are so good you'd follow them through the Sahara, while others are so dreadful you consider quitting from your first day on the job. And if the boss isn't up to snuff, the conversations between the two of you will almost always be difficult. This chapter deals with handling those communications.

In the Eye of the Beholder

Whether a boss is good or bad often depends on you. If a boss is brusque, do you see him as rude or simply a no-nonsense person? When a boss is demanding, do you view her as a tyrant or someone who wants high-quality work? We all have filters and screens through which we view the actions of others. I don't advocate putting on rose-colored glasses when a boss is behaving irrationally, but I do suggest you view your boss as a human being and not just a figurehead to fear and dislike. Unless he's an ill-mannered boor who also happens to be insane (and some of them are), you can probably develop a positive working relationship.

Every boss is a learning experience. Taskmaster bosses can teach you about getting the details right. Shy bosses will help you become more outgoing. Micromanager bosses force you to hone your assertiveness. The belligerent boss can teach you patience. And the bully boss will no doubt be your instructor in how much you're willing to accept before you take action on your own behalf.

Look around your workplace. If you can't stand the boss, but everyone else in the office can, the fault, dear Brutus, may be in you. You might ask those who get along well with the supervisor to share their secrets. Don't run down the boss or list the unpleasant exchanges you've shared with him. Just mention that you'd like to have some insight into working more effectively with the manager. Most colleagues are happy to give you what you need because it makes the office a more pleasant place to be.

A Catalog of Bad Bosses

Some bosses are truly dreadful. In the movie *9 to 5*, Dolly Parton's pig of a boss drops papers on the floor so he can stare at her cleavage and derrière as she crawls around to pick them up. That example probably was taken from life, because many employees report that similar things have happened to them. There's the boss who asks staffers to tell her husband she's in a meeting when she's having a tryst with the partner in her extra-marital affair.

Some bosses clip their toenails at their desks; snap their fingers to call staff members; throw things, including furniture, at employees; make disparaging remarks about appearance or weight; lie to staff; refuse to honor commitments; don't allow people to leave the office to tend to family emergencies, up to and including death; and even in this day and age believe it's their right to sexually harass both men and women who work for them.

These types of outrageous bosses don't deserve the service and loyalty of good employees, and if you're working for one, get out as soon as you can (unless you know he's about to be canned himself), because they rarely change. Keep your eyes and ears open, however, because sometimes even in the most untenable situations, you can pick up a great deal of useful information. Treat every office, even the most intolerable, as a learning laboratory. The only thing you might pick up is how not to treat people, but that's good to know when you become a boss yourself.

The Most Common Bad Bosses and How to Handle Them

Dishing about bosses is a favorite office pastime, and various firms and online sources delight in surveying people about what goes on in the office. When it comes to terrible bosses, the same types make an appearance on nearly every survey. They include:

- The Micromanager

- The Inexperienced Boss

- The Wimpy Boss

- The Explosive Boss

- The Bully Boss

Each of these bosses may seem impossible to work for, but a little insight into why they are the way they are can help you understand and approach them. And that's a much better use of your time than sitting around the break room moaning and complaining.

Managing the Micromanager

Micromanaging bosses behave that way for a variety of reasons. People are often promoted because they have mastered the technical challenges of departmental jobs. For example, a director of communication may be a good writer, a competent designer, an adequate photographer, an expert in digital image editing, and a talented interviewer. Because she is proficient at these tasks, those up the chain assume she'll be talented at supervising others who do the same tasks, and they promote her to head the communications department.

But the ability to supervise is learned; it's not an inborn trait. If the boss has been given no training in how to manage others, she probably won't do it very well. She will instead fall back into her comfort zone, scrutinizing details instead of concentrating on the big picture. She'll demand to see every picture, approve every word, and oversee every interview. She can't lead because she can't let go of her previous tasks.

It may be that the micromanaging boss is being micromanaged herself. She may be under tremendous pressure from those above her. Maybe she's managing the most important project of the year—and she's scared to death it won't get done on time or that it will be incomplete. Because the buck stops with her, no matter what her staff does, she's responsible. It's enough to make almost anyone overly cautious.

There's also the possibility that she's been burned by substandard subordinate performance in the past and found it necessary to take back the reins to protect her own job. Now she rides herd on staff to make sure that every picayune detail is roped and tied—and drives employees batty in the process.

Managers sometimes don't understand that delegating a task means delegating the authority for it as well. They give the job to a staffer, but watch so carefully they smother the employee's initiative and creativity.

You might approach a boss like this by saying: "You know, I've watched how hard you work at supervising so many details. I'd like to help relieve some of that stress and develop my skills at the same time. You assigned me responsibility for the grand opening of our client's flagship store. I'm very good at event planning, and I also know that you like to know how things are going.

"How about this? I'll prepare a schedule of all the tasks that need to be done and a timeline for them and present that to you for your approval. That way, if I've neglected anything, you can pencil it in.

"Then, every Friday, I'll send you an updated project report in any format you'd like. I'll check off each detail on the timeline so you can see that I'm maintaining the schedule and finishing the jobs you've approved."

The weekly check-in may be of sufficient comfort to allow the boss to let go. It won't happen overnight, but if you acknowledge her need to keep a spoon in the soup, while at the same time asserting your need to take responsibility for your job, she may slowly relinquish some control.

This strategy works only if you're willing to attend to every detail. If you let her down, she'll be back in the driver's seat so fast it will make your head spin. A string of successes will encourage her to trust you and hand over more responsibility and authority.

Experiencing the Inexperienced Boss

Bosses may be inexperienced because they're young and haven't had much time on the job. They might be experienced managers, but new to the company—or even to the industry—and on a steep learning curve.

Inexperienced bosses often have received no management training—a problem they share with many other types of bad bosses. Companies promote them and provide no assistance in how to do the job of management, which is a different job from the one they may have been doing before they were promoted.

The key to dealing with a young or inexperienced boss is not to grouse about your luck, but get down to the business of training him. You do that, not by confronting him about his inadequacies, which he's probably aware of, but by asking questions that will force him into developing a management style. You could ask:

> **Don't Do It!**
>
> Don't mistake inexperience for incompetence. Some people have a flair for working with others, even if their skills are a little shaky. Even the most inexperienced manager can have great ideas. Put your assumptions on the shelf and give the manager your support. As he climbs the ladder, he may take you with him.

- ◆ "What are your goals for the department? Do you have short-term objectives as well?"

- ◆ "How will you measure whether we're being successful in reaching goals?"

- ◆ "How do you prefer to work? Do you like to handle the big picture and delegate details? Or do you prefer to delegate entire projects?"

- ◆ "How often do you like people to report on projects they're responsible for? Do you like weekly reports, quick summaries, or a check-off sheet?"

- ◆ "If people have questions, do you want them to come to see you or would you prefer e-mail?" (Some introverted managers can be very effective without a lot of face time; they like e-mail and use it well to provide direction.)

- ◆ "Do you anticipate having frequent staff meetings or do you like to meet with managers individually?"

- ◆ "Is there anything I can help you with as you get acclimated? I've been with the company for seven years and I know the policies and procedures well."

These questions will make the new manager think about how he wants to run the shop, and you may see a big improvement in his abilities in just a few weeks.

Because you've been around awhile, you might be able to help your boss if you see him going down a blind alley. However, be gentle in your approach. "Yikes, you can't do that!" could generate resentment and close down further communication. But if you share history or examples or ask an open-ended question ("You know, it seems that management has always preferred …" or "Have you thought about …" or "Do you think it might be wise to …?"), you'll be able to steer the boss in the right direction and do yourself some good in the process.

Supporting the Wimpy Boss

Like the inexperienced boss and the micromanaging boss, the wimpy boss may tiptoe because she has been promoted above her level of comfort. Some companies provide new manager training; unfortunately, it may not be comprehensive, and the manager has to feel her way into being at ease with supervising other people.

Some wimpy bosses never take a stand because they want everyone to like them. Because they seem to have no opinions, no one can take issue with them. They don't support their employees, especially if there's a difference of opinion between work groups. They'll tell you to figure it out on your own, but they won't give you the tools to do it.

A wimpy boss usually doesn't know what she wants. She can't give consistent direction because her opinions change with the politics of the organization. Staff members are confused by her lack of leadership; they can become demoralized and demotivated because they aren't getting the feedback they need to do their jobs effectively.

You can help the tentative boss by being decisive yourself and asking for details when you need them. If you need feedback, solicit it actively and document it as well. It will help at your performance review.

- ◆ "I'm working on the interviews for the annual report. Can you tell me what day you'd like to have them? I can finish them today or Monday."

- ◆ "Could you tell me what approach you want me to take with the photography? Do you want a journalistic approach with a lot of black and white photography or would you prefer an edgier look with more design elements and fewer pictures?"

- ◆ "What did you think of the work I produced last week for the operations staff? Is there anything I should have done differently?"

Although it may not look that way from the outside, some bosses really aren't tentative at all; they're hands-off. They keep the ship afloat by concentrating on the horizon and expect the deck hands to do the work of keeping everything in working order.

If you're used to greater direction, you might have to ask for what you need:

Words to the Wise _____

It's surprising but true. You don't have to like your boss. All you have to do is respect his position and do the best job of which you're capable, even if he's not your personal cup of tea.

- ◆ "There are several ways we can structure the financing of the client's equipment. I think it might be wise to recommend a lease this time. Do you concur?"

- ◆ "What is the deadline for this project? I need to get it into my schedule, and I don't know how much time I have."

- ◆ "I'm feeling confused about how you want me to work with Carlos. Which one of us do you want to work directly with the client?"

Avoiding the Explosion

The boss who explodes is a familiar part of the business landscape. Some people yell because it's their nature. When they get excited or passionate about something—good or bad—the volume goes up. It means nothing. Ignore it.

Others yell because they lack self-control or have no other way to meet untoward situations. These people holler at waiters in restaurants, scream at customer service people, and shriek at family members. Growing up, they probably were taught no coping strategies except to talk louder than the other guy, especially if they're unsure of themselves. They embody the phrase, "Doesn't work and play well with others." And if, by chance, they get rewarded for their behavior—if people cave in and give them their way to stop the yelling—it reinforces their belief that losing control is an effective strategy. It might work, but it doesn't engender respect or liking.

Whatever the reason for a supervisor's going ballistic, it's no fun to be on the receiving end. If the explosion is private, don't cower and slink away, but don't answer yet, either. Responding to a screamer just turns up the heat. Face the boss, make eye contact, sit up straight and stand in a relaxed, open posture. Don't look intimidated; keep your face neutral. Don't be drawn in. Let her run down.

Then speak up, but don't say the first thing that pops into your brain, which probably is some variation of, "You dumb jerk. How dare you speak to me like that!" What you say instead is, "I understand" or even, "Message received." Then excuse yourself and walk it off, get a drink of water, and calm down.

In the next day or so, ask for a meeting with the boss and confront the behavior, using the three-step approach. "Yesterday, I made a mistake in the way I presented the sales figures, and you yelled at me for several minutes" (I see). "When I'm yelled at, I become angry myself and it affects my productivity for the rest of the day" (I feel). "If I need discipline or correction, I'll certainly accept it, but please speak with me rather than yelling at me" (I want).

If the boss is childish and can't take even this mild confrontation, it's possible she'll go off again. Follow your former strategy and get away as quickly as possible to contemplate your options, which may include rethinking your employment. Some bosses will listen, however, and scale back the temper—and some may even apologize and offer explanations.

Suppose the boss dresses you down in a meeting, on an elevator, or in the break room where other people are around. You can't take a poke at her when there are witnesses. Attractive though it may seem, eliminate that option from consideration. You also can't quit, unless this is the last straw and you've already cleaned out your desk in preparation for leaving immediately. If you're being asked to explain yourself, do so calmly and rationally. Under no circumstances should you allow yourself to behave as badly as the boss. When you descend to his level, you give away all your power. He wins. You confront him later.

> **Talking Points**
>
> All is not lost. A 2003 survey released by Ajilon Finance found that 79 percent of employees say they respect their bosses a great deal. On the other hand, some 30 percent of Americans feel they are more competent than their current managers.

Of course, you carry out your confrontation technique when it's appropriate, and this time you ask that the boss comment on your performance privately.

Stay or Go? The Bully Boss

One rung up the ladder from the screaming boss is the bully, and this boss is far and away the worst of the worst. Bullies demean, abase, and threaten. They call employees names, and some have been known to attack them physically as well. We often think of bullies as screamers, too, and sometimes they are, but a bully also can be quiet, inflicting torture below the surface. They are a scourge to employees and to business itself.

A former employee of an ad agency says, "I had a boss who was abusive. Although he was an incredibly talented man, he liked to scream and swear at people in person or on the phone. He'd use their names frequently so everyone in the office knew who he was humiliating.

"He was also a serial sexual harasser. The end came for me when I decided to put a clock on him and see how long it took for him to make the first salacious remark after he entered the office. The day it was 17 seconds was the day I quit. I just couldn't listen to it anymore. Everyone, including his wife, said he was going to get into hot water for his language and attitude toward the women who worked for him, but he wouldn't listen. I think he was honestly shocked when he was sued for his behavior and lost a court fight over it.

"This man was also a Jekyll and Hyde. One minute he was the office daddy and the next minute a leering satyr. You couldn't tell the players without a score card, and it was a sick workplace. It was also strangely productive because of his incredible talent. If you could handle the atmosphere you could learn a great deal from him, and in the six months I could tolerate working there, I learned a lot about copywriting and design, but I also learned the limits of my tolerance."

Bullies bully because they can. Most bully bosses pick on only a few people, usually those they perceive as unable to stand up for themselves. Bullies revel in the uneven balance of power, and they always have excuses—and because they eschew responsibility for their actions, most of their excuses begin with the word "you":

- "You made me lose my temper."

- "You can't find your butt with both hands."

- "You have nothing to say about it. I'm in charge. Now shut up and do what I say."

- "You'll stay all night if you have to. This will get done before tomorrow, and I don't care if it is your daughter's birthday. You work for me, not for her."

Many employees are unwilling to confront a bully boss because they are immobilized by what-ifs. "What if I do this and it just makes things worse?" "What if he threatens to fire me?" "What if he does fire me?" The secret to dealing with what-ifs is to play them out to the end and take action to mitigate the consequences.

Don't Do It! _____

No matter how bad the situation, don't immediately go over the boss's head to his supervisor or to HR. Keep your powder dry and work within the chain of command. If things don't improve, then do what you have to do.

For example, when you first become aware of bullying, document everything abusive that's been said to you. Write down the details of every confrontation. Keep these records at home, not in your desk. Document what you see happening to others as well. Draw a complete picture of your toxic work situation. Stick to the facts—use actual words and real situations. Resist the temptation to embellish. Shading the truth will come back to haunt you if the boss can prove that what you've said isn't true.

With your documentation available, you can confront the bully with confidence, telling him what is bothering you and asking for a change of behavior. If he heaves a lamp at you or there's no appreciable change in his behavior over time, you take your paperwork to his supervisor or HR. Sit back and see what happens.

What if he does fire you? Remember you can collect unemployment for a time while you look for another job, but also remember that if you think firing is likely, it's best to have another job offer in your pocket before you confront. Having the upper hand gives you the freedom to leave if you have to.

You confront bully behavior the way you confront anything else, but you may have to replace the "I want" portion of the three-step approach with an "I will not tolerate" statement. Be prepared to be shown the door. But sometimes simply drawing a line in the sand makes a bully back down. When he discovers that you have a spine, he may give up the reign of terror.

What You Must Remember

When you're dealing with a bad boss, the one thing that doesn't work is silence. Silence is consent. Speaking up in a mature, professional manner might alleviate the current situation and it might also help the boss. Many bosses don't know that their behavior is ineffectual or offensive because no one has ever told them. If you confront them, you may start a chain of events that results in greater productivity and a better workplace for everyone. That can only be a plus.

Also keep in mind that even if you're the most incompetent employee on the planet, you may deserve to be fired, but you don't deserve to be walked on and mistreated. If respect and courtesy aren't forthcoming and never will be, leave. Life is far too short to waste any of it being persecuted and denigrated. You will find another job, and the wear and tear on your health isn't worth it.

The Least You Need to Know

◆ Bad bosses are a fact of business life, and you'll probably have to deal with at least one in your business career.

◆ Bad bosses and toxic work environments are major factors in declining productivity.

◆ Some bosses may be unaware that they're ineffective leaders, and blame everything on bad employees.

◆ You should confront a bad boss, but always have a back-up plan in case you get fired for telling the truth as you see it.

◆ Maintaining your poise may be hard, but it's essential in dealing with a bad boss.

Chapter 18

Giving Great Service

In This Chapter

- The link between service and productivity
- Why customer service fails
- How word of mouth affects your business
- Common service problems in person and on the phone
- Solving customers' problems

One measure of a business's productivity is customer loyalty. All other things being equal, when customers return again and again, the business will be productive, profitable, and successful. But if business owners have to spend their time and money courting new customers because previous ones are staying away, the business is in danger. It's always less expensive to retain current customers than it is to recruit new ones, so customer satisfaction has a major economic impact. In the next two chapters, we'll look at customer service from both sides of the desk: how to give great service and how to get it.

When Customer Service Is an Oxymoron

My father-in-law used to have a sign on his door. It said, "Don't bother the help. Good help is hard to find. Customers? Forget about 'em. They're a dime a dozen." In his case, the sign was a joke, because the service he gave his customers was legendary, but today that sign appears to signal the way many businesses really feel.

Talking Points
In a 2006 Harris Interactive survey reported by RightNow Technologies, 96 percent of those responding reported a bad customer service experience within the previous 12 months, and 80 percent said they had stopped doing business with an organization because of poor service.

Every consumer has had the experience of being treated badly. Setting aside obvious scams that rob consumers of their money, dignity, and sleep, even legitimate businesses often disappoint those who try to use their products and services. Wretched customer service can happen in person or on the phone, and wherever it occurs, it leaves a bad taste in customers' mouths and makes them less likely to buy from the company in the future.

Customer service has deteriorated because …

♦ There aren't enough customer service people.

♦ Customer service representatives are neither well-selected nor well-trained.

Not Enough People

In an era of shrinking margins, customer service is often one of the first areas to be cut. That's short-sighted. Customers are the lifeblood of a business and treating them shabbily is ill-advised. One of the chief complaints people have about shopping is that there's no one to help them. They enter a huge store and there's no one on the floor, or if there is, that person "doesn't work in this department," doesn't know the merchandise, and seems to have little interest in finding out what the customer needs to know.

Poorly Selected and Trained

It takes a certain set of skills to serve the public well: knowing the products, listening with attention, speaking appropriately, possessing a problem-solving mentality, and caring about both the business and the customer. Customer service people, particularly those on the front line—from sales clerks to cable installers to car salespeople—should be carefully sought out and given the tools, authority, responsibility, and financial incentives to do their jobs well.

After-the-sale employees should be trained at least as well as sales personnel. Once a purchase is made, it's far more likely that customers will interact with technical staff, support personnel, or customer service than they will with the person who sold them the product or service. Yet training dollars may be lavished on sales staff, with only the leftovers given to those who might matter most in developing customer loyalty.

Too often these folks are treated as interchangeable cogs in a giant wheel, taken for granted and paid poorly. It doesn't take a genius to figure out that those conditions contribute to the lack of service that's a feature of most businesses today.

To keep customers loyal, service representatives must be given the leeway to make decisions that favor the customer on the spot. "Yes, I can do that for you" is refreshing after a day of "No, I can't, because that's not our policy." Nothing beats a customer service person who can deliver real customer service.

What Angry Customers Do

When customers are treated rudely, they walk out. Why shouldn't they? There's no one on the floor to complain to anyway, and even if they do complain, the supervisor is often as obnoxious and uninformed as the employee. But it's what happens after a customer leaves that can have the greatest impact on a business. Customers' actions can cost people their jobs and put a big crimp in profits for a long time to come.

If customers feel they've been kicked around, they:

- Go to the top
- Spread the word

Go to the Top

Contrary to popular opinion and with a few notable exceptions, upper management does care about how customers are treated, and if they receive a carefully crafted letter of complaint or a well-reasoned phone call, they often will investigate the incident. Heads sometimes roll.

Spread the Word

The most damaging thing customers can do is to tell others how badly they were treated. If you're unkind to my sister, you'll lose her as a customer, but you'll also lose her husband, her two daughters, their husbands, their three children, me, my husband, our children, and their husbands and wives—as well as some assorted cousins and their families. That's a lot of potential sales to give up for the thrill of being rude. And of course, that figure doesn't count all the people outside the family who will hear about your lousy service.

Grapevines are not restricted to offices. Because people don't hesitate to use the Internet to post their stories on sites that gather opinions about products and services, the grapevine now reaches everywhere. Many consumers check these sites religiously before making a buying decision. If your customer service people don't know what they're doing, it won't be a secret very long. Sometimes web sites offer photographic evidence of bad service through cell phone cameras or personal video that can be uploaded and beamed around the world in a matter of minutes. It's time to clean up your act.

Talking Points

It's estimated that one dissatisfied customer tells 11 people and that each of those people tells 5 more. In a very short time, 66 people are aware of your service snafu. A recent Canadian survey indicated that negative word of mouth is powerful. When people hear negative things about a store from other people, a whopping 51 percent of them don't shop there.

Things That Drive Customers Away

The common annoyances that cause customers to tear out their hair? There are plenty.

Not Looking at or Speaking to the Customer

A friend of mine bought a shirt at a local store. The clerk never looked at him and never spoke to him, concentrating only on ringing up the purchase and examining his credit card. "I needed the shirt right away," he says, "or I would have left."

What he did instead was to stand quietly after his purchase was rung up and bagged, preventing the next person in line from getting to the cashier. When she realized her line wasn't moving, the clerk looked up. He said, "You really need to look at the people who are at your counter. If I'd come in to rob the place, you wouldn't have been able to give the police a description." He then apologized to the woman behind him for keeping her waiting in line an extra minute and left the store. He has never been back.

Customers are the reason you have a job. The very least you can do is acknowledge their presence and act as if you're glad to see them.

"No."

Here's a dialogue that drives customers nuts.

Customer: "Do you have this item in stock?"

Service Person: "No."

Customer: "Can you tell me when you expect to get it?"

Service Person: "No."

Customer: "Do you have anything similar?"

Service Person: "No."

It's not what the customer service person is saying that's so offensive; it's the way she's saying it. How about:

"I'm sorry that item is out of stock right now, but we expect a shipment on Thursday. Would you like me to reserve one for you and give you a call when it arrives?"

There's no doubt the customer will be momentarily annoyed that what he came in to buy isn't available, but he'll also be impressed with your willingness to help. You've salvaged a customer relationship by speaking appropriately. In the first instance, the customer service person simply provided information. You made no attempt to actually serve the customer's needs. In the second instance, you placed the customer front and center. He got the same information and was given the same message—"no"—but in a way that was palatable.

If you want to deliver exceptional, superior customer service (and some companies are noted for it), you have the item delivered to the customer's door as a thank you for his patience.

> **Talking Points**
>
> A 2006 survey by the National Retail Federation and American Express reported by CNNMoney.com listed Amazon.com as the top performer in customer satisfaction. The company was followed by Nordstrom, L.L.Bean, Overstock.com, Lane Bryant, Boscov's, Kohl's, REI, Lands' End, and Macy's.

"You Have to Understand."

Want to make customers' ears turn red? Tell them they have to understand. Here's a news flash. Customers don't have to understand. "You have to understand that we only get a delivery once a week." Or "You have to understand that only a security person can enter the area where we placed your property and there's no security person here right now." Those may be the facts, but the customer isn't required to understand your delivery schedule or your security policies.

It's at least slightly better to say, "We're out of what you want, and our truck comes only once a week. I'll be happy to call our other stores to see if they have the item and have it sent here for you to pick up. Otherwise, I can put one aside for you next Tuesday when we get our shipment." Or, "I'm so sorry. We locked your wallet in our security area after we found it on the counter, but now there's no one here who can unlock it. I know it's frustrating to make another trip back, but our security personnel will be here this evening at 9 and back in the morning at 10. Do either of those times work for you? I'll leave a note that you'll be here to pick it up. I wish we could just deliver it, but it has to be identified before we can release it."

In neither of these cases has the customer been asked to understand, and that's good.

> **Words to the Wise**
>
> Keep explanations simple, especially if you're dealing with technology. When customers ask for help, speak slowly and steer clear of jargon. And don't laugh if what the customer did was forget to plug in the new device, turn it on, or charge the battery. By that point, she feels stupid enough. There's no need to rub salt in the wound.

Inappropriate Behavior

Silly behavior can run the gamut from talking on a cell phone while you're serving a customer; carrying on a personal, angry, or profanity-laced dialogue with another employee while the customer is within earshot; chomping on a wad of gum; eating or drinking during a conversation with a customer; or rolling your eyes, sighing, and looking impatient when a customer has a question. None of these things makes a good impression, and if they have a choice, customers will choose a vendor who is polite, friendly, and professional.

Forgetting Your Manners

A customer who enters your store should receive a polite and pleasant welcome from everyone she encounters, not just from some paid greeter. Smile when you direct people to the right department, and say "You're welcome" when someone thanks you for your help. Let your body language convey warmth and approachability. Don't be closed off and rigid.

Any customer who has purchased from you deserves some eye contact and a genuine thank you, not a "ThankyouforshoppingatSurlyMart." That person's purchase helped provide your paycheck. Look at her and say thank you—and mean it. Appreciating the customer is a big part of customer service, and it's little things, like a thank you, that people remember.

No Better on the Phone

Customers often become angry about those they can't see: notably call center employees who are incompetent, rude, and seemingly hate their jobs.

"Can You Hold?"

It's nice to ask people if you may place them on hold, but it's not nice to actually do it before they have a chance to grant permission. I recently called my doctor and in the nanosecond between, "Can you hold?" and the time the receptionist punched the hold button, I said, "No, I can't." I was tempted to tell her I was bleeding out the eyes, but I refrained and explained the medication side effect that was the reason for my call. It turned out to be a biggie and the doctor immediately took me off the drug.

One of the biggest customer complaints is that nobody listens. Start listening the minute you pick up the phone. If you ask a question, have the courtesy to wait for an answer.

"What's Your Account Number?"

Last week, I had to call a utility about a service problem. The phone was answered, "Great Big Utility Company, may I have your account number?"

I waited two beats and said, "Good morning." The customer service representative was so shocked she didn't say anything for a couple of seconds. Then she said, "Good morning. What can I do for you?" That's better.

Don't Do It!

Never put a caller on speakerphone without permission. A caller has some expectation that a phone call is a private communication. She might not want her voice amplified and blasted to the far corners of the call center.

Then I asked her name and told her mine and we were off to the races. The service situation went very smoothly, in part because I was friendly, but also because I refused to let her be curt and dismissive.

It takes only a moment to say, "Good morning. Great Big Utility Company. How may I help you?" Help is what you're there to do. Say so.

"I'm Putting You on Ignore."

If you must put a customer on hold while you work to resolve an issue, try to keep wait time to a minimum. If it will take a while, share that information with the customer at the outset, and get back on the line occasionally to see if he's alive or dead. Report your progress on fixing the problem.

I suppose ignoring a customer might eventually make him go away, but he'll be back and he'll be angry. Music on hold is often intrusive, but at least it's a way to let the customer know the connection hasn't been broken.

Language Issues

When companies send their customer service work overseas, they open a can of worms. If the representative doesn't speak English well or has a heavy accent, calls can be interminable, as the caller and the customer service person struggle to understand each other.

If you don't want to antagonize clients, your customer service people must understand English and speak it fluently. They must be able to answer questions or field concerns that aren't in their scripts, and they can't do that without English proficiency. My friend Liz had an encounter with an outsourced service department that was a textbook example of everything that can go wrong.

The call was a collection matter and the customer service representative told Liz that payment needed to be made right away. And then it went downhill.

> Liz: "I'm expecting a check today or tomorrow. When it comes, I will go to one of your branch stores and make the payment immediately."
>
> Rep: "So you'll be mailing a check today?"
>
> Liz: "No, I have to wait for my check to arrive. Then I'll make the payment at the store."

Rep: "You will make the payment today?"

Liz: "No. Please listen to what I'm saying. I will make the payment at the store itself. I will not mail it and I can't give you a precise date. The check I am expecting should arrive today. I will put it into the bank. It will clear overnight, and then I will take a check directly to the store."

Rep: "So you will make the payment online?"

Liz: "No, and if you won't listen to me, this conversation is at an end. You'll receive the money at one of your stores within a couple of days. Goodbye."

She was steamed for several hours, all because a company had decided its customer service function wasn't important enough to hire a person who could understand what was being said to him. It wasn't his fault; it was the company's fault. Liz made the payment as soon as she received her check, as she had promised to do. She then tore up her store card and vowed never to do business there again.

On the other side of the coin is the incoming call from a customer with a heavy accent. Be polite and explain to the customer that you are having trouble understanding him. Ask him to speak slowly. You do the same. And don't shout. The customer has a language problem, not a hearing problem.

Keep any trace of annoyance out of your voice. No matter how accented a customer's speech, he has the same rights to service as a customer who speaks standard English.

Many call centers now have associates who speak a variety of languages. Try to enlist the help of one of these agents or transfer the call right away. You might also send the call directly to a supervisor who has access to language sources you might not know about.

Resolving a Complaint

Resolving a customer complaint is relatively easy if the customer is reasonable. Here's what you do:

Take Responsibility

If an error is the company's fault, say so. Don't double shuffle and try to blame someone else. "It appears we didn't ship when we said we would."

Listen

Let the customer vent until he runs out of steam. Don't interrupt, saying, "Sir?" every time he takes a breath. He will interpret that as interrupting and it will fuel his annoyance even more.

Empathize

"I can understand why that would be upsetting," is a powerful phrase. It gives the customer a sense that the two of you are in this together, rather than in an adversarial relationship.

Stay Cool

Never lose your head. Never shout or hang up on the customer, even if you're tempted to.

Generate Options

"There are a couple things we can do to take care of this problem. I see that we've made the shipment now, so if you like, you can refuse it and send it back at our expense, or I can subtract all the shipping charges from your order, and you can keep the merchandise. What would be best for you?"

Solve the Problem

"It sounds as if you want to keep the merchandise. Then I'll be happy to adjust your invoice to remove all the shipping charges. And how about this? I'll send you a coupon for 25 percent off your next purchase as a thank you for your patience."

Underpromise and Overdeliver

If you know beyond a doubt that the merchandise will be in the customer's hands by Monday, promise it by Tuesday. It will be a happy surprise when it arrives "early."

Check Again

"Here's where we are now. I can guarantee your shipment by Tuesday and it will be free of shipping charges. Does that resolve this situation satisfactorily?"

Say Thank You

"Thank you for bringing this situation to my attention. If you should have any more problems, my name is Pam and my customer service number is 87652. You can call back and ask for me personally any time." Once again, you've joined forces with the customer against the problem.

Words to the Wise

If a customer asks to speak to a supervisor, transfer the call. There seems to be a move afoot to tell customers, "I don't have a supervisor." That's silly. Someone has to be in charge of a call center, and it's usually not the first-line employee. Help the customer move up the chain, rather than hacking him off even more.

Venting, Yes: Abuse, No

What if the customer isn't reasonable? He's screaming, swearing, and threatening. You don't have to take that. Here are some ways you might calm down the rhetoric or get out of the situation.

Use the Customer's Name

Show him that you know who he is. It might snap him back to reality. "Mr. Williams, it sounds as if you're very upset with us, and I'm here to see how I can help. My name is Pam. Let's figure out what we can do to get your issue resolved."

Set Limits

Out-of-control customers who are having the equivalent of a two-year-old's tantrum need to understand that you do not tolerate personal abuse. But stay away from "you" statements, such as, "You don't get to speak to me like that," or "You're being so rude I can't deal with you." Try, "I can hear you're very upset and I'd like to help solve your problem. I can't do that until I know what it is. Please stop swearing at me so we can begin working on whatever has made you so angry."

If the customer continues to rant, rave, scream, and otherwise be impossible, your stress and anger will rise, and you won't be effective. You can say that. "Mr. Williams, I don't think I'm going to be able to help you. I can't seem to get you to tell me why you're angry, so perhaps it would be wise to let you speak to someone else. I'm going to transfer you to my supervisor, Ms. King, who will try to resolve the problem." If you have the capability to let Ms. King know what's coming her way, do that. You might even stay on the line to introduce the two of them.

Close It Down

If there's no one to transfer the call to and the customer bellows on, berating and demeaning you, call a halt. "Mr. Williams, we're not getting anywhere. I'll be happy to help you at another time, but I cannot allow you to continue speaking to me this way. I'm going to terminate this call now. Please get in touch with us later when you can tell us what the problem is."

Most customer service issues can be resolved if you keep your eyes on the prize—a satisfied customer—and avoid getting sidetracked by insignificant issues along the way.

The Least You Need to Know

- ◆ Dissatisfied customers cost your business both money and time.
- ◆ Most customer service personnel have not received sufficient training to do their jobs well.
- ◆ One-word answers and curt responses annoy customers and should be avoided.
- ◆ Off-shore customer service can hurt you if service personnel cannot speak English well enough to solve customers' problems.
- ◆ Customer service representatives should be taught how to handle difficult customers, but they should not allow themselves to be abused.

Chapter 19

Getting Great Service

In This Chapter

- Bad customers get bad service
- Complaining effectively
- Quotas and customer service
- Why complaints matter
- Short circuiting the complaint process

And now we come to the other side of the desk: being the customer others want to help. What is your responsibility in the consumer/customer service representative equation? Why do some people get great service while others always seem to find the nastiest service people in the world? This chapter will answer some of those questions and help you find the right words to use.

Don't Be a Difficult Customer

Customer sales, service, and support staff are employed to sell you products and resolve legitimate issues, and when you abuse these people, you make it tougher for everyone, including others who need service. They won't thank you for that.

Are you one of these three types of difficult customers?

Marty the Manipulator

Do you always try to get something for nothing? There's nothing wrong with a little negotiation. If you've hired a design firm to create an ad for you, you can ask them if they'd touch up your home page, too. They might do it to keep your business. But don't get all offended and huffy if they say no. They're in business to make money, not give you free service. And don't expect perks every time you pick up the phone. You're not entitled to them.

Bob the Bully

Do you scream, insult, and belittle others, and then blame them for your all-around nastiness? You may get what you want just because people want to shut you up; generally, however, it takes longer to deal with your complaint because no one feels like helping someone who's calling her names. If you're behaving badly over the phone, you may find yourself listening to a dial tone, and if you're berating someone personally, you may look up and discover security or the police ready to escort you from the premises. Neither of these solves your problem. And, frankly, what makes you believe you have the right to abuse another person? The customer service rep didn't cause your problem and she doesn't deserve your out-of-control wrath and bad manners.

Liz the Liar

Have you worn that new cocktail dress to a charity event, spilled wine on it, and then taken it back for a refund, saying you put on the dress and it had "this big stain on it." Have you returned "defective" merchandise without mentioning that you dropped it before it stopped malfunctioning? Most stores will let you get away with it a couple of times. Now, however, some retailers are using their computer capabilities to pinpoint habitual return-policy abusers; they either refuse to take the merchandise back or charge a restocking fee.

Intangible Assets

There are other ways to make the service experience more productive. First, and perhaps most important, enter into the experience believing that your problem can be worked out. If you start out with the expectation that getting what you need will be a battle, you set up a negative situation from the outset. Your tone of voice is more strident than necessary, the words you choose may be more combative, and the look on your face may invite an adversarial response.

A smile and a lighter touch can go a long way toward making the conversation work, as can the expectation that the service person is someone who has your best interests at heart. It's some kind of karmic law that we get back what we put out, so put those positive vibes out front and see what happens. There's lots of time to fight later, if it becomes necessary.

Turnabout

You know how mad it makes you when the clerk or salesperson talks on the phone while you're standing right there? Well, talking on a cell phone while you point and snap your fingers for service is just as rude and thoughtless when you do it as when it's done to you. Get off the phone and give your attention to the person who's trying to help you.

Keep It to Yourself

Don't involve other people if you're in a set-to with customer service. It's not necessary for you to roll your eyes at other customers and say, "Can you believe this? What an idiot!" It serves no purpose except to make you look like a tyrant, and while you're playing to the crowd, you're slowing down the resolution of your problem. Pay attention and handle your dispute in a mature fashion.

Hands Off

Here's one you might not have thought of, but customer service people know about. Keep your hands to yourself. Don't touch the person who's waiting on you or trying to resolve your complaint. I have a friend who worked her way through school as a cocktail waitress. "The job of a cocktail waitress," she says, "is to serve you drinks and food, not to be your plaything. Most customers know that, and they're great people who understand the rules and tip well. But one night I was serving a man who decided that he could put his hands in the most inappropriate places just because I was wearing a short skirt. I told him to stop and then I went to my manager and asked to have the jerk thrown out. I was stunned when he told me that behavior was okay; it went with the territory and I should just smile my way through it.

"I did as I was told and put up with an evening of groping. But I had my revenge a couple of weeks later. It was New Year's Eve, the busiest night of the year. The place was bedlam, and even a full staff wasn't enough to take care of everyone. Midway through the evening, when things were especially crazy, I went to the manager, took off my name badge and said, 'Oh, by the way, I quit. You should have backed me up when I asked for your help.' And then I walked out. I lost a lot in tips that night, but I never felt better. A manager should support employees who are being abused. The customer is not always right when the customer is being an insulting creep."

> **Words to the Wise**
>
> The most important rule to remember in any customer service interaction is the golden one. Are you treating the service staff the way you would want to be treated?

By the way, it's also improper to throw merchandise—or anything else—including paperwork, your telephone, or your handbag, in the clerk's face. That verges on assault and can get you in big trouble. No customer service problem is that important.

Why Customer Service Is Frustrating for Everyone

In a word, quotas. Customer service people are stressed and overworked because they are expected to clear a certain number of calls a day or write a certain number of orders. Complaints may take time to resolve, and if the service rep really tries to help, she's going to hear from management that she's not processing enough calls during her shift. Some companies put a clock on every call or customer interaction, and a rep or salesperson can lose his job if he exceeds the time limit too often. It's very efficient, but the focus of the job then becomes to get you off the phone or out of the store, not to solve your problem.

The following worksheet gives you some clues about whether the company values speed above service.

Ain't No Service Here

When you call for customer service, does the company representative:

		Yes	No
1.	Sound rushed?	❑	❑
2.	Ask you to call back when he's not so busy?	❑	❑

	Yes	No
3. Refuse to give you his name or employee number?	❏	❏
4. Tell you all the reasons that your solution won't work or is against policy?	❏	❏
5. Suggest solutions other than what you want?	❏	❏
6. Tell you there's no one of greater authority available to take your call?	❏	❏
7. Speed through explanations and become impatient if you don't understand everything the first time?	❏	❏
8. Put you on hold several times during your call?	❏	❏
9. Transfer you again and again?	❏	❏
10. Ask you to repeat details of your complaint several times?	❏	❏

If you've answered "yes" to three or more of these questions, customer service is a low priority.

Complaint Central

Most unpleasant conversations about service come about because the original product is substandard or a previous interaction has been unsatisfactory. The current conversation is therefore a complaint.

Good customer service people understand that a complaint can be an opportunity and that those who complain are doing the company a favor. Those who complain rather than going public with their unhappiness allow businesses to …

- ◆ **Improve their products.** If customers are having trouble using a product, manufacturers need to correct those defects.

- ◆ **Detect patterns.** Is the same problem occurring again and again? Are there service bottlenecks? Too much wait time? Too many instances of products being out of stock? A service person who's particularly good—or bad?

♦ **Build loyalty.** Customers whose complaints are resolved quickly (within 24 hours) have been proven to be more loyal than average customers who have never complained.

In fact, smart businesses actually solicit complaints by making follow-up calls or mailing surveys that invite customers to comment on their shopping or service experiences. And they resolve complaints on the first contact.

The Nonsqueaky Wheel

You don't have to be annoying to complain well and get what you want. In most cases, all you have to be is assertive, specific, and courteous.

Go to the Right Person

If you have the flu, you don't consult a plumber. Same thing with a service problem. You need to find the person who can actually help you. Sometimes that's a customer service representative and sometimes it isn't. If the people on the phone haven't been given the authority to make decisions and offer real assistance, your call is useless. It's not the representative's fault; he's often as irritated and impatient with policies as you are. Don't waste your time venting your anger on him. Just thank him and ask for the supervisor.

If you're told there's no supervisor available, ask to speak with the center manager. Don't be put off. You can say, "I'm quite sure your whole center is not working without supervision. I would like to speak to the person who is in charge of this shift, and I'd like to do that immediately." Keep your tone pleasant but businesslike.

I once called a store to complain about a box of cookies that had worms in it. You know what's worse than finding a worm in your food? Finding half a worm. And that's what happened. After I had stopped squealing and checked with my doctor to see if I was in danger of imminent death, I didn't mess around. There was no sense in telling the check-out person or even the store manager. It might have been a system-wide issue, so I went straight to the regional manager of the grocery chain and notified him of the incident.

The next morning, I was astonished to find a representative of the cookie company on my doorstep. He explained what had happened and how that box of cookies ended up at the store. He gave me a zillion coupons for their products—and I continued to buy them because clearly this was an isolated incident.

Getting to the right person made a difference. Yes, he got off cheap, but I had no reason to sue or to be vindictive. I didn't have monetary damages or lasting health issues. Just a case of the creeps.

Get on a First Name (and Number) Basis

When you reach any representative, ask for her full name. If she's not permitted to give you anything but her first name, ask for her employee number. Tell her your full name, too. Be aware that some customer service people feel offended if you ask for their names, but try to get some identifier. Exchanging names reminds both of you that you're each talking with a person, not a machine.

Ask for Help

I've found that the phrase, "I need your help," sometimes works wonders. Customer service reps often have to listen to rude demands, and a simple request for help may be a refreshing change. "I'm having a problem with one of your products, and I need your help," may engage them and enlist their support.

Be Clear About the Problem and the Desired Solution

Be respectful of the fact that the service representative has to accomplish his quota for the day, so don't waste his time. Don't talk about how long you've been a customer and how sad it is that quality is so poor today. Get to the point: the problem and how you want it solved.

> "I bought a Squash-It Sandwich Maker, Model 495, from your website on January 8 of this year. It arrived January 15. Unfortunately, after the first month, it stopped heating. I would like you to replace it or refund my money. I returned my warranty card on January 16; it should be in your system."

This is a straightforward request any frontline person should be able to handle, but because some businesses are focused on things other than service, this may be just the opening few bars of a complicated dance.

You may be told that you can return the merchandise only at your own expense. Or maybe it's not the appliance at all. You're probably not using it properly. Perhaps it just needs a new power cord, and they'll send you one. This is a fine, inexpensive solution for them, but if the power cord isn't the problem, you still have a non-functioning sandwich maker and you've wasted a lot of time.

Whenever the service rep suggests a solution that isn't to your liking, agree with whatever you can, but continue to restate your position. You might say:

- ◆ "You're right. I suppose it could be the power cord, but I'd like you to replace the unit or refund my money."

- ◆ "It's true that sometimes people don't know how to use what they buy. But the sandwich maker worked for a month so I must have been doing it right. I bought the merchandise only thirty days ago, and now it doesn't work. I'd like you either to replace it or refund my money as spelled out in the guarantee. You have my completed warranty card."

def•i•ni•tion

Fogging is an assertive communication technique in which you agree to portions of the other's position while retaining the right to your own opinion. **Broken record** is a simple repetition of your point in response to whatever the other person says.

This type of communication is a combination of two assertiveness techniques called *fogging* and *broken record*, and they can be very effective when time is limited. You don't need to raise your voice. In fact, the calmer and more positive you are, the greater your chances for success. You're showing you understand the representative's point of view, but don't agree with it. You're also eating up minutes, and he might do what you ask just to get rid of you.

If not, ask for the supervisor. Start again.

Remain Calm and Be Polite

When describing your problem, there's no reason to be unpleasant. That puts the other person on the defensive. But there's no reason to be diffident and toe-in-the-sand, either. If you've been sold a defective product or been mistreated, don't apologize for holding the company's feet to the fire. But don't be rude. Remember that the person on the other end of the phone didn't make the product and isn't the one who first treated you badly. Your disagreement is with the company, not with her personally.

Don't Settle

If you've asked for compensation of some sort, don't be fobbed off with an apology. "Oh, we're so sorry that happened," should be the starting point in your negotiations, not the end.

Know Your Rights

Yes, fraudulent businesses do exist, but most people are honest and try to do well by their customers. Therefore, if you need to rectify a situation with a business, begin by assuming it was an error rather than a deliberate attempt to defraud you.

In the sandwich maker case, your rights are in the warranty. "The guarantee indicates that the product is warranted for one year against defects in workmanship. I bought it a month ago, and it's defective. Therefore, I'd like you to replace it or refund my money."

Sometimes government regulations protect your rights. In the matter of collections, for example, the law states clearly what collections personnel may and may not do. For example, they cannot call you at "inconvenient times and places," such as before 8 A.M. or after 9 P.M. Collectors may not threaten you or use obscene language. They aren't allowed to call repeatedly to annoy you. There's more spelled out in the Fair Debt Collection Practices Act. If you're a victim of harassment or violations of the law, you have recourse.

In dealing with a service issue, be reasonable and don't demand compensation you aren't entitled to. But if you're within your rights, keep at it until you've made yourself understood.

Words to the Wise

If you wonder if a business is legitimate, there are the tried and true ways to check it out, such as seeing if the company has been reported to the Better Business Bureau or to your state's Attorney General. Sometimes it's faster to hop onto a search engine and type in the name of the company and then the word "scam" or "lawsuits." That will lead you to sites where others may have reported fraudulent activities.

Persist

If your problem is even remotely complicated, you're going to have to explain it more than once—to the rep, the supervisor, the manager, and maybe others. All these repetitions take time and effort. You might short-circuit this process if you anticipate it. "I have a somewhat complicated situation and I need to speak to someone who has the authority to solve it today. You're probably going to have to escalate this call anyway, so may I please speak to your manager?"

Don't be surprised if your strategy doesn't work. You may have to start at the bottom and work your way up. If you think you're going to run out of steam—or patience—consider whether you're willing even to begin the complaint process. Some companies use excessive wait times and transfers to make you give up. Do you have the patience to persevere?

It helps to have your statement of the issue written out so your presentation of the facts never varies. For example:

> "My son has been attending classes at the Hearing Centre to deal with a speech delay. When I precertified the classes, I was told that I would be reimbursed for the classes because they were covered under my policy. Now the company is refusing reimbursement. I have discovered that there is a coding error that indicates my son has cerebral palsy. He does not have cerebral palsy. I already have documentation from his pediatrician that he has a speech delay, not cerebral palsy. I would like this coding error to be rectified immediately and to be reimbursed for the classes."

This complaint will have to go up the chain for sure, so be prepared to use all your tact and patience. You'll be in the process for a long time.

Take Notes

Keeping detailed notes is one of the most important things you can do if you're trying to resolve an issue. In the situation above, for example, the first question you'll be asked will be, "Who told you that the class fees would be reimbursed?" If you can answer, "I spoke with Ms. West, whose employee number is 7654, on May 7, at 10:30 A.M., and she assured me that my policy covered this situation," you're in a much stronger position than if you say, "I don't know, but someone did."

Next, the representative may question how you know the coding is wrong. "I spoke with my son's pediatrician, and her billing department checked it for me. That was on

August 6. The reimbursement specialist's name is Abigail Browne. Her phone number is 614-555-1234. The codes for these conditions are very similar, but the two numbers in the middle—6 and 8—have been transposed. I'd like to fix that right away because I'm sure it's going to have an effect on his coverage in other situations as well."

Questions can go on and on, and good notes make it possible for you to answer them succinctly and accurately. More than any other technique, taking notes puts you in the driver's seat; you can't be rattled because you have the facts. Keep relevant paperwork, such as credit card receipts and warranty information, in a file. You may be asked for documentation to prove that what you're claiming is true.

Words to the Wise

If you're caught in complaint hell, you can sometimes jump over several layers of middle managers by going to the company website. Search for the company officer in charge of the area you're complaining about. E-mail that person directly, appealing for her intervention. You can also communicate with the PR department. They don't like dissatisfied customers and may direct you to the person who can help.

Reward Good Service

There are some wonderful customer service people out there. When you run across one, thank her and tell her that you'd like to commend her to her supervisor. It's amazing how quickly she'll put you through. When the news is good, there's no baloney about the call center not having any management people available. Be specific in your commendation, and make sure that the supervisor will note it in the employee's file. Offer to write a letter. Good service, which is rare, should be noticed and rewarded.

The Least You Need to Know

- Sometimes poor customer service results from customers' bad behavior.

- To solve a problem, you must be polite but not wimpy.

- Every complaint should include a clear statement of the problem and the actions that you want to see taken.

- Know your consumer rights, but don't try to exceed them.

- Use websites for information about company officers you can contact if customer service is poor or nonexistent.

Chapter 20

Stress and Burnout

In This Chapter

- ◆ The nature and effects of stress
- ◆ Common reasons for stress
- ◆ The relationship between stress and burnout
- ◆ Addressing burnout as an employee
- ◆ Addressing burnout as a manager

In the American workplace today, it is estimated that as much as 80 percent of medical costs may be traced to stress complaints and serious physical problems that are exacerbated by stress. Obviously stress is a productivity issue, but stress also causes communication problems. Stressed people are likely to blow up or shut down. People who are tense and on edge often converse only with great difficulty. In this chapter, you'll learn what to say when you or others are struggling with stress.

The Effects of Stress

Stress affects the body, the mind, the soul, and the spirit.

In the body, stress can cause:

- Sweaty palms
- Rapid heartbeat or a feeling of flutteriness
- Debilitating headaches
- Stiff neck and shoulders
- Low back pain
- Extreme fatigue
- Lightheadedness, dizziness, fainting
- Intestinal complaints ranging from nausea and diarrhea to vomiting and constipation

Continual, unrelieved stress floods the body with hormones that keep it in a constant state of readiness for fight or flight and can cause serious damage to the heart and other organs. Why do you think more heart attacks occur on Monday mornings than any other day of the week? On Monday morning, we turn up the stress level, and for some people, that additional stress is the factor that overwhelms the heart's ability to cope.

In the mind, stress can trigger:

- Frustration
- Confusion
- Obsession; that is, thinking about the same things over and over again
- Irritation
- Panic
- Worry about real issues and what-ifs
- Mental exhaustion
- Inability to concentrate or listen effectively
- "Jumpiness"
- Inability to respond quickly to changing conditions

Stress and Behavior

When the body and mind are disorganized, behavior suffers. Stress makes us quick to criticize and take offense. It often leads to anxiety and depression. It can make us suspicious and short-tempered, and as we take our frustration and anger out on others, the workplace becomes more unpleasant, which ratchets up the stress even further. Resentments build up, teams break down. Productivity disappears. Conversation is often difficult and understanding sometimes nearly impossible.

These issues are common in most businesses today. It seems that nearly every American is carrying not only a workload, but also a big load of stress. Common causes are things over which the average worker has little say: mergers, layoffs, jobs being sent overseas, and other changes in the overall business climate. But even the most stable job may have its stressors.

Talking Points
Executives are not immune to stress. The Institute for Management Excellence estimates that stress-related executive illnesses cost American industry approximately $10 billion per year.

Too Few and Too Much

The workload continually increases as people strive to cover their own work and that of those who've been laid off in companies' attempts to become more efficient. Stress levels rise as employees try to manage a multitude of competing deadlines, projects, and priorities. Very well-organized employees with excellent time management skills may thrive for a time in a fast-paced atmosphere, but as more and more work piles up, even these hardy souls begin to buckle under the load.

Lack of Privacy

Cube farms make it nearly impossible for employees to get away from each other. Personal conversations are overheard, and people "prairie dog," popping their heads over the top of the partitions all day long to talk with one another. Interruptions are constant. Because there are usually no doors on cubes, bosses, team members, and other employees barge right in, sometimes interrupting work at exactly the wrong moment. If there's nowhere employees can work uninterrupted and at a pace they can manage, fatigue and stress increase and jobs go unfinished.

Talking Points

As reported by *Science Daily* in 2001, scientists at Cornell University discovered that low-level noise found in open-plan offices can result in higher levels of stress. Even though workers in a study didn't report feeling greater stress, their bodies created much higher levels of stress hormones than did the bodies of their colleagues who were assigned to quieter offices.

Ineffective Communication

Poor communication leads to uncertainty about priorities and expectations. A dearth of information contributes to inaccurate rumors. Rumors bring about confusion and distrust, both of which result in stress. Communication that flows only one way—from the top down—makes employees feel bewildered and resentful, both emotions that also create stress.

Powerlessness

Employees who have little say about how they do their jobs are candidates for massive amounts of stress. Autonomy, input, and participation in decisions that affect them give people a sense of power and authority. Take those away and the workplace is populated by a gang of stress-ridden automatons whose primary goal is to get out of that workplace—or to sabotage it.

What to Say About Stress

If you're under great stress, you may resist talking about it except to grouse and commiserate with co-workers. That may confer some temporary relief, but it doesn't solve the problem. To relieve stress, you have to get to the root, and the root is often the boss. It's the boss who can change working conditions, provide support, help solve interpersonal issues, and deal with a whole host of other problems.

Talking with the Boss

You might find yourself hesitating because you worry that confessing you're suffering from stress may target you as weak and unable to deal with the realties of the workplace. The solution is to talk not about yourself, but about the issues that cause the stress in the first place. You might say:

- ◆ "There appears to be a series of deadlines on multiple projects, all of them coming at the same time. Can you help me set priorities? What do you need first, and what deadlines might be more fluid?"

- ◆ "The Chicago project is critical and I need some time and space to finish the implementation phase of the plan. Is there a place other than my cubicle where I might go to think it through? Or would it be possible for me to work from home for the next two mornings? The work will go much faster if I have some uninterrupted time, and the quality will be higher, too."

- ◆ "With so much going on, I want to make sure I'm not missing crucial steps. Could we set up a weekly time to meet for feedback—at least until we get through this extremely busy period?"

Continue to peck away at what underlies the stress rather than whine to the boss about the stress itself. Couch the stress issues as productivity barriers; explain that you want to do the best job you can, but you need to have some of the barriers removed. Chances are the boss will be responsive. If you're a good employee, she won't want to lose you and go through the hassle of breaking in someone new. That's a stress *she* doesn't need.

You aren't powerless. If stress is interfering with your ability to work productively, you must be active on your own behalf. Seek help from the people who have the ability to give it.

Dealing with Co-Worker Stress

Sometimes you're coasting along pretty well, but you notice that a co-worker is struggling. There's no need to keep your mouth shut. Ask about it.

> "Meg, I notice that you seem to be floundering a little bit. I was expecting the story you were working on for the magazine yesterday, and I've never known you to miss a deadline. Is everything okay?"

Share observations, not accusations. See if you can unearth the problem. If these are simply a couple of isolated incidents, the issue may self-correct, but a pattern of missed deadlines, confusion, tension, physical complaints, and quick temper point to something more serious. Meg may be facing problems at the office because of a crisis at home: an illness in the family, a marital problem, or a financial shortfall. Sometimes all she might need is someone to talk to, and you might serve as a sounding board for a while. If the problem is beyond you, and your company has an *Employee Assistance Program (EAP)*, you might suggest she turn to them for help.

def•i•ni•tion

A company-sponsored counseling service, an **Employee Assistance Program** offers help with personal problems that affect job performance and productivity. It is a confidential service provided by a contracted company.

Burnout or Just a Bad Day?

Burnout and stress, although related, are not exactly the same thing. You might think of burnout as stress squared or what happens to a stressed body when it doesn't get relief. If you nip stress relatively quickly, you may not proceed to a stage of burnout, but if you allow stress to run unabated, you're a serious candidate for burnout. More than stress, burnout includes a feeling of helplessness and loss of hope. You feel you can't handle what's demanded of you. Your coping mechanisms are so strained, you feel there's nothing left of you, and you're likely to be resentful as well as exhausted.

def•i•ni•tion

Burnout is a term that describes overwhelming physical and emotional exhaustion, coupled with a diminished capacity to care about work and activities.

If you're feeling stressed, take this little quiz to assess how close you are to burnout.

Are You On the Way to Burnout?

Do you routinely:

	Yes	No
1. Try to go to work late and leave early?	❏	❏
2. Find yourself looking forward to lunch at 9:00 in the morning?	❏	❏
3. Feel anxious and depressed on Sunday night?	❏	❏

	Yes	No
4. Watch the clock obsessively, thinking about how long it is until you can escape?	❑	❑
5. Feel so tired you can barely drag yourself into the office?	❑	❑
6. Not care that you're turning in work that's less than your best?	❑	❑
7. Find your company's priorities warring with your own values?	❑	❑
8. Feel yourself becoming less interested in every aspect of your work, even parts you used to enjoy?	❑	❑
9. Feel unable to cope with what you used to handle with ease?	❑	❑
10. Feel negative about many aspects of your life?	❑	❑

More than three yes answers may be danger signals of impending burnout.

How to Address Burnout

Burnout is a complicated issue and if you believe you're headed for it, get help immediately from family, friends, and professionals. Burnout often requires a systematic revamping of one's entire life, including beliefs about self, work, service, limits and boundaries, family, and responsibilities. Many fine books and websites explain how to cope with burnout, but it is far better to address burnout before it happens.

Although burnout is most common in helping professions, such as the clergy, social work, health professionals, and caregivers, it's certainly not rare in business and industry. After all, the very behaviors that cause

> **Don't Do It!**
>
> Don't suffer in silence. Seek medical attention. Stress ailments are real and need real treatment. Don't work yourself into a stroke, a heart attack, or an emotional breakdown because you think you should be able to handle stress on your own.

burnout—working too many hours, burning the candle at both ends, taking on too much responsibility, and expecting perfect performance on every project—are the behaviors that business typically rewards.

A taskmaster boss says, "Thomas was on vacation with his family—his first one in three years. There was a snag in one of his proposals, and when I called to tell him about it, he was on the next plane home. He worked nonstop for three days to get everything fixed. The competition got the job, but he was willing to sacrifice family time and work like a maniac. That's real loyalty." It sure is, but Thomas's life is so out of whack that he's going to burn out down the road. Count on it.

The One-Word Answer

To protect yourself from flameout, there is a word you must learn to use. That word is "no." If the thought of saying no to a request—or an order—from management makes you shake in your shoes, realize that if you burn out, management will probably say no for you by removing you from your job. Of course, you don't march into your boss's office and shout, "No" to every request. Be diplomatic, but be firm as well:

> "Norm, I appreciate your thinking of me for the Wilkinson team, but with the merger documentation and the audit, my plate is full right now. If you think the Wilkinson situation is more pressing, I'm going to have to hand off some of the other responsibilities. Or I can stay on those duties, and you can put someone else—maybe Robin—on the Wilkinson team. I'm open to whatever suggestions you have, but I can't maintain the level of performance you want if I add another top-priority project. How would you suggest we move ahead?"

You must take care of yourself because no one else will do it for you. If you present yourself as being a) invincible or b) a patsy because you need to be liked, you'll be overburdened in a heartbeat.

Reporting What You See

At work, if you notice burnout occurring in your department, you owe it to your supervisor to say so. That takes guts, but most companies today are aware of the syndrome and want to avoid it. Once again, place your observations in the context of time and money. You may find a more sympathetic hearing than you anticipate. Avoid naming those you believe may be suffering unless you have their permission to bring it up to your manager. You might say something like:

"Henry, I've noticed a downturn in the quality of work we're turning out. People are sniping at each other, and there's more absenteeism than before. I think these issues are stress related. What do you think we can do to take some of the pressure off? I'm concerned that we're going to have a mass exodus of talented people if we don't get a handle on structuring the work differently and getting the staff some relief."

Setting an Example

If you are the manager, you have a responsibility not only to keep work flowing, but also to guard the health and productivity of those who report to you. You need to keep an eye on employees who look as if they might crash and burn. You have to encourage them to do the things that are good for them and keep them well and eager to work. You may run into resistance with people who believe they must work constantly to gain the regard of higher-ups. Here are some powerful work/life balance messages:

◆ "June, I see you haven't taken any vacation so far this year, and you know you're supposed to use it during the year you earn it. The year is winding down, and I want you to get away for a while. Your work is just fine; there's no slippage, but for you to maintain that level, you have to have some downtime. Please schedule at least some of your vacation within the next six weeks."

◆ "Jill, I notice that you've been putting in a lot of extra hours. I'd like you to be able to go home at the end of the day and relax. Work is important, but it isn't all there is to life. Are you staying because you love what you're doing or because there aren't enough hours in the day to handle what we've piled on you?"

◆ "Rob, you've put in a tremendous amount of effort and overtime on this project, and I think some comp time might be in order. I'd like you to take two days off next week."

What these types of messages do is convey respect for the totality of the employee's life, and respect is what keeps employees motivated and satisfied. You also show respect by giving employees as much autonomy as possible in how they schedule and complete their work and as much input as possible into decisions that affect their on-the-job performance. People who are burned out believe that others control their lives. Restore their power to them and you relieve that perception and release enormous pent-up energy.

Finally, you have to set the example. If you're killing yourself, your employees will believe that's what's expected of them, too. If you want a healthy workplace, take care of yourself first. Lip service means nothing. You have to walk the walk.

The Least You Need to Know

- Stress and burnout impede productivity and communication.

- If you are under extreme stress, you must take action to ameliorate it, rather than waiting for someone else to do it for you.

- If you don't want to talk about stress, talk about quality and productivity.

- To relieve stress, managers must take care of themselves and insist that employees do the same.

Chapter 21

Substance Abuse and Domestic Violence

In This Chapter

- The costs of substance abuse
- Detecting substance abuse
- The wrong way to approach the issue in the workplace
- Substance abuse and the family
- Helping victims of domestic abuse

The National Clearinghouse for Alcohol and Drug Information estimates that American companies lose $100 billion a year due to alcohol and drug-related abuse by employees. Obviously, it's a massive productivity issue and also one that's hard for co-workers and supervisors to discuss with those who may be drinking or using drugs on the job. Domestic abuse also takes a toll not only on the victim, but also on the bottom line. This chapter highlights some ways to talk about these life-altering issues.

Drunk or High on the Job

No doubt you've seen lists of signs and symptoms of alcohol or drug abuse, and reading the lists has led you that to conclude that a co-worker or someone you supervise (or are supervised by) has a *substance abuse* problem. Sometimes you don't need a list; the issue is clear. The person staggers in from the three-martini lunch several times a week, is late every Monday, reeks of alcohol, and can't remember being in meetings because of blackouts. This situation requires immediate action by supervisors, an Employee Assistance Program (EAP) if available, and treatment programs if necessary. It must be made very clear to the employee that continuing this behavior will cost her her job.

def•i•ni•tion

Substance abuse is using alcohol or other drugs to the point of causing continuing problems for the user.

If her behavior has been particularly outrageous—insulting customers, threatening co-workers, spitting in the president's eye—you have grounds for immediate dismissal.

Even if you're firing your employee on the spot, make arrangements for her to be taken home or even to a hospital if necessary. Do not allow her to drive or take public transportation. Call a family member, a taxi, a car service, or security to transport her.

Fortunately, not every substance abuse problem is so dramatic. The issue is often insidious and the signs, which are sometimes subtle, may include …

Talking Points

According to the National Institute on Alcohol Abuse and Alcoholism, nearly 17.6 million adult Americans—that's one out of every 16—abuse alcohol or are alcoholic. Several million more adults engage in "risky" behavior, such as binge drinking.

- Frequent short absences from the work space with a change in mood upon return.

- Mood swings from day to day—expansive and optimistic one day and depressed and irritable the next.

- Dilated pupils, red eyes.

- Passivity and sleepiness, often combined with a desire to snack.

- Loss of inhibition; reckless behavior.

- Hallucinations.

The problem with these signs and symptoms, however, is that most of them also can be attributable to something else. For example, dilated pupils and red eyes can mean that an employee just returned from the optometrist or is using drops for an eye infection; frequent absences from the work space may be quick breaks an employee takes to clear his head and remain highly productive; mood swings can result from stress and worry. Sleepiness and confusion might be signals of overwork. Even something as dramatic as hallucinations could be a side effect of prescribed medications.

More accurate than a list of potential signs is an obvious decline in performance or productivity, coupled with other suspicious behaviors.

Bringing It Up

If you suspect that someone you employ or supervise is struggling with substance abuse, confront the issue, not the employee. Make sure you are in a private place where you will not be disturbed. As you open the discussion, don't focus on *dependency* or *addiction*; emphasize only the way the declining performance is affecting you and your department. You might start off this way:

def•i•ni•tion

Dependency is continuing to abuse the substances in spite of the problems they cause, while **addiction** is the compulsive use of the substance without the ability to stop.

> "Joanne, I'm becoming very concerned. You've missed the last three task force meetings because you were two hours late to work each time, and when you finally arrived, you were distracted and confused. When I came into your cubicle last week for our meeting, you were unprepared because you were asleep with your head on your desk. And, frankly, you don't look like yourself. You're disheveled, and that's not like you. I feel that something must be seriously wrong. Is there anything I can do?"

If Joanne says she's fine and offers a reasonable explanation for her behavior (all-night hospital vigils with a relative, for example), your suspicions might have been misplaced. Nonetheless, keep observing her behavior and document anything that indicates a continuing problem. If her performance remains less than satisfactory, have another meeting. Once again, share your observations and back them up with your documentation. Ask her why she believes her work is suffering.

The reason for treading carefully is that if you come on strong with an accusation of alcohol or drug abuse, even if you're right, several bad outcomes—denial, rage, threats—are likely.

Denial

Denial is a universal feature of abuse. Abusers will continually deny that they have any problem at all with their use of drugs or alcohol. You may hear such statements as:

- "I know what I'm doing."
- "I'm on top of it."
- "I can stop anytime I want."
- "It's a very stressful time right now and I'm just taking the edge off."
- "I need a vacation."
- "I'm fine. You're the one with the problem."

If Joanne senses that you're onto her, she may deny the problem, but continue the behavior more secretively. The treatment she needs will be delayed.

It's possible she denies your allegation because she really isn't abusing anything. If you accuse her of it, that's probably the end of your relationship. The real problem, which may be stress or worry or a physical ailment, doesn't get addressed because she's too angry to confide in you. It's likely she'll begin looking for another job because you've insulted her.

Rage

Joanne may fly into a fury and lash out at you, deflecting your concern by saying that other employees are jealous or spiteful and you should deal with them rather than her. Should you be diverted by her tactics, she's dodged the bullet; she doesn't have to deal with the real issue. It's imperative that you keep the focus on her and her performance. If she blows up, wait quietly for her to calm down, and then restate your concerns and the steps you expect her to take get back on track.

Threats

Joanne may threaten legal action or to quit on the spot. She tosses out these diversions to keep you from getting to the truth. Once again, don't allow yourself to go down a blind alley. Remain relaxed, let her vent, and tell her that you'd rather she allow the company to offer assistance.

Tell her that whatever is causing her work to deteriorate needs to be addressed and see if she'll make a counseling appointment with the EAP. Explain to her that such meetings are confidential and that what happens there is not disclosed to you or placed in her file. Stress that she is valuable to you and your team or you would not be making these efforts to help her. If there is no EAP, make sure you have a list of counselors available and check with HR to let Joanne know what her treatment options are and what's paid for under her health plan.

As the supervisor, you have to make it clear to Joanne that if her performance doesn't improve, you'll need to begin disciplinary steps; this meeting is an attempt to avoid harsher measures. The choice is hers. If she won't face her problem and refuses assistance, you'll have to follow up on the process that eventually will result in her dismissal.

By being firm but not judgmental and concerned rather than condemning, you've opened the door to help. You can't make her walk through it, however, so don't be too hard on yourself if she refuses your aid. You have done what you could. You are her supervisor, not her counselor, and you have to do what's best for your entire department and the company. Jobs are important to people, and when faced with the loss of employment, some people do seek help and go on to lead better, more productive lives.

Safety for Everyone

Those who come to work under the influence of drugs or alcohol cost their employers money and time, and they are sometimes a danger to themselves or others. While drunkenness in a white collar office may be only repulsive and counterproductive, drunkenness on a shop floor or in a laboratory, a cockpit, or a hospital can be deadly. Manage the risks or face the consequences. While managing the risks usually includes uncomfortable confrontations, a little discomfort is a small price to pay for the safety of all your employees.

Surprising Facts

While most of the attention about alcohol and drugs is focused on those who abuse these substances on the job, the greatest hit to productivity comes from those who are hung over, rather than actively drunk. Employees who are hung over may take a sick day, and if they come to the office, their work may be substandard. Researchers have shown that hung over employees' cognitive and technical abilities may be impaired long after their blood alcohol levels are normal. It's as important to be on the lookout for morning-after syndrome as it is to ferret out on-the-job use.

It's a Family Matter, Too

Conversations with addicts are as difficult at home as they are at the office. The addict may deny the problem, become angry, violent, or self-pitying, make threats, or walk out. And sometimes he doesn't even hear what the family is saying because he's under the influence at the time of the conversation. It's frustrating and frightening.

The Toughest Conversation: The Intervention

In days not so long ago, alcohol or drug abuse was not discussed. It was considered too shameful a subject to be talked about outside the family—and often inside as well. Today, however, we know that these conditions are treatable, but for treatment to occur, the problem has to be brought to the surface. In some cases, the path to assistance is through *intervention*. Interventions are often most useful when the user recently has experienced a consequence directly traceable to the use of alcohol or drugs: an arrest, an injury, or a disciplinary action at work.

def•i•ni•tion

An **intervention** is a planned, structured interaction with a person who is abusing, dependent, or addicted to alcohol or other drugs. Its function is to break down the abuser's denial and to persuade him or her to begin treatment.

Getting Ready

Substance abuse specialists have differing views on intervention. Some believe strongly in the process, while others think it may make things worse in the long run. If you and your family feel an intervention is the way to go, don't try to do it by yourself. It's essential to find a professional who can help you structure the process and provide pre-intervention counseling for the family. Addiction is a family problem, and family members may have unintentionally fostered the addiction with their own behavior.

Professional help is also needed so the family knows what to do if the intervention goes badly. In television depictions of the process, the addict almost always agrees to treatment. In real life, he may storm out and refuse even to talk about it. The family is left wondering what steps to take next. An *interventionist* can participate in the process or coach the family in the techniques that will allow them to do it themselves.

def•i•ni•tion

An **interventionist** or intervention specialist is an alcohol or drug counselor who has specialized training in the intervention process. Interventionists organize the intervention and prepare families, co-workers, supervisors, and others for participation.

Planning for Intervention

An intervention cannot be a spur-of-the-moment occasion. Planning is required. There are insurance considerations to deal with. There are different treatment plans and locations to think about. If you're going to ask the alcoholic or drug abuser to enter treatment "today," transportation must be arranged and a suitcase packed.

The purpose of all the planning is to determine each person's role in the intervention and also to find answers to any objections the abuser might raise. Objections can run from the real ("What about my job?") to the ridiculous ("Who will feed the fish?"), but objections must be anticipated and resolved.

In addition, the plan must encompass the possibility that the person will refuse treatment, which can leave those who intervene confused, angry, and ready to blame one another. Those who have stated consequences and limits must be prepared to carry them out, and that can lead to further conflict. Therefore, many interventionists counsel against an intervention unless everyone involved is prepared for failure.

What Intervention Sounds Like

Although there's a great deal of preparation that precedes the actual intervention, it's the conversational part of the process that causes the greatest anxiety. It can be heart-wrenching. You (and others) have to be honest about the effects the abuse is having on your lives, but you also have to steer clear of blaming the victim. That's quite a tightrope to walk if you're angry and want to strike back for things that have hurt and embarrassed you. Writing down what you need to say is very helpful and can keep you from veering off into accusatory statements.

As the intervention begins, it's important to place your observations in the context of the love or regard you have for the person in trouble, and to help him understand that the intervention is not a punishment, but a desire to keep him from having to "hit bottom." Too often, hitting bottom can mean a long-term illness, financial ruin, or even death.

During the intervention, you state or read what has caused you to be uneasy or afraid and what you are willing or not willing to do in the future. Never state a consequence you are not really committed to carrying out. For example:

- "When you're drinking, I worry you'll have an automobile accident and hurt or kill yourself or someone else."

- "Jenny doesn't invite her friends over anymore because when you're drinking, you're rude to them. She feels isolated and alone and embarrassed."

- "I'm frightened when you drink because you get out of control. I worry that you're going to hit me or the children. I should feel safe in my own home and I don't."

- "I'm worried that you're about to lose your job. I know you love your work, and I'm afraid of the impact losing your job would have on you."

- "If I see you getting into a car drunk, I will call the police and ask them to pull you over."

- "If you are arrested for drunk driving or fighting, I will not bail you out."

- "I've become so worried about the children's safety—and my own—that I will have to look at other housing arrangements."

- "By covering for you with your boss, I've made it easier for you to deny that you have a problem. I'm not going to do that anymore. When she calls, I will no longer lie to her. I won't tell her you're sick or have a doctor's appointment or car trouble. If she calls, you'll have to speak with her or I'll just tell her the truth myself."

Often, an intervention results in the person's immediate entry into treatment, and many who initially refuse treatment because they are angered by the intervention process seek help within a matter of weeks. Whether the person stays in recovery is another issue, but the difficult conversation that characterizes intervention may be a step in the right direction.

Domestic Violence Comes to Work

Domestic violence is an epidemic in the United States, and though there are some male victims, those who suffer are predominantly women. In fact, battering is the most common injury in American women. More than five million women are abused each year, more than 500,000 are stalked by an intimate partner, and more than 1,000 are killed. The leading cause of women's death in the workplace? Homicide, and 16 percent of those killings are at the hands of a domestic partner.

Beyond the toll in human suffering is the economic impact. More than half of the victims of violence miss work and nearly three-quarters of them are harassed at work by their abusers. Clearly, these situations are detrimental to productivity and cost business several billion dollars each year.

def•i•ni•tion

Domestic violence, or battering, is a pattern of coercive, controlling behavior rooted in violence: physical, sexual, emotional, psychological, and economic. The behavior allows the abuser to feel strong, superior, dominant, and powerful, while causing the partner to feel worthless and powerless.

Because domestic violence is so prevalent, you have to be prepared to deal with it. You may work with or supervise employees who already are being abused and whose abusers may show up and wreak havoc.

Because they feel ashamed, isolated, and frightened, most victims will not tell you about the abuse. Once again, if you notice declining performance, you must look for clues. In this case, the clues may be easier to see than in the case of alcohol or drug abuse. As you observe the employee, look for …

- ◆ Unexplained bruises or reports of repeated "accidents"—walking into a door, hitting one's head on an open cabinet, falling downstairs, tripping over a rug.

- ◆ Crying, fear, or anger during or after phone calls from the spouse or domestic partner.

Don't Do It!

Don't assume that only women are battered. Researchers have found that 50 percent of the men who batter their wives also abused their children. And gay men are sometimes battered by their partners.

◆ Unexplained and unwelcome visits to the workplace by the domestic partner.

◆ Depression, anxiety, or irritability.

◆ Absenteeism and lack of ability to concentrate while on the job.

◆ Reports by co-workers that the victim has alluded to being abused or talked frequently about marital problems.

Talking It Over

Once again, a discussion of so personal an issue as abuse may be brushed off, and if that happens, you must respect the victim's decision but offer her options.

> "Kathryn, I've noticed that your boyfriend makes frequent visits to the office, and that these visits seem to upset you. These visits are disruptive and have an effect on your performance. Is there any action I need to take?"

If the victim denies a problem, you might gently press the issue.

> "I also notice that you appear to have frequent accidents that keep you from working, and that's having an impact on how effectively you're able to do your job. I'm concerned about your physical health, as well as the fact that you seem to be upset and anxious a good deal of the time. I'd like you to consider a consultation with an EAP counselor to see what they might recommend. Those consults are completely private and confidential. They don't report anything to me. If you don't want to do that, there are community resources to help you, too."

If She Tells the Truth

In the face of even gentle probing, the victim probably will continue to deny violence because she is frightened or has been threatened with further abuse if she discloses the truth or tries to escape. Sometimes, however, realizing that others have noticed the situation and are willing to help may allow her to admit the problem.

As the supervisor, you have to let her know that you believe her and have concerns for her safety. Explain that the EAP can help her plan what she should do next. If there is no EAP, direct her to community agencies or counselors that specialize in domestic violence.

Because of the controlling nature of most abusers, the victim may not be able to go to counseling except on company time. Let her know that you can rearrange her work hours to allow her to attend her sessions. Explain that in order to do that you'll need to consult with Human Resources about how she might use vacation time or time off to handle her situation, and let her know that Security must be involved, too, to make sure that violence doesn't endanger co-workers, customers, or others who do business with the company.

Disclose nothing to anyone else, even to the co-workers who might have brought you the issue in the first place, unless she gives you permission. She may tell others, but you should not.

Many women stay with abusers for reasons that make no sense to those outside the situation. Even if she stays, continue to offer your nonjudgmental support. You can't force her to leave, and making critical or disparaging remarks makes the situation worse.

The Wrong Things to Say

Domestic violence is a complicated issue and simplistic pronouncements from others aren't helpful. Steer clear of such statements and questions as:

- **"Why don't you leave?"** There are many reasons women stay: threats against their children, economic considerations, difficulty finding another job or a safe place to stay. As one battered woman says, "One day I was on my last nerve when someone asked me why I stayed. I said, 'Why don't you ask him why he doesn't stop?' I stayed because I was an alcoholic and not thinking straight. When I got sober, I left."

- **"What are you doing that's making him violent?"** That's what every woman needs to hear. Her black eye and broken ribs are her fault. Abusers have choices. Battering someone—man or woman—is the wrong one.

- **"You have to get out of there today."** Unless you're prepared to take in the victim and her children and deal with the repercussions of that, this is a useless statement. She knows what she needs to do; she might need time to do it.

Domestic violence is a multifaceted problem that requires time, careful handling, and an understanding of the power of words.

The Least You Need to Know

◆ Alcohol, drugs, and domestic violence are serious productivity issues for American business.

◆ When confronting these issues, concentrate on the poor performance rather than the reason for it.

◆ An intervention is often an effective way to get a person into rehabilitation, but an intervention is not foolproof and may fail.

◆ Most of the time women are abused by those they know rather than strangers.

◆ Some of the things we say to victims of domestic violence are understandable, but very damaging.

Part 5

The Stages of Life

Difficult conversations occur everywhere, often with family and friends. What do you say to the mother-in-law who rearranges your kitchen and takes umbrage when you put it back the way you want it? How do you hold on to your sanity when your teen wants purple hair and a pierced tongue? And how do you talk to a parent with diminished capacities?

Situations like these—and more—are the subject of this part, and you'll find practical tips on dealing with tough conversations close to home.

"We think it's time you moved out."

Chapter 22

The In-Laws and the Outlaws

In This Chapter

- ◆ Who is the family?
- ◆ Kindness first
- ◆ Boundaries and how to set them
- ◆ Respecting the differences
- ◆ Special issues with grandchildren

Families can be hard places to live. Once you establish a new family, how do you handle in-laws' intrusions into your life, or, conversely, their total lack of interest? Where does the spouse-in-law—your spouse's first husband or wife—fit into your current family? Normal differences between families of origin, in-laws, and stepfamilies can loom large; family ties may not only bind, but also chafe. This chapter helps you learn to respect differences, draw appropriate boundaries, and live happily with people who may be very different from you.

Can't We All Just Get Along?

Once the wedding is behind you, you become part of a new extended family of in-laws. Often that relationship goes swimmingly, with in-law children and parents loving each other and valuing the kinship. In other families, the parties are anything but kindred spirits and don't relish spending time together. In my opinion, what makes the in-law relationship difficult is the inability of in-law parents and children to establish and recognize boundaries. Because parents are older and often see their children as youngsters, even if the children are in the 30s and 40s, they may not respect the "kids'" autonomy; they still may be trying to impose their own ideas and views and attempting to use disciplinary techniques that were outmoded when the children were 13.

Some parents say and do things to their children that they'd never dream of doing to anyone else. They barge into their children's houses at will, read their mail, rearrange their furniture, and comment on every aspect of their lives. For some inexplicable reason, they feel free to criticize their child's spouse, dishing up negative remarks on everything from style of dress to discipline to cooking—and that criticism may be unrelenting, even when the younger couple has been married a long time. Troublesome in-laws trample right over the physical and verbal boundaries that make a relationship work.

> **Words to the Wise**
>
> Insulted by an in-law? If you have it in you, you might try to laugh it off. "Oh, I know, but if I cleaned up, I'd have to resign my membership in Sloppy Sisters United, and they're such a nice group." Then cool down by going to get glass of water or taking the dog for a walk.

On the other side of the coin, adult children may deal in extremes. In an effort to establish their own enclave, they sometimes close themselves off too quickly and too harshly. The walls are too high, and if they feel intruded upon or slighted in any way, they may disregard the boundaries of courtesy and understanding. Rather than confronting their parents in a positive manner, they often explode, whine, and behave in a less-than-mature fashion, which, of course, confirms the parents' suspicion that the kids need guidance—and the spiral continues.

Get It On the Table

In most cases, when all the parties are grown-ups of good will, boundary-setting is easy and involves the use of the word "prefer":

◆ "Grace, I'd prefer that you let me know when you're in the house. You don't have to telephone ahead or even ring the doorbell, but when you come in, please call out and make me aware that you're here. It might save us both some embarrassment someday."

♦ "Son, I'll lend you any tools you need, but I'd prefer that you bring them back in the same condition you received them. If you break something, please have it repaired or replace it before you return it to me."

♦ "Jasmine, Ed tells me you're angry about a remark I made about your dinner party. You're right. It was inappropriate and I apologize. In the future, though, I'd prefer that if you have a problem with me, you talk with me about it face to face. I don't like putting Ed in the middle."

These positive statements place a fence around what's okay and what isn't in a non-threatening way and even the prickliest in-law shouldn't find them hard to take.

When simple confrontations have been avoided for the sake of family harmony or fear of consequences, however, issues may go underground, festering and gaining power—sort of like a subterranean tornado. After a time, the energy has to be released and the lid blows off. Everyone may say regrettable things and the relationship is impaired, perhaps permanently. It's better to deal with small problems when they occur, and if things have already gone too far, boundary-setting is a much more unpleasant chore.

> **Talking Points**
>
> The worst complaints about in-laws include criticism of the spouse, too much incursion into the marriage, misunderstanding of roles, and privacy. In seriously dysfunctional families, these complaints can assume operatic proportions.

The Rules of Engagement for In-Laws

If you're the in-law parents, or you have to deal with intrusive in-laws, here are some important ground rules:

Nobody Messes with the Marriage

When you and your spouse took your wedding vows, you promised to "leave your father and mother" and be loyal to one another. Naturally, you want to retain a relationship with both sets of loving parents, but that relationship now becomes secondary to the one you share with your spouse.

The new *family system* is sometimes hard for parents to take, and they may fight like broncos to win back their original position. One way they may choose is to constantly criticize their in-law child. They find fault with everything he or she does, no matter

def•i•ni•tion

Family system theory includes the belief that the family is a single emotional unit whose interactions form a complex system. That is, the actions of each family member may have profound effects on every other member.

how innocuous it may be. They harp on his or her shortcomings and suggest that their child has made a terrible mistake. Some actively try to break up the marriage. If things come to this point, you must protect your husband or wife against the assaults launched by your parents. They're *your* parents; it's your job.

It does no good to rant and rave at your parents. All that does is confirm their suspicion that your spouse has turned you against your own family. My friend Julie says that her mother-in law once said, "Ron was always such a thoughtful person before he met you. I don't know what you've done to him." (Her mother-in-law also made Julie call her "Mrs. Whittington" for twenty years, but that's another story.)

Keep your composure. If you're serious about changing your parents' behavior, speak quietly, politely, and firmly. Lay out the consequences that will ensue if your parents don't knock it off. Saber-rattling gets you nowhere, so never threaten to impose a consequence you aren't willing to carry out. Here's an example:

"Dad, I know you don't like Randy and you never have. You're entitled to your opinion and neither he nor I can change it. It makes me sad because I love you both very much. I've asked you to be kinder to him, but you continue to be rude. On top of that, you often suggest that I should kick him to the curb, and you usually make that suggestion when the children are around. It frightens them, and I can't allow that anymore.

"I've decided I'm not going to listen to any more criticism of Randy. I need you to show him the respect he is entitled to simply because he is my husband and the father of your grandchildren. If you can't do that, then we can't be around you.

"I won't cut my ties to you, and I will still see you, but I won't bring Randy here nor will I bring the children because you speak to them so disrespectfully about their father. You and Randy don't have to be best friends. I don't expect that, but I do expect that you will be civil to my husband and do what's best for our children. It kills me to have to do this, but my relationship with my husband comes first, and what you're doing hurts me as well as him.

"I'm not going to do this right away because I want to give it one more try, but if it continues, Randy and I will take the children and leave any situation in which I feel he's being abused."

These statements are going to be met with plenty of resistance, and while it behooves you to listen to what the other person has to say, don't get dragooned into a vitriolic exchange. A calm resolve on your part may bring about the desired change.

After this boundary-setting session, see what happens when you're all together again. If the undesirable behavior crops up again, apply the consequence. No matter what, don't get into a shouting match. Be rational, quiet, and firm.

> "Dad, we're going to leave now. I explained what would happen if this nastiness continued, and I meant it. We have no choice but to go. Yes, I know it's Thanksgiving, but we'd like to have a pleasant Thanksgiving, too, and this isn't it."

I won't minimize the difficulty of making consequences stick or how rough it might be the first time you do it, but for the sake of your spouse and children, you have to give it your best shot. Drawing a firm boundary may make things better, and if it doesn't, you're no worse off than you were.

By the way, parents don't have the corner on interference. Siblings and extended family often butt in with their opinions, too. Unless they are presenting you with absolute proof that they saw your spouse in a disreputable bar handing money to a drug dealer (and your partner is not an undercover detective), thank them for their concern and explain that you and your spouse are doing fine, thanks, and if you need advice, you will certainly ask them for it. Otherwise, you'd appreciate their silence regarding your marriage.

Keep Private Issues Private

If you've had a good relationship with your parents and shared intimate thoughts and details with them in the past, it's hard to realize that that behavior might not be in your best interest now. As my young neighbors Beth and Mark tell it, "Both our mothers were young widows, and we each sort of grew up with them. Both of us are close to our moms. We love them very much, so when we began having marital problems, it seemed logical that each of us turned to our own mother for support. It might have been logical, but it wasn't smart. My mother said awful things to my husband, and his mother treated me like dirt. Then they fought with each other. It was horrible."

The couple eventually sought counseling and discovered that "in turning to our mothers instead of each other, we set up an inevitable conflict. After all, what mother isn't going to fight for her own cub? We're trying to repair all that damage now and to establish a new relationship with our mothers. It's not easy. They both feel left out and hurt, but we have to stand on our own and renegotiate how we deal with them. My mother is coming around a little bit, but Mark's mom isn't—and that's so painful.

"We've learned the hard way. If we have problems now, we see our counselor and don't involve other family members. We wish we'd been smarter earlier. It would have created a much less confusing environment for us and our three little girls."

Zip Your Lip If You Can

My mother was a saint. (That's not a unilateral opinion. My husband would tell you the same thing.) I can't remember her ever offering unsolicited advice. She let my husband and me make our own mistakes, although I now know that she must have lain awake many nights while we did it. I've tried to emulate her example, but I'm afraid I'm not as successful as she was.

How your children rear their children is their business, unless the children are in real danger of physical or emotional abuse or neglect. Discipline, bedtimes, diet, and homework are no longer your decisions to make. You had your chance with your own children; let your kids mess up their children in their own way.

There is no more critical time to withhold unsolicited opinions than around the birth of a couple's first child. The new mom has raging hormones and only theoretical knowledge about being a parent. She may feel very tentative about her ability to do the job. The mother-in-law is experienced, but may be out of touch with today's childrearing methods. For example, when I was a young mom, we put babies to sleep on their stomachs to keep them from aspirating if they spit up in their sleep. Today, babies sleep on their backs or sides to help prevent *Sudden Infant Death Syndrome (SIDS)*. And that's just one change.

def•i•ni•tion

Sudden Infant Death Syndrome (SIDS) or "crib death" is the sudden, unexplained death of a child up to one year of age.

"It's my baby," the young mother says, "and all she does is horn in, telling me to put him on a schedule and let him cry rather than pick him up. And I'm never, ever supposed to rock him to sleep!"

It's wise for the mother-in-law (and the other grandmother, too, for that matter) to hold her tongue as much as possible. In the new mom's fragile state of mind, any suggestion you make probably will be interpreted as criticism. You might not mean it that way, but that's what she'll hear. The less you offer advice, the more often you may be asked for it.

Look for Pure Motives

If your mother-in-law offers you some gift cards for beauty salon services, don't immediately jump to the conclusion that this gift is her oh-so-subtle way of telling you you're a slob. She might just be trying to do something nice for you because she appreciates how hard you work and thinks you might enjoy some time just for you. Don't take everything the wrong way; don't run to your husband and moan about what you perceive as slights. If there's a real problem, take it up with her or ask him to, but don't be surprised if you find out you're imagining things.

If your son-in-law wants to take you to a baseball game, don't get all bent out of shape because "that idiot doesn't even know I hate baseball." Go anyway. Talk about why he likes baseball. Have a hot dog with lots of mustard. Get into it. You might surprise yourself by having a great time.

In short, lighten up. Don't ascribe motives to other people's actions. You can't possibly know what they think unless they tell you. These people are your family now. Give them the benefit of the doubt. Be kind. They may be quirky, but that doesn't mean they're impossible.

There are very few of those Dr. Phil in-laws who put a hit out on their daughters-in-law or try to run over their wife's father. (I always tell my in-law children to be sure to watch those shows; I may not do everything right, but I look darn good in comparison.) Can't we all just get along? Of course we can if we're willing to listen, compromise, overlook a thing or two, speak up when we need to, and occasionally bite our tongues. Life's too short for families to be at each other's throats.

Words to the Wise

Remember one important thing. No matter how annoying you find your in-laws to be, remember that you love your spouse—and those nutty parents produced the person you chose to spend your life with. They must have done something right, at least occasionally.

The "Outlaws"

"Outlaws" explains the relationship—or lack thereof—between the two sets of in-law parents. If you and your spouse grew up in the same town or city, all your parents may know each other well. In other cases, the parents may not meet until the wedding day and after that may see each other rarely, if at all.

The outlaw relationship, which would seem to be easy to manage, is sometimes fraught with difficulties. Jealousy, although it may be disguised, is common. One set of parents may have far more money and time to travel to see the children and grand-children, which makes the others pine for the same privilege. One pair of parents may be geographically closer to the younger family and be more involved in their daily lives, which makes the others feel shut out.

The parents also may be very different: Republicans vs. Democrats, churchgoers vs. agnostics, retired vs. working. These differences can create tension and hard feelings when everyone's together.

Here's a tip: There's nothing in the Great Big In-Law Manual that says the outlaws have to have a deep, meaningful relationship. Although you may all end up bosom companions, the only thing you really have to be is polite. If you have little in com-mon, you can make small talk and gush over the accomplishments of your mutual grandchildren. You can agree to disagree on various topics and still be pleasant to one another. Between family occasions, it's not required that you seek each other out, go to dinner, or even speak on the phone. While it might be polite to include these folks if you're planning a big bash of some sort, it's not impolite if you don't. You may have absolutely nothing to talk about but your children, so why force what isn't there?

In-law status is involuntary; it comes with the wedding ceremony. Outlawhood is dis-cretionary. Take it or leave it.

The Spouse-in-Law

Many families today are blended, which means that somewhere in the bushes there's an ex-husband or ex-wife. In many cases, there's no longer any connection between your spouse and his or her ex. When they share children, however, the ex-spouse will be part of your life, too.

The emotions in spouse/ex-spouse/new spouse relationships are so complex that sometimes it helps for everyone to seek some guidance from a neutral third party. Serious questions have to be answered. Is the step-parent allowed to discipline the child? What happens if the styles of discipline are very different? What does the child call the step-parent? Many a parent's heart has been ripped open when he hears his child call a step-parent Daddy. Can all the parents stand to be in the same room with one another at holidays or would it be better to celebrate separately? Will the new spouse have any financial responsibility for the step-child? It's a tangled web.

For the sake of the children, spouses and ex-spouses need to get along as best they can. In optimal cases, they become friends or at least colleagues who work together in the child's behalf. That doesn't happen very often, though. There's usually jealousy, anger, disappointment, disillusionment, and a host of other feelings that get in the way. Because of the potential for confusion and hot words, it's preferable for the spouse-in-common to deal with his or her own ex-partner. If that's not possible, however, you should approach the former husband or wife with as much diplomacy as you can muster.

> **Talking Points**
>
> More than 50 percent of American children live in non-traditional families, and 30 percent live in step-families (www.rainbows.org).

- ◆ "Dave, I understand you're asking Jimmy what his mom and I say about you. I'd prefer that you not force Jimmy into the role of informant. I can assure you that Jane and I would never say anything negative about you to him. You're his father. I certainly don't want to mess that up and neither does Jane."

- ◆ "Samantha, when Ken and I were married, we agreed we wouldn't use physical punishment with our children. Madison says you spank her. I understand that not everyone feels the way I do about spanking, but it's a big issue with me, and I'd prefer that you not do it. I use a time out or take away a favorite television show or activity she likes. That seems to work. Would you please try those things instead?"

Of course, these examples are only opening shots and the conversation may not go well at all. The other spouse may be unreasonable or respond in a less than helpful manner. You may have to involve the spouse-in-common or, in extreme cases, your lawyer, but if you can keep your temper in check and your wits about you, you probably can avoid some unpleasantness. It's about the child, isn't it?

And speaking of the child, if you have been presented with a step-grandchild through the marriage of your child, treat that little person as well as you do any "natural" grandchild. You may not feel a great connection to the child, but that's not the child's fault. Ignoring the step-grandchild, refusing to buy her birthday presents, or obviously favoring your blood grandchildren is uncalled for and guaranteed to stir up trouble between you and the child's parent, who is now your son- or daughter-in-law. There's no reason to make the child feel awful just because he wasn't born into your family. The old definition of family is passé, and you have to live with new realities.

The Least You Need to Know

◆ Marriage blends families who may be very different from one another.

◆ In-law relationships that work are a source of strength and comfort to young people, but when the relationships are toxic, boundaries must be set.

◆ Boundary-setting conversations tend to be stressful and difficult.

◆ In-laws should give as little advice as they can—and sometimes that's a really hard thing to remember.

◆ Step-parent relationships are part of many American families and roles and rules must be carefully negotiated and spelled out.

23

Big Issues with Kids

In This Chapter

- The scientific reasons teens drive parents crazy

- When to start important conversations

- Yes or no and the reason for both

- Talking about sexuality

- Why your child may underachieve in school

Most parents and children love each other very much, but at certain predictable intervals—notably during the toddler period and the teen years—they also drive each other crazy. In this chapter, we'll learn the reasons for the turbulent teens and how you can reduce the number of head-butting conversations that accompany that time of life and make the conversations that remain more productive.

Brain's Note to Parents: I'm Not Finished Yet

A child is born with approximately 100 billion brain cells, and in the early years, the brain builds connections, called synapses, at a nearly unbelievable pace. During what scientists call the "period of exuberance," between the ages of six and twelve months, the brain may construct as many as two million synapses every second. You didn't misread that. Every second. Once that period calms down, the brain begins to rewire itself based on how it experiences the world. Brain scientists often say that "what fires together wires together"; that is, *neurons* that are active at the same time become more strongly connected. Weaker connections are *pruned*.

Scientists once believed that the period of growth and pruning was a once-in-a-lifetime occurrence. It isn't. Longitudinal brain imaging studies demonstrate that there is a similar period of dramatic change in adolescence. The changes that occur—and where in the brain they take place—explain why adolescents can be as volatile and tantrum-prone as toddlers. Add surging hormones to the mix and it's easy to understand why behavior can go haywire and make parents throw up their hands in frustration and sometimes in despair.

Becoming Their Own Persons

The tasks of adolescence are many: discovering what it means to be a man or a woman, both physically and socially; developing a set of values; preparing for independence; and making decisions about a future career. This is also the time when children search for their own identity apart from their parents. They try their wings and make some of their own decisions about how they will live their lives. This experimentation is essential if children are to grow up and take their place in society. But it can be painful and worrisome to parents if the children decide to pull away by indulging in risky behavior.

Many of the teenage battles can be avoided if parents have been actively involved in their children's lives from the outset. If children have been told what they need to know about health, bodily changes, sexuality, and peer pressure at developmentally appropriate times and have been given some coping strategies to deal with life, the kids will still pull away from the parents, but they'll do it without so much damage to the relationship.

When children are young, parents also have the opportunity—and duty—to impart and reinforce their values. "In this family, we tell the truth. If you've done something wrong, just let us know and we'll work it out. If you lie about it or don't tell us, the consequences will be more severe."

It's crucial that parents pick their battles, such as drugs, alcohol, smoking, or accelerated sexual behavior. If you feel the need to impose your will on every aspect of the child's life, you're in for a series of difficult and seemingly endless conversations, almost certainly peppered with phrases such as "You don't understand anything" and "You don't trust me."

"It's My Body!"

If there's one thing teens—and parents—argue over, it's how the kids choose to express themselves bodily and sexually.

Hair and Clothing

Until the 1960s, hair wasn't much of a battleground, but then along came the Beatles and "Make Love, Not War." In family after family, hair became a symbol of rebellion. Today, fewer parents become exercised about hair because they remember what theirs looked like and are more accepting of their children's choices. They also remember that hair does grow out. Nonetheless, even today, Mohawks, spikes, and purple hair can make a parent see red.

If freaky hair is the only overt symbol of rebellion, ask yourself if it's even worth talking about. If it is, screaming at the child that his hair "had better be grown back in tomorrow" is unrealistic. If the child's head is shaved, the hair will take time to reappear. While regrowth is going on, there's time to talk reasonably with your child about his choice and to help him understand that everything he does has consequences in the real world.

> "Sam, there are whole lot of reasons I wish you hadn't gotten that haircut, but the bigger issue is the consequences of it. You said you wanted to get a job and save for a car. We think that's a good idea, but you've taken a step that narrows your options. There are some places that won't hire you now, especially if you're going to work with the public. Most workplaces have standards for employee appearance, so if you're serious about wanting a job, think twice about your hair. You'll want to give yourself as many choices as you can."

Clothing also can be a source of disagreement. Many schools have now instituted dress codes to get rid of gang colors, baggy pants, midriff-baring tops, and skirts that barely clear the buttocks. While it's good to allow your child some say in clothing choices, you can certainly decree that choices will be within the bounds of taste that you establish.

"Hayley, t-shirts are okay, but none that that contain vile language or graphics. I won't spend my money on clothing I consider offensive, and I won't allow you to wear it even if you buy it with your own money. It gives people the wrong idea about the kind of person you are."

Children, though they may deny it, want boundaries and direction, and even when they push against the limits, they will usually acquiesce after a time—sometimes a protracted period—of testing.

Piercings and Tattoos

These forms of self-expression are more permanent than haircuts, and if they're performed incorrectly, there can be long-term damage. For example:

◆ Piercing the cartilage of the upper ear is dangerous. The cartilage does not have a blood supply of its own; if serious infections arise, antibiotics may be ineffective and the child can end up with a disfigured ear, which is hardly the effect she was after.

◆ Blood-borne disease is a significant risk if piercing and tattooing instruments are not properly sterilized between each use or if the person doing the procedure does not observe correct technique. Diseases that are possible include pneumonia, blood stream infections, Hepatitis B and C, and HIV. Infections of the skin may also occur; some of these can be debilitating and, in very rare cases, fatal.

def•i•ni•tion

Keloids are bumpy, thick, raised scars caused by excessive tissue growth.

◆ Scarring is possible, and *keloids* may form in those who are susceptible to them.

◆ Allergic reactions to jewelry or to tattoo dyes sometimes occur.

The fact that these procedures are not necessarily benign means that a serious conversation is in order prior an adolescent's getting a tattoo or piercing. Parents can negotiate what they will allow and what's off limits.

"Jacqui, when I was a child, the only people who pierced things and had tattoos were gang members. I realize times have changed, but I still have reservations about it. I know kids do it for self-expression, but what you want to express now might not be what you want to express when you're going to college or working. And there are some health issues you may not have thought about.

"It seems okay to me if you want to pierce your earlobes, or even double-pierce them, but no other part of your ear because of potential complications. And there are some things I absolutely don't want you to do."

Then lay out the actual medical issues that can arise from a botched piercing or tattoo.

"Therefore, at this stage of your life, I can't allow you to pierce your tongue, your nipples, or your genitals. If you want to do that when you're an adult, that will be your choice, but you don't want to be dealing with a bunch of infections to your reproductive system—and that might happen. If you want children some-day, it's something to think about. And if you want to pierce your ears, we will find a place that will do it right so there's minimal risk to your health."

This conversation acknowledges what the child wants while spelling out concerns she might not have considered. The prospect of Hepatitis C can be a strong counterbalance to peer pres-sure, and finding a middle ground makes the negotiation easier.

If you are absolutely opposed to bodily altera-tions for any reason, you can explain that, too. The most important part of the discussion is reason. Becoming hysterical or laying down the law without backing up your decision is a sure way to make the forbidden activity even more attractive.

> ### Talking Points
>
> In most states, it is illegal to tattoo a minor. A few states allow the procedure with parental consent when a child is younger than 18. Only two states and the District of Columbia have no regulations regarding the age of consent for tattoos.

Sexuality

Sexuality is a big concern for school-age children and becomes even more critical for teens. They want to know if and when to become sexually active, how to keep from becoming pregnant or impregnating a young woman, and how to prevent disease. It's at this point in their lives that many boys and girls also question their sexual identity.

By the time a child has reached adolescence, there shouldn't be too much she doesn't know about issues related to sexuality. These conversations should have begun when the child was old enough to ask about the differences between boys and girls. Little children become curious about how babies are born and how they are made, and they may have many fanciful ideas about both. Their questions should be answered factually, but you don't have to include every detail about intercourse, pregnancy, and birth when they're three years old. Keep it simple, but be honest. No storks. No cabbage leaves.

The reason for beginning early is that laying a foundation of trust and honesty makes it more likely the kids will continue to check things out with you as they grow. When they become teens, they often prefer to get their information from peers, but if they know you will talk with them about their concerns and confusions, you have the opportunity to correct misinformation they got from the kid next door. It also gives you one more chance to inculcate your values concerning sexual behavior.

Sometimes kids' reactions to sexual information are surprising. When young girls first hear about menstruation, many of them cry, even if the facts are presented sensitively by either mother or father. And both sexes can be appalled when they first hear about how pregnancy happens. "Ick," said 9-year-old Chris. "Isn't there a more natural way?" And the thought of their parents' having engaged in such unseemly conduct is sometimes terribly embarrassing for children and young adults.

The Questions

As your children get older, they can handle more information—and they should have it. Don't fool yourself that these conversations can wait or that innocence about such matters is a good thing. The media have opened up subjects that were once taboo (what adults ever believed that the words "oral sex" would be a staple of the evening news for weeks—and that they'd have to explain it to their seven-year-old?). Before the kids have taken sex education classes in school, they may have surprising questions about sex, some sophisticated and some off the wall. For example:

- ◆ "What's a homosexual? How do you know if you are one?"

- ◆ "Why do boys get erections if they aren't having sex with someone?"

- ◆ "Can you get pregnant if you have your clothes on?"

- ◆ "Do birds have sex?"

- ◆ "What's a three-way?"

- "Does having sex take a long time? It did for the dog, and she cried. Does it hurt?" (So much for the theory that letting children watch breeding in the animal kingdom helps them understand human reproduction.)

- "What's a vibrator?"

- "What's the best kind of condom?"

- "How many times do you have to have sex to have a baby?"

By the time the students reach high school, the questions and statements, if they come at all, may be more confrontational in nature:

- "I know you think I should wait to have sex, but why? Everybody does it."

- "I would never have unprotected sex. I carry condoms with me."

- "I think I should go on the pill. I'm going to marry Jerod, and he wants to have sex now."

- "I don't see anything wrong with oral sex. It's the best form of birth control, isn't it?"

Answers, Not Evasion

To deal with this kind of confrontation, you'll need to have real answers, which may require that you do some research. It's critical that you have your facts straight and report them accurately. Teens will turn off completely if you tell them some horror story that turns out not to be true. Here are some examples of fact-based answers:

- "It's interesting that you'd say everyone does it. Studies are showing that fewer teens are having sex. In 1991, 54 percent of high school students said they'd had sex. Ten years later it was 46 percent. That's less than half, so everyone really *isn't* doing it. We think at your age, having sex is risky, both physically and emotionally."

- "Do you know that there are almost a million babies born out of wedlock every year? I'll bet that some of the parents meant to use birth control every time. When you're in the midst of it, though, sometimes you forget about protection. You think you're safe just this once. And even if you're responsible every single time, you might use the condom incorrectly—and every method of birth control has a failure rate."

Don't Do It!

Don't close down conversation just because a subject is embarrassing or unpleasant for you. Keep the lines of communication open at all times, even if you hear things that disturb you. Putting your head in the sand is not the way to help a child figure out the right things to do.

♦ "I'm glad you're thinking about the consequences and not just the sex. The pill is effective birth control, but it doesn't protect you against HIV or other sexually transmitted diseases. There are all kinds of infections you can get, and some of them can have serious consequences if you ever want to have a child."

♦ "You're right. You can't get pregnant from oral sex, but you can get a sexually transmitted disease, like herpes or gonorrhea, even if you aren't having intercourse. Oral sex can be riskier than you might imagine. It's even possible to get HIV that way, although it's rare."

Be respectful of the fact that your teen has chosen to discuss these issues with you, but also be firm in stating beliefs that have arisen out of your greater experience.

"I'm glad you're talking to me about this, but some of what you're saying worries me. If you get pregnant or get someone else pregnant, there are very difficult decisions that have to be made: abortion, adoption, or keeping the child—and all of those decisions have their own repercussions. If you contract a disease, it can affect your ability to have children and ruin your future sex life. I don't think you're fully informed about everything that can happen. I'll be happy to go online with you and find some sites that will give you accurate information.

"Sex isn't just for now; what happens in one sexual encounter can affect the rest of your life. That's why I've always thought it was best to wait until you and your partner have thought everything through and know what you would do if something went wrong. At 16, I don't think you're ready to do that."

The most important thing you can do for an adolescent is to listen, even if what they're saying seems nonsensical or ill-informed. If you join with your children to confront issues, the kids will probably make the right decision, even if there are a lot of slammed doors in the process.

Drugs and Alcohol

The world can be frightening for kids and their parents. Every day it seems there's a new designer drug, some so powerful that addiction can be almost instantaneous. The waste of life is incalculable and the strain on relationships nearly intolerable.

Prevention of substance abuse requires the same techniques you use with sexuality issues. Conversation about drugs and alcohol should begin early, and they don't have to be great big pow-wows. Just slip the message in when it's appropriate. Maybe you see something on television that projects a positive image of drug or alcohol use or depicts smoking as desirable. That's the time to engage your child in conversation. How does she feel about what she just saw? Does she agree that smoking looks like something cool to do?

Once again, you must get the facts and you have to be accurate in your presentation of them. Know the language kids use when talking about drugs. Know the signs of abuse and don't be afraid to confront your child if you see those signs. You may save his life. Don't accuse. Instead, share your observations.

> "Dan, your eyes are red and you seem dazed and sleepy a good deal of the time. We were so concerned that you were using that we searched your room. We know that's a violation of your privacy, but your life is more important than your privacy right now. We found marijuana, and we know you're not holding it for someone else. We love you and we're scared. We need to know how often you're smoking marijuana and if you're using anything else. In this house, illegal drugs are absolutely forbidden, so we have to talk about it now."

Are You a Hypocrite?

What if you experimented with drugs when you were a teen? Many parents did. Do you disclose your use to your child or keep it a secret? There are two schools of thought about the best course of action. Most physicians say that telling the truth can help open a useful discussion because you know from experience that drugs can mess you up.

Other experts believe that confessing your own use condones your child's use and that you should keep your past to yourself. That can be done if there is no chance whatsoever that your child will ever find out. If he stumbles across the truth, however, all your pronouncements about drug use seem hypocritical.

If you decide to share your story, you can also say that the past is the past and you do not use any illicit drugs now nor do you ever abuse a prescription drug. You're not proud of your previous behavior and you want your child to keep from repeating your mistakes. You will help him find treatment to get himself clean and sober before he ruins his future.

Understand that no matter how powerful the peer group, you are the most important model for your child. If you talk about "needing a drink" after work or binge drink on the weekends, you're setting a potent negative example—and there's no conversation in the world that can undo that.

School Performance

Children often don't do as well as they should in school, and some of the reasons may be surprising. Although it's true that some kids are lackadaisical about schoolwork, others underachieve for a variety of other reasons, including test emphasis, school conditions, economics, and curricular mismatch.

Test Emphasis

Because educational policy now rewards school districts for students' test performance rather than their learning, too many teachers are forced to drill the same facts again and again until every student has at least a rudimentary understanding. Rote learning is boring and stifles curiosity and engagement.

School Conditions

Some schools are not places for learning. They are violent institutions, complete with armed guards and metal detectors. The stress can be so great that students find it almost impossible to learn. They're too busy worrying about surviving to the end of the school day.

Economics

Many school districts, urban and rural, are so cash-poor they can barely maintain school buildings. Textbooks often are out-of-date and don't reflect the latest research in various disciplines. The school may have outmoded computers, and be woefully lacking in the basic equipment students need for learning.

Curricular Mismatch

This country has approximately three million gifted children, but only about half have been identified. These children languish in a curriculum that offers them no challenge, and after their talents are stifled for several years, they may give up on academics altogether. These same students often demonstrate exceptional talent in community work, theater and art programs, book groups, athletics, leadership activities, or other outlets.

Steps to Take and What to Say

If your child is underachieving in school, the best person to talk to (after the child) is the teacher. Some parents dread these conferences, and so do many teachers. Both are on edge. Parents might believe that the teacher is going to judge their parenting, while the teacher is waiting to be attacked for her teaching style.

The parent-teacher dyad can be powerful in igniting the child's desire to learn, but only if you work as a team. If you're the parent, approach the teacher respectfully. Don't swoop in with a bundle of accusations. Here's what doesn't work:

> "I don't understand why Taylor is failing your class. She does fine everywhere else. What are you doing that's making it so hard for her to learn?"

Here's what might:

> "I'm worried about Taylor's performance in your class. She seems a little confused at home, so we're wondering if there are some basics she doesn't understand. What do you see? How can we work together to get her back on track?"

Let's face it. There are some really bad teachers out there, and nothing you say is going to make a particle of difference to them. But even the best teachers face tough odds: overcrowding; highly diverse classrooms with a variety of learning needs; and discipline restrictions that seem to reward bad behavior. In general, teachers appreciate and will work closely with parents who are interested in collaborating rather than pointing fingers.

When you're dealing with the child, it's equally important to step carefully. Grounding, threatening, and other power plays often fail because they create stress that makes learning even harder. It's best to ask questions.

> "What do you think is going wrong in this class?"

The answers to this question are varied:

- ◆ "The teacher doesn't like me."
- ◆ "I'm bored."
- ◆ "This stuff has nothing to do with real life."

"The Teacher Doesn't Like Me."

Although that's usually a misconception or an excuse, if your conference with the teacher reveals that he's punitive, sarcastic, rude, or otherwise inappropriate, it might be difficult for your child to learn in that classroom. A change of teacher could make a difference.

"I'm Bored."

Be careful of this one. Kids may trot it out just to shut down further conversation. Sometimes, though, they're telling the truth. Seek out the reasons for the boredom. If it's because the teacher drones on and on, help your child understand that in the real world he'll have to deal with dull bosses, dull customers, and dull colleagues. You expect him to give his best effort in spite of the teacher's style.

If the child says his boredom arises because he already knows what's being taught, take that seriously. If he can demonstrate mastery of the curriculum, the school might be able to place him in accelerated programming; he'll find much greater challenge there.

"This Stuff Has Nothing to do with Real Life."

He could be right. If he's studying history, and all he's learning are the facts and dates that will be on a test, his coursework is irrelevant. Parents often have to be co-teachers today, so challenge him at home. Show him how events of the past have shaped his life today. Give him real-world examples of ways he'll use algebra or composition when he's an adult. Help him make connections.

Part of the responsibility of parenting is preparing your children for life. That means taking their concerns seriously and helping them navigate challenges. It means setting high standards, requiring adequate performance, and administering suitable discipline. But it also means engaging in meaningful conversations throughout the child's growth and development. The more you do that, the easier those conversations are.

The Least You Need to Know

- ◆ Adolescents are beginning to form their own identities and it's appropriate for them to challenge you.

- ◆ There are biological reasons, as well as psychological ones, for teens' sometime inexplicable behavior.

- ◆ It's important to pick your battles with teens, saving your heavy ammunition for important issues such as alcohol, smoking, or drugs.

- ◆ Sexuality is a significant concern for teens and an area in which they require guidance.

- ◆ School performance can suffer for reasons having nothing to do with the child's ability.

Chapter 24

When the Roles Are Reversed: Talking with Aging Parents

In This Chapter

- ◆ Is age only a number?
- ◆ Expectations that cause misunderstandings
- ◆ Medical and end-of-life issues
- ◆ Maintaining their independence
- ◆ When to take the keys

In Chapter 23, we talked about being the parents and talking to your kids; in this chapter, the focus shifts to being the adult child who must talk about important issues with those who have probably been the authority figures in your life: your parents. Even if the relationship has been plagued with misunderstandings and acrimony, very few people simply abandon their parents—and those who do may saddle their siblings with full responsibility for dealing with the issues of aging, illness, financial hardship, and death. As you can imagine, many of these conversations have pitfalls. This chapter deals with avoiding the snares.

The Issues of Aging

More parents are living longer and remaining in better health than ever before.

Nonetheless, many older parents are affected by a variety of age-related issues including:

◆ Healthcare

◆ Housing

◆ Legal and financial concerns

◆ Independence and care needs

def•i•ni•tion

Adults who provide care for both their own parents and children have been dubbed the **sandwich generation**.

As members of the "*sandwich generation*," you may be faced with helping your parents through these concerns as you also grapple with bringing up your children. The financial and physical costs of managing both responsibilities can be very great and sometimes overwhelming.

Expectations and Realities

Your parents may have expectations you know nothing about. They might believe, for example, that if they become infirm, you will:

◆ Take them into your home.

◆ Provide assistance with home chores or meals.

◆ Offer financial help or even support them completely if they cannot make ends meet.

◆ Keep them out of a nursing home or care facility at all costs.

Talking Points

According to the 2000 census, the third-fastest-growing age cohort was those 90 to 94 years; this group showed an increase of 45 percent from 1990.

The realities of what you might be able to do, however, may be far different from what your parent has in mind. If you are paying two college tuitions and downsizing to smaller living quarters, you probably won't have money or space to house another person, let alone one who has special needs, such as one-floor living. You and your spouse may work full-time and not be able to give up one job so you can care for your parent at home. If you have an illness yourself, you may not have the physical ability or stamina to see to the needs of another person. Even if you fully intend to care for your parents as they age, circumstances change as life rolls on. Caregiving at a distance is very difficult and caregiving for members of your family and your spouse's at the same time can be impossible.

Unmet (and unfortunately often unspoken) expectations can trigger explosive arguments and eventual estrangement; the only way to forestall such disputes is to talk about expectations and plans openly and honestly—and early.

Every expert in eldercare issues urges that these conversations begin before a crisis happens. Crises can trigger hasty decisions with long-term negative consequences.

Bringing Up the Issues

You don't one day waltz into your parents' house and say, "Mom and Dad, you aren't getting any younger, and I want you to know I'm not going to be able to offer you much help if one or both of you gets sick. I have my own life to live. See ya!" And if possible, it's best not to use the holidays as an opportunity to remind your parents of their impending decrepitude.

Words to the Wise _____

If it's your parent who brings up end-of-life or inheritance issues, don't brush it off with, "I hate talking about this. You're not going to die tomorrow." Such things as heroic end-of-life medical treatments or who gets the family heirlooms are important to older folks. Put aside your discomfort in favor of your parent's peace of mind.

It's best to pick a time when everyone is in good health to sit down with your folks. You might say, "You know, Sara and I have begun talking about getting our affairs in order—updating our wills, signing *advance directives*, letting the kids know about our financial situation and what inheritance plans we've made for them. It got us to thinking that we don't know much about the kinds of planning you've done and what you want and expect from us."

def•i•ni•tion _____

Advance directives are documents a person fills out and signs that explain his or her medical wishes in advance and allow someone else to make treatment decisions on his or her behalf.

Once they get over the shock that their own children are acting in such a responsible manner, your parents may surprise you by telling you that their advance directives are signed and on file with their doctors, their wills are with the lawyer, their investments are in order, they have put down a deposit down on a retirement community that offers a full continuum of care, and all their funeral plans have been made and prepaid. If that's what you hear, you can all relax and go out to dinner.

Such extensive preparation, however, is not common. People resist thinking and talking about infirmity and death, and you might find that your parents have done little, if any, planning. Therefore, some conversation is in order. How you handle that conversation can go a long way toward preserving a good relationship with your parents.

Don't try to resolve every issue in one gulp. Start small. For example, "Mom, if you were hurt or in an accident, would it be up to me to give the hospital your medical information? I'm not sure we're up to date. Could we talk about it?" Here are some things you need to know:

- The names and phone numbers of your parents' doctors.

- What medications they take, in what dosages, and any medications they're allergic to or that cause them other problems, such as vomiting.

- Medical conditions for which they're being treated, such as diabetes or lupus, and any surgeries they've undergone, such as having a defibrillator implanted.

- Whether they've signed advance directives and where they are.

- What insurance they have beyond Medicare (if any) and where the paperwork is located.

Even this small bit of information will give you considerable peace of mind and will make it easier to move on to other topics, such as where and how they want to live if they become less able to care for themselves, and what end-of-life plans they've made. If your siblings don't live near your parents, make copies of all the medical information in case a parent becomes ill while visiting them.

"So When Did You Get So Smart?"

This question can be an expression of admiration for your acumen in dealing with elder issues; it can also be a sarcastic comment on your attempts to help your parent. It's all in the tone of voice.

If your parents are gratified by your assistance, it's probably because you've remembered some important rules in dealing with the people who brought you up.

Don't Give Them Advice

Your parents may need information, but unless they are confused or suffering from dementia, they don't need you telling them what to do. If you find your elderly parent standing at the top of a ladder changing light bulbs, don't think you have to jump in and tell him to get down. Old doesn't necessarily mean infirm. Yes, a fall from the top of a ladder might be serious, but if your parent is in good health, active, and doing what he's always done, let him alone.

If your parent is in ill health and having dizzy spells, of course you don't want him on the ladder, but there's a way to say that. "Dad, it worries me to see you up so high when you've been in the hospital so recently. I'm afraid you'll fall. I'd rather change that bulb myself, but if you want to do it, I'll hold the ladder. That will make me feel better." You may still get the brush-off, but at least you haven't treated your father like an infant.

> **Don't Do It!**
>
> Don't assume that every episode of forgetfulness means that your parent has Alzheimer's disease. Don't you sometimes forget, too? If your parent can't find his glasses, that's one thing. If he doesn't know what to do with his glasses, that's something else. A specialist in geriatric medicine can help you sort it out. There are many reasons for memory issues.

Collaborate, Don't Dictate

This one goes hand in hand with the point above. You may have good ideas, but if you try to tell your mother how to live her life—don't eat so much salt, put on a coat, stop staying up late—prepare for war. Unless she's incapacitated or already demoralized by your constant hovering and instruction, she's going to resist. She's an adult; you're her child. What makes you the arbiter of her life?

But if you can make your suggestions gentle and ask for her input, you might find success. "Mom, I know it's hard to have to deal with the salt restrictions in your diet right now. I'm probably going to face the same thing some day, so why don't we learn about this together? I'm sure there are some good cookbooks and there's a dietician who gives talks at the library about meal planning and special diets. What would you like to do to make this whole situation easier, since so many prepared foods seem to be off-limits now?"

You might give her some options, but listen to what she has to say. And if she says butt out, then butt out. When she comes to dinner at your house, you can serve the sorts of meals she should have, but you can't control what she does when you aren't around. People tend to do what they want to do, and if they don't follow their doctors' orders, the results can be serious or even catastrophic, but in large measure, it's out of your hands.

Foster Continuing Independence

In this mobile age, we often underestimate the comfort of home. The house where your parents live may be where they brought you home as babies. They know every nook and cranny. They welcome the spring tending a garden they've planted every year, and they enjoy the brilliant color of the foliage in the fall. Even if the house is long paid off and would provide enough for a move to retirement center, your parents may prefer to remain where they've been happy for decades.

You may believe that they should move because the house is becoming increasingly difficult for them to manage or they're having trouble handling the activities of daily living in a large house. Elderly people who have difficulties with any of these activities needn't be given the bum's rush out of their homes. There are adaptations that can be made: lift chairs, grab bars, and elevated commode seats are simple, inexpensive solutions to some of these problems. Other universal design elements can be incorporated even into older homes and include such things as:

◆ Lever handles rather than doorknobs to make doors easier to open.

◆ Bright task lighting to enhance meal preparation and reading.

◆ Buttons on control panels that allow a person to distinguish them by touch as well as by sight.

◆ Flat panel light switches that are easier to manipulate than small toggle switches.

More expensive accommodations include installing ramps, showers that are flush to the floor, and bathtubs with doors that allow easy access.

You'll have to investigate ways to fund these modifications; some may be covered by various state and local programs that promote independent living. There are also visiting nurse programs, meal delivery services, and other agencies that help keep seniors on their feet and in their homes. If they are at least 62 years old and own their home, a reverse mortgage may allow them access to funds for making the house more elder-friendly and hiring some services that will allow them to remain at home and independent.

You can approach the need for some of these services by saying, "Mom, I think this house is getting to be a lot for you to handle, but I know how much you love it and want to stay here. There are little things we can do to make it safer and easier for you to get around. Why don't I bring some brochures over and we'll talk about what's possible."

That's a far superior approach to, "Mom, I've watched you trying to take care of yourself here and it just isn't working. Tom and I think you should find a nice retirement center because you might need assisted living soon. I've picked three. Let's go look at them this week."

During the discussion of adapting the house, it may become clear that your parent really can't stay by herself any more, but if she comes to that decision by herself, she'll accept it far more easily than if she has one—and only one—option shoved down her throat.

A Tough Decision: Taking the Keys

Giving up the car keys is one of the hardest things a senior has to do. When they were children, they looked forward to the independence driving affords, and just because they've gotten old doesn't mean they've lost that desire for self-sufficiency.

Don't jump to the conclusion that one fender-bender means that your parent shouldn't drive anymore. My last fender-bender occurred when I was 53, and it was the result of inattention, not age. I also had a similar accident when I was 16. When should the keys have been taken from me? At 16? At 53? Or any year in between?

What you should look for is a pattern of behind-the-wheel problems that signal the inability to handle the job. Do you notice your parent misjudging distances, running red lights or stop signs, hitting curbs, missing freeway exits, being confused at one-way streets or roundabouts, or driving far too slowly?

These add up to a need to begin talking about alternative forms of transportation. Speak with the parent's doctor; it's possible that medication is affecting coordination or reaction times. See if other prescriptions might have a beneficial effect.

When my sister and I had to make the decision for our mother, we enlisted her physician. He told her that the physical changes she was experiencing put her and other people at risk on the road. Although she was broken-hearted at losing this part of her independence, she acquiesced because of her fear of hurting others. When she was much younger, she had hit a child on a bicycle. Although she was totally blameless and the youngster was not seriously injured, the horror of that day never went away, and she saw that it could happen again if she continued to drive.

If you have to do the job yourself, don't come on like a storm trooper. State the facts. Your parent may come to the right conclusion without assistance.

> "Daddy, when I was driving with you the other day, I noticed that you ran the red light at the Five Points intersection. Then I had to stop you from going up the one-way ramp at the airport. When we left the parking lot, you got into the wrong turn lane. Once we were on the freeway, you did just fine, but there were a lot of near misses, and you appeared to be very tentative. I'm concerned about that and I think it would be good for you to have your driving evaluated by someone other than your child. I'd like you to take a driving test with an instructor. Maybe you were just having a bad day, but if a neutral party says you're making serious mistakes, we have to think about options."

If the senior is physically able and bus transportation is available, it's a safe and convenient alternative, but for those who live far from public transportation, giving up the car will be a great inconvenience and may curtail his personal and social life. As the Baby Boomers age, transportation will achieve greater prominence as a public policy issue, but you have to deal with it one-to-one. And when your parent cries or tells you you're overreacting and heartless, you'll find it's truly one of the most bruising conversations you'll ever have to deal with. You may have to weep right along with your parent, but if you and a neutral third party agree that this is the right course of action, you'll have to harden your sympathy because the risk is too great, both for your parent and for innocent bystanders.

The Least You Need to Know

- Many seniors are healthy and of sound mind throughout their entire lives.
- All family members should be aware of the senior's medical history, and the family and physician should have a copy of his advance directives.
- Helping seniors maintain their independence is a worthwhile use of your time.
- The time to talk about issues is far in advance of a crisis and cooperation among siblings is important.

Good Fences, Good Neighbors

In This Chapter

- ◆ What do neighbors fight about?
- ◆ Avoiding extremes
- ◆ The ladder of complaints
- ◆ Are you sure about the law?
- ◆ Living with homeowners' associations

Sharing boundaries with others isn't always an easy proposition. You probably expect that your neighbors will respect the boundaries, but often they don't, allowing dogs and children to ruin your landscaping and disturb the peace. They're noisy. They don't take care of their own property, causing nuisances and hazards, and their neglect can affect your property value, too. When you have troublesome neighbors, you have plenty of opportunities for confrontation. When should you take those opportunities and when are things best handled by others—or ignored? This chapter gives you some things to think about.

How Neighborly Are You?

Many problems with neighbors can be avoided by performing some simple acts of consideration. Here are a few. Do you do them?

	Yes	No
1. I know my neighbors' names and I say hello to them when I see them.	❏	❏
2. I keep an eye on my neighbors' property when they're away.	❏	❏
3. I keep my property neat.	❏	❏
4. I participate in neighborhood traditions, such as a July 4th block party.	❏	❏
5. I consider the effects my property decisions have on the neighborhood.	❏	❏
6. I keep my car garaged or in my own driveway or designated parking space.	❏	❏
7. I keep my animals under control and do not allow them to destroy my neighbors' property or peace and quiet.	❏	❏
8. I respond promptly to any neighbor's complaint.	❏	❏
9. I assume the best about my neighbors and approach them politely with complaints.	❏	❏
10. I complain only about matters that are continually annoying, not about every minuscule issue.	❏	❏

Answers:

1. Knowing your neighbors can go a long way toward fostering communication and solving problems that might arise.

2. Watching each other's property makes neighborhoods more cohesive and safer. That's good for everyone.

3. Keeping property tidy lessens animal incursions and enhances property values.

4. You don't have to attend every activity in the neighborhood, but showing your face and talking to your neighbors at meetings or events makes it less likely they'll consider you stand-offish and hard to deal with.

5. Does your new outside lighting shine directly into your neighbors' bedroom? Will the trees you want to plant block his view of the lake, the ocean, the mountains, or any other feature he might enjoy? Does your son's garage band practice at the time your neighbor is trying to sleep? Thinking about how your actions affect others makes neighborhood living much more peaceful.

6. If you annoy your neighbors by making it difficult for them to enter and leave their property or grabbing their parking place, be prepared to hear from them.

7. Don't allow your cat to use the neighbors' Japanese garden as a litter box or let your dog bark incessantly.

8. A quick response, such as turning down your music late at night (especially if you like building-shaking bass), helps preserve harmony. If the issue is something you can't fix immediately, respond anyway, offering a time to talk about the problem.

9. Don't get paranoid and decide your neighbors are out to get you. In many cases, they may not even know they're causing a problem.

10. Nosy Nates who have nothing better to do but complain about everything their neighbors do cannot expect much cooperation when there's a real issue to be resolved.

What Are You Complaining About?

Neighbors can get upset about all sorts of things: trees, fences, animals, children, land use, and décor. You name it and some people will fight about it. Although some neighbors truly believe that the world is their private preserve and don't care whose rights they trample on in their quest to enjoy the world on their own terms, most people will attempt to rectify situations that impinge on their neighbors' quality of life.

If you have a beef with your neighbor, make sure that what you're complaining about is what you're really upset about. Don't get into an uproar about their cat if what you're really mad about is that they had a big barbeque and didn't invite you. Be honest with yourself and them.

The Process of Complaining

Neighborhood residents may be unaware that what they're doing bothers anyone else. Let's say your lawn-proud next-door neighbor, Pete, gets up early every Saturday morning, and by 6 A.M. the dulcet tones of his power mower are wafting through the breeze. You, hoping to avoid a confrontation, say nothing, but you become angrier every time he mounts his beast of a mower. Six weeks later you blow like Mount Saint Helens.

You stomp over to his house in your pajamas and scream at him that he's in violation of about sixteen noise ordinances and if he keeps it up, you're calling the cops. He tells you to get your derrière off his property and so begins a dispute that eventually involves other neighbors. People take sides, start gossiping about each other, and the quality of life in the neighborhood declines.

I once lived in a neighborhood where a noise problem drove a wedge right down the middle of the community. Warring neighbors turned their backs if they encountered one another on the street. It was childish, silly, and actually affected property values as potential buyers heard about the problem. Who wanted to move into a situation like that?

It's much easier and more politic to …

♦ Keep quiet, but not forever. Let the first annoying instance pass so you can see if it was a one-time occurrence.

♦ Keep resentment at bay. Once you've discerned a pattern of behavior that's bothersome, don't let your exasperation grow to the point that you can't be civil. Speak up quickly but politely.

♦ Have a quiet talk with your neighbor when you're calm and rational and the behavior is not occurring.

♦ Approach the situation as a problem to be resolved. Don't attack your neighbor personally.

An attack, especially an ambush, doesn't work well and positions you as a grouch and a bully. Try to stay away from character assassination:

> "Listen, Pete, that obnoxious lawn mower of yours is a real pain. Do you think the first thing I want to hear every Saturday is that thing right next to my bedroom window? Cut it out!"

What will work better is a statement of the problem, why it's a problem, and a request that you work it out together:

> "Pete, I've been admiring your lawn since I moved in. It puts everybody else's to shame. I'd like to ask you a favor, though. I go to work every morning at five o'clock, and on Saturday I like to sleep later. My bedroom is right at the property line, and sometimes it sounds as if the mower is coming right through the wall. Can you help me out by starting later in the morning?"

Pete may say he didn't know the noise was an issue and instantly acquiesce to your request. On the other hand, he may tell you it's his property, his mower, and he'll do whatever he pleases. "Get some earplugs."

You now have a couple of choices. You can get into a shouting match with him right then and there or you can say, "I'd really appreciate it if you'd think about it and get back to me. Maybe together we can come up with something that satisfies both of us."

Occasionally, people who are caught off guard overreact to what feels like a reprimand. Once they've thought it over, they modify their behavior and peace returns. They may even apologize both for the original offense and the way they acted. Or they may never mention it again because they're embarrassed by their own response to your request.

Words to the Wise

When a neighbor's behavior seems continually irritating, keep a log of when each incident occurs. You may discover that the troublesome incidents are not as frequent as you think. Because each occurrence raises your annoyance factor, you may overestimate how often he engages in the offensive activity. A log also gives you the real evidence you need to confront your neighbor constructively.

How to Involve the Neighbors

If your neighbor continues to play hardball, you'll need some back-up. Research your community's noise ordinances. Running an ear-splitting piece of machinery at 6 A.M.

probably violates at least one of them. Copy and highlight the ordinance and send a pleasant note along with the citation. When people see a violation in writing, they often tone down the rhetoric and become more cooperative.

You might also check with other neighbors and see if they, too, are bothered by the noise. Be careful with this strategy. If Pete's a popular guy and has lived there longer than you have, you can open a can of worms. The neighbors may begin to view you as a troublemaker and rally around Pete. Alternatively, if Pete's widely known as a short-tempered tyrant, people may not want to share their feelings with you for fear of retaliation. Make it clear that you're not out to get Pete; you just want to know if the mower bothers anyone else.

As you negotiate with Pete, listen to what he has to say as well as to your own voice. Pete's rude suggestion of earplugs might actually have some merit. Give them a try. Maybe they'll work. Problem solved.

Mediation

When you've tried everything and Pete refuses to make any compromise, you might think about *mediation*.

def•i•ni•tion

Mediation is a process in which a trained neutral person helps you and another person communicate with one another and understand one another's positions. A mediator does not give legal advice or recommend courses of action.

Mediation is successful between 75 and 95 percent of the time, and it's an effective way to avoid the costs and hard feelings that can arise from a lawsuit between neighbors. Having to put your gripes out there in front of a mediator can also bring perspective to a situation that might have gotten out of hand.

As those involved in the dispute try to avoid what are becoming increasingly difficult conversations and rely on written communication, it's easy to forget that the argument is between people, not faceless nonentities. When you're together in a room, that fact becomes much more apparent, and when you have to say out loud what the problems are, you can sometimes get to agreement with nearly lightning speed—and then you wonder what took you so long.

Local Authorities

As a second-to-last resort, you can involve the police or other local authorities. Police, animal control, or code enforcement personnel can be called in to put a stop to the offensive or illegal behavior. It will create hard feelings, but if things have reached this stage, good feelings are probably long since past anyway. And at the end of the road, you can consider a lawsuit. You may not have a case, but you can find that out by talking with an attorney.

Get Your Facts Straight

Before you get all high and mighty with your neighbor, or call in law enforcement, or decide to take matters into your own hands, be sure you know what you're talking about. For example, suppose your neighbor owns a tree—that is, the tree trunk meets the ground entirely on his property. Now suppose she doesn't trim the tree and branches overhang your property. You politely ask her to trim the tree. She doesn't. You ask her again. Same response.

So one day you pick up your loppers and go trim the tree. Surprise! Your neighbor now may have a cause of action against you. Perhaps she didn't trim the tree because it was sheltering a shade garden of expensive rare plants that will wither and die in the sun. You might have had the right to trim the part of the tree that was hanging over your yard, but maybe not. Tree law is complicated. Just because something is a nuisance doesn't mean it's legal for you to take unilateral action, even if you've tried to resolve the situation through conversation.

When asking your neighbor to help you out, offer the rationale for your request and really listen to his response. In the example above, if you had had a real conversation with your neighbor instead of simply asking her to trim her tree, you might have learned why she didn't, and she might have learned why it bothered you. That's the basis for fruitful negotiation.

How to Respond to a Complaint

Realize that it takes some bravery for one person to confront another about a neighborhood problem. The complaining neighbor doesn't know if you're going to blow her off or be angry. Surprise her with civility. She probably doesn't expect it.

Complainers are occasionally vague. "Your dogs make too much noise" doesn't give you enough information to address the issue. Seek understanding of the real problem by asking questions.

"I'm sorry the dogs are bothering you. What is it they're doing?"

Perhaps you hear it's the dogs' barking that's disturbing the peace. Next, find out when the barking is a problem. The more details you have, the more solutions you can generate.

"Is there a specific time when the barking bothers you?"

It's astonishing how many working singles and couples have dogs and aren't aware that the animals bark from the moment the humans leave in the morning until they return in the evening. In shared living arrangements, such as co-ops and condominiums, this never-ending racket is intolerable, to say nothing of being exhausting to the dogs. Boards of directors will move quickly to protect the other residents from noise pollution.

Often, however, the problem is more limited, and by asking questions, you can discern how difficult the solution will be. For example, when I had my first baby, I always tried to put him down for a nap about 1 P.M. That was exactly the time when my neighbor would put her two yippy, yappy schnauzers out in the yard. I had a yippy schnauzer, too, but he couldn't hold a candle to this pair. They would run back and forth under the baby's window and bark and bark—and bark. If I could get my son to sleep before they came out, the yipping didn't wake him up, but if the dogs were out first, it was tough for him to drift off, and I was in for a long afternoon of infant crankies. At other times of the day, I didn't care if the dogs barked their brains out, but those few minutes were a real problem for me.

I told my neighbor about my concern, and we came up with a couple of compromises. I would try to put the baby down a bit earlier and she would let the dogs out a bit later. That freed up about a half-hour when things were quiet. My son got his nap, the dogs got their exercise, and I got to do other things while the baby slept. A winning situation all around.

Keep Your Part of the Bargain

If you've arrived at a compromise, be sure to live up to your part of it. My friend Lynne lives on a farm that backs up to a small sheep ranch. Lynne has three large dogs that roam her property. Sometimes, though rarely, they wander over to bother the sheep next door. They have never harmed the other animals, but enjoy barking at them and chasing them a bit. Her neighbor called her and threatened to shoot the dogs first and ask questions later.

Lynne requested instead that he alert her if the dogs got onto his property and she would immediately remove them.

A couple of weeks later, Lynne's son looked out the kitchen window to see the neighbor on their property, his shotgun by his side. He marched up onto the porch and told the boy he was going to shoot the dogs right then. "They'd strayed," Lynne said, "but they hadn't hurt the sheep, and there was no need for this show of force. He didn't notify me or my husband as we had agreed. He came on to our property with a lethal weapon and took the matter up with a 14-year-old—and threatened to kill his dog in the process. Obviously, our son ran over and got the dogs, but that's not what the adults had all agreed to. It was a sticky situation that we've had to renegotiate. He's definitely not allowed to bring a gun onto our property again."

> **Don't Do It!**
>
> Whatever side of the problem you're on, don't attempt to reason with someone who is drunk, high, abusive, or threatening. In these situations, the wrong word can bring about violence.

Sharing the Walls

One neighborly disagreement that's highly unpleasant and sometimes disillusioning is what happens when people move into a shared living arrangement, such as a condo or co-op, without reading and understanding the rules and regulations that govern such communities. Because of ignorance, they break by-law after by-law, and the boards seem to be on their case every other week. The conversations can degenerate into warfare, with groups of people joining up to discipline the offender or throw out the condo board.

Unquestionably, some condo and co-op boards are populated with martinets who enjoy throwing their weight around and enforcing every rule to the limits of tolerance. Others, though, are trying to do the thankless job of keeping property values high for everyone. They often take tremendous heat just for doing the job other residents elected them to do.

You have no right to abuse these people nor do they have the right to be rude to you, but remember that in moving to a co-op or condo, you give up some of your autonomy. Once you're a resident, trying to do your own thing is very difficult. What are called covenants, conditions, and restrictions—the rules—dictate many of your decisions about your home. Structural changes will require not only a variance from the city, but also written permission from your homeowners' association.

If you don't mind someone else's telling you what color to paint your garage door or how much square footage you must cover with carpet, condo living may be right up your alley, but if you have to have eggplant-colored trim, you're not a good candidate for shared living arrangements.

In short, neighbors can get on your nerves, and it may take all your civility and tact to manage your interactions with them. Weigh your options carefully because what you choose may make it impossible to continue living in your present home. Situations that can't be rectified usually end up with someone's moving. That's a big price to pay for an argument.

The Least You Need to Know

- Neighbor disputes are among the most distressing conversations because of repercussions that can affect the entire neighborhood.

- If you have an issue with a neighbor, attack the problem, not the neighbor.

- Mediation may be useful in resolving long-simmering neighbor disputes.

- Code enforcement or animal control officers might be more helpful than police in dealing with neighborhood annoyances.

- Shared living arrangements such as condos and co-ops are not for everyone.

Appendix

Glossary

active listening   A way of listening concerned with discerning the speaker's meaning and state of mind. It involves listening and clarifying what is heard.

activities of daily living   Activities such as bathing and eating that adults must be able to carry out alone or with assistance to live independently.

ADA (Americans with Disabilities Act)   A law that prevents discrimination against those with physical or mental challenges.

addiction   Psychological and physical dependence on a habit-forming substance.

adrenaline   A stress hormone that prepares the body to fight or flee.

advance directives   Legal documents that tell the doctor and family what a person wants for future medical care, including when or whether to start life-saving treatment and when to end such treatment.

broken record   An assertiveness technique that involves continually repeating the outcome or desires.

central tendency error   The belief that most workers fall into the center of a bell curve, and therefore, do not deserve outstanding or negative reviews.

civility   Showing courtesy and respect for others, both in word and in deed.

compromise   A solution to a dispute that involves each person's giving up a portion of what he or she wants.

confrontation   Facing another person with the intent of arguing a position.

conflict   Heated argument caused by disputants' inability to accept one another's positions.

debate   A formal argument in which one side argues for an idea and the other side argues against it.

dependency   A physical need for a habit-forming substance.

diatribe   The vilification of another person.

discipline   Training that is expected to produce certain behaviors.

domestic violence   Abuse of one domestic partner by another.

emoticons   Icons that give a clue to the intent of the writer of an e-mail. When emoticons are turned sideways, the reader can see a face that expresses the writer's emotions. For example, ;) means a wink and :(indicates a frown.

employee assistance program (EAP)   A company-sponsored counseling program that deals with personal problems that contribute to poor job performance.

empathy   The ability to feel what another person is experiencing.

executor   A person appointed to carry out the terms of a will.

extrinsic motivation   Motivation that comes from an outside source, such as the promise of a reward or promotion.

face   Positive self-regard that can be enhanced or damaged by the acts of others.

family system   The theory that a family is an emotional unit and that each member's actions affect other members of the group.

feedback   An evaluative response to an action or series of actions.

fogging   An assertiveness technique in which you agree to portions of the other's position while retaining the right to your own opinion.

gossip   Talking about others, usually in a disparaging manner, when they are not present.

gunnysacking   Holding onto grievances for an extended period of time and using them in a current argument.

halo effect   Believing that competence or skill in one area is proof of competence in all areas.

haptics   The science of touch, especially as related to technology or conversation.

hospice care   Care provided in the home or in a facility for those who have a terminal diagnosis. Services include medical care, pain and symptom management, and supportive psychological and spiritual counseling for the patient and family.

hostile work environment   A workplace in which it's difficult for people to do their work because of threat or harassment.

high-context   A culture in which communication is carried nonverbally, in gestures, tone of voice, or facial expression.

I-message   A message that explains how one is affected by the actions of another.

Intervention   A carefully structured conversation designed to help a substance abuser see the need for treatment.

interventionist   A professional who is skilled in intervention techniques.

intrinsic motivation   Motivation that arises internally when people find an optimal mix of challenge, control, and commitment in their work.

keloid   An overgrowth of scar tissue.

ketosis   A build-up of ketone bodies in tissues and fluids.

low-context   A culture in which words carry the meaning of a conversation.

mediation   A process in which a neutral third party helps those involved in a dispute improve their understanding and communication.

monochronism   An ability or preference for carrying out individual tasks in sequence.

multi-tasking   To work on a variety of different tasks simultaneously.

neuron   The nerve cells that make up the central nervous system. They send and receive messages by means of a weak electrical current.

oculesics   The study of the way the eyes are used in communication.

paralanguage   In conversation, everything but the words.

perceived value   The value attached to a product or service by the person receiving it.

pitchfork effect   The belief that incompetence in one area means incompetence in every area.

polychronism   The ability or preference to work on a variety of tasks at once.

progressive discipline   A series of increasingly harsh steps designed to elicit better employee performance.

proxemics   The study of the effects of spatial distance in personal interactions and conversation.

pruning   The weeding out of certain synapses in the brain.

recency error   Giving too much weight to recent performance and behavior.

repartee   Witty speech.

reverse mortgage   A loan against your house that isn't paid back until the property is sold or the property owner dies. You must be a least 62 years old and own your home to apply for such a mortgage.

sandwich generation   Adults who have primary responsibility for raising their children and caring for their aging parents.

substance abuse   Misusing chemicals that can alter bodily or mental functioning.

Sudden Infant Death Syndrome (SIDS)   The abrupt death of an apparently healthy infant while the child is asleep.

teachable moment   Particular times when people are most susceptible to learning something new.

universal design   The design of environments and products that allow the greatest number of people to use them.

Appendix B

Read More About It

Anderson, Peter. *The Complete Idiot's Guide to Body Language*. Indianapolis: Alpha Books, 2004.

Brinkman, Rick, and Rick Kirschner. *Dealing with People You Can't Stand: How to Bring Out the Best in People at Their Worst*. New York: McGraw-Hill, 2002.

Burley-Allen, Madelyn. *Listening: The Forgotten Skill: A Self-Teaching Guide, Second Edition*. Hoboken, NJ: Wiley, 1995.

Davidson, Jeff. *The Complete Idiot's Guide to Assertiveness*. Indianapolis: Alpha Books, 1997.

Faber, Adele, and Elaine Mazlish. *How to Talk So Kids Will Listen and Listen So Kids Will Talk, 20th Anniversary Edition, Updated*. New York: Avon, 1999.

——— *How to Talk So Teens Will Listen and Listen So Teens Will Talk*. New York: HarperCollins, 2005.

Forward, Susan. *Toxic In-Laws: Loving Strategies for Protecting Your Marriage, Reprint Edition*. New York: HarperCollins, 2002.

Harkins, Phil. *Powerful Conversations: How High-Impact Leaders Communicate*. New York: McGraw-Hill, 1999.

Hirsch, Gretchen. *Talking Your Way to the Top*. Amherst, NY: Prometheus Books, 2006.

Hynes, Geraldine. *Managerial Communication: Strategies and Applications, Third Edition.* New York: McGraw-Hill/Irwin, 2005.

Jay, Jeff, and Debra Jay. *Love First: A New Approach to Intervention for Alcoholism and Drug Addiction, New Edition.* Center City, MN: Hazelden, 2000

Kübler-Ross, Elisabeth. *On Death and Dying.* New York: Scribner's Reprint Edition, 1997.

Martin, Judith. *Miss Manners' Guide to Excruciatingly Correct Behavior, Freshly Updated.* New York: W. W. Norton, 2005.

Orman, Suze. *The 9 Steps to Financial Freedom: Practical and Spiritual Steps So You Can Stop Worrying, Third Revised and Updated Edition.* New York: Three Rivers Press, 2006.

Patterson, Kerry, Joseph Grenny, and Ron McMillan. *Crucial Conversations: Tools for Talking When Stakes Are High.* New York: McGraw-Hill, 2002.

Patterson, Kerry, Joseph Grenny, Ron McMillan, and Al Switzler. *Crucial Confrontations: Tools for Resolving Broken Promises, Violated Expectations, and Bad Behavior.* New York: McGraw-Hill, 2004.

Pell, Arthur. *The Complete Idiot's Guide to Managing People, Third Edition.* Indianapolis: Alpha Books, 2003.

Post, Peggy. *Emily Post's Etiquette, 17th Indexed Edition.* New York: Collins, 2004.

RoAne, Susan. *What Do I Say Next? Talking Your Way to Business and Social Success.* New York: Warner Books, 1999.

Selak, Joy, and Steven Overman. *You Don't Look Sick: Living Well With Invisible Chronic Illness.* Binghamton, NY: Haworth Medical Press, 2005.

Stone, Douglas, Bruce Patton, Sheila Heen, and Roger Fisher. *Difficult Conversations: How to Discuss What Matters Most.* New York: Penguin, 2000.

Tannen, Deborah. *I Only Say This Because I Love You: Talking to Your Parents, Partner, Sibs, and Kids When You're All Adults.* New York: Ballantine, 2002.

Truss, Lynne. *Talk to the Hand: The Utter Bloody Rudeness of the World Today, or Six Good Reasons to Stay Home and Bolt the Door.* New York: Gotham, 2005.

Whitney, Carol Strip, and Gretchen Hirsch. *A Love for Learning: Motivation and the Gifted Child.* Scottsdale, AZ: Great Potential Press, 2007.

Index